THE WAY OF THE WORLD
A FESTSCHRIFT FOR
R. H. STEPHENSON

CULTURAL STUDIES AND THE SYMBOLIC, 4

Previously published

Cultural Studies and the Symbolic, 1. Edited by Paul Bishop and R. H. Stephenson. Leeds: Northern Universities Press, 2003.
ISBN: 1 904350 03 8

Cultural Studies and the Symbolic, 2. *The Paths of Symbolic Knowledge*. Edited by Paul Bishop and R. H. Stephenson. Leeds: Maney Publishing, 2006.
ISBN: 1 904350 27 5 (978 1 904350 27 9)

Cultural Studies and the Symbolic, 3. *The Persistence of Myth as Symbolic Form*. Edited by Paul Bishop and R. H. Stephenson. Leeds: Maney Publishing, 2008.
ISBN: 978 1 904350 29 3

THE WAY OF THE WORLD
A FESTSCHRIFT FOR
R. H. STEPHENSON

Edited by

PAUL BISHOP

Maney Publishing

2011

Published by Maney Publishing, Suite 1C, Joseph's Well, Hanover Walk, Leeds LS3 1AB, UK; www.maney.co.uk

Maney Publishing is the trading name of W. S. Maney & Son Ltd
Printed and bound by Charlesworth Press, Wakefield, UK

ISBN 978-1-906540-95-1

Front cover: A diagram accompanying Goethe's letter to Carl Friedrich Zelter of 24 November 1804, representing 'an old picture, unfortunately lost', depicting Meles and Cretheis (the river god and the nymph he marries). In his previous letter, Zelter had described Carl Ludwig's painting, *The Damnation of Judas Iscariot*.

In Memoriam

Bernard Ashbrook

1939–2009

and

John Michael Krois

1943–2010

With thanks for the support of
Dr Helen Bridge
Hedy Harsam
Selena Hunter
Dr Gautum Pingle
Dr Gordon Barclay
University of Glasgow, Library
Ms Maire Davies
Dr Shona Allan
Prof. Sir Drummond Bone

CONTENTS

INTRODUCTION

Inaugurated with a collection of 'intercultural readings' of Goethe on the occasion of the 250th anniversary of his birth, the series *Cultural Studies and the Symbolic* has to date examined various aspects of Ernst Cassirer's theory of symbolic forms, including 'the paths of the symbolic' — how to symbolize is to have culture — and 'the persistence of myth' — the ubiquitousness of that 'symbolic form' Cassirer described as 'lurking in the dark'. In its fourth volume, we turn attention to the 'world', in the sense in that Nietzsche — in section 109 of *The Gay Science* (*Die fröhliche Wissenschaft*) (1882; 1887) — contrasts 'the astral order in which we live' (*die astrale Ordnung, in der wir leben*) as opposed to 'the total character of the world' (*der Gesamtcharakter der Welt*) which is, he tells us, 'in all eternity chaos' (*in alle Ewigkeit Chaos*).[1] For Cassirer, the function of the symbol was to give form and thus, ultimately, to give birth to the world: as he put it in volume 1 of *The Philosophy of Symbolic Forms* (*Philosophie der symbolischen Formen*) (1923–1929), 'the function of linguistic thinking, the function of mythical and religious thinking, and the function of artistic perception' (*die Funktion des sprachlichen Denkens, die Funktion des mythisch-religiösen Denkens und die Funktion der künstlerischen Anschauung*) lay in bringing about 'an entirely determinate formation, not exactly *of* the world, but rather making for the world, for an objective meaningful context and an objective unity that can be apprehended as such' (*eine ganz bestimmte Gestaltung nicht sowohl der Welt, als vielmehr eine Gestaltung zur Welt, zu einem objektiven Sinnzusammenhang und einem objektiven Anschauungsganzen*).[2] And yet the world has, as the title of a famous Restoration comedy puts it, its 'ways'; after they have created it, even the symbol forms inhabit a specific politico-cultural context. In other words, how do we negotiate the 'symbolic forms' and the bureaucratic world of application forms? How do we, to paraphrase Nietzsche, bring reason to its senses? Or how do we, in the title of a paper by R. H. Stephenson, make sense of sense?

This volume is offered as a *Festschrift* for Roger Stephenson, who recently retired from the William Jacks Chair of Modern Languages (German) at the University of Glasgow. It consists of a collection of essays written by a wide range of scholars, reflecting his interests in various aspects of modern German and European literature, and in particular his engagement with Weimar classicism, the so-called *Meisterdenker* tradition of ideas, and his commitment to close reading — illuminated by theory — within a broad cultural context. The papers collected in this volume reflect the wide range of Roger's scholarly interests.

The first section contains three papers devoted to key figures of the German eighteenth century: Gotthold Ephraim Lessing (1729–1781), Wilhelm von Humboldt (1767–1835) and Friedrich Schiller (1759–1895), as well as the man who lent his name to the period known as the *Goethezeit*, Johann Wolfgang Goethe (1749–1832). In the first paper, Barry Nisbet, the author of a major biography of the German dramatist, philosopher, and critic, discusses the figure of Lessing. In *The Birth of Tragedy* (*Die Geburt der Tragödie*) (1872), Nietzsche cited the famous passage from *A Reply* (*Eine Duplik*) (1778), in which Lessing wrote:

> Not the truth in whose possession any man is, or thinks he is, but the honest effort he has made to find out the truth, is what constitutes the worth of a man. For it is not through the possession but through the inquiry after truth that his powers expand, and in this alone consists his ever growing perfection. Possession makes calm, lazy, proud. —
>
> If God had locked up all truth in his right hand, and in his left the unique, ever-live striving for truth, albeit with the addition that I should always and eternally err, and he said to me, "Choose!" — I should humbly clasp his left hand, saying: 'Father, give! Pure truth is after all for thee alone!'

> [Nicht die Wahrheit, in deren Besitz irgendein Mensch ist oder zu sein vermeinet, sondern die aufrichtige Mühe, die er angewandt hat, hinter die Wahrheit zu kommen, macht den Wert des Menschen. Denn nicht durch den Besitz, sondern durch die Nachforschung der Wahrheit erweitern sich seine Kräfte, worin allein seine immer wachsende Vollkommenheit bestehet. Der Besitz macht ruhig, träge, stolz. —
>
> Wenn Gott in seiner Rechten alle Wahrheit und in seiner Linken den einzigen immer regen Trieb nach Wahrheit, obschon mit dem Zusatze, mich immer und ewig zu irren, verschlossen hielte und spräche zu mir: 'Wähle!' — ich fiele ihm mit Demut in seine Linke und sagte: 'Vater, gib! Die reine Wahrheit ist ja doch nur für dich allein!']³

In so doing, Nietzsche argued, Lessing had shown himself to be 'the most honest theoretical man' (*der ehrlichste theoretische Mensch*), inasmuch as he had revealed that 'he cared more for the search after truth than for truth itself' (*daß ihm mehr am Suchen der Wahrheit als an ihr selbst gelegen sei*).⁴

In 1794 the German philosopher Johann Gottlieb Fichte (1762–1814) delivered his famous lecture in Zurich under the title, *Concerning Human Dignity* (*Über die Würde des Menschen*).⁵ As if in response to the Idealist stance of his (soon, erstwhile) colleague in Jena, Schiller contributed the following (bitingly satirical) poem to the collection (written with Goethe) of *Xenia*:

> No more of that, I beg you. Give him some food, give him shelter,
>   Once you have covered bare need, dignity comes by itself.

> [Nichts mehr davon, ich bitt euch. Zu essen gebt ihm, zu wohnen,
>   Habt ihr die Blöße bedeckt, gibt sich die Würde von selbst.]

Jim Reed's paper — all the more timely in the wake of the global credit crisis of 2007–2010 and the subsequent reductions in public spending planned by governments across Europe — addresses itself to issues of literary responsibility, social justice, and human dignity. It demonstrates well why, in the enthusiastic words with which Hans-Jürgen Schings (in his review in the *Frankfurter Allgemeine Zeitung*) greeted the publication (in the year commemorating the two-hundredth anniversary of Schiller's death) of Rüdiger Safranski's biography,[6] *Schiller ist immer noch da — und wie!*

In his contribution Martin Swales uses Cassirerian principles as a basis for his consideration of two poems by Goethe. (Swales's recent study, together with Erika Swales, of Goethe's literary work constitutes a plea for the retention or return of Goethe's texts as part of a university German curriculum, in the face of their gradual disappearance from *Germanistik* as taught in the UK.)[7] Cassirer's admiration for Goethe was legendary: after a visit to Weimar with her husband, Toni Cassirer (according to her account in her biographical work *My Life with Ernst Cassirer* [*Mein Leben mit Ernst Cassirer*] [1981]) understood that 'Ernst's relation to Goethe stood on a completely different basis from his relation to the other great names with which his work connected him' (*daß Ernstens Verhältnis zu Goethe auf einer ganz anderen Grundlage beruhte als sein Verhältnis zu den anderen großen Erscheinungen, mit denen seine Arbeit ihn verband*).[8] In fact, she goes so far as to say that 'I came to know Goethe through Ernst, and Ernst through Goethe' (*Ich habe Goethe durch Ernst und Ernst durch Goethe verstehen gelernt*).[9] Beyond the anecdotal, however, substantial principles link Cassirer's corpus to Goethe's, as Toni Cassirer explains:

> Cassirer's view of history; his feeling for nature; his increasingly noticeable efforts to widen his field of interest, to extend his knowledge to almost all fields, in order to be secure in his judgement and to avoid one-sidedness, to keep it pure from the influences of personal experiences and at a distance from the events of the moment — all this points to Goethe. His firm belief in the value of the human personality, his desire for structure and harmony, his rejection of violent destructiveness, be it of one's own self or of the world around one, his dislike of all slogans (political, religious, or of a world view) — in short, everything that constitutes the essence of being points in the same direction.

> [{Cassirers} Geschichtsauffassung; sein Naturgefühl; sein immer stärker hervortretendes Bestreben, sein Blickfeld zu erweitern, seine Kenntnisse auf fast alle Gebiete zu erstrecken, um sein Urteil zu sichern und vor Einseitigkeit zu schützen, es rein zu halten von Einflüssen persönlicher Erfahrungen, es zu distanzieren von den augenblicklichen Zeitgeschehnissen — dies alles weist auf Goethe hin. Sein fester Glaube an den Wert der menschlichen Persönlichkeit, die Sehnsucht nach Formung und Harmonie, die Abwehr gegen gewalttätige Zerstörung — sei es des eigenen Ichs oder der Umwelt —, sein Abscheu vor weltanschaulichen, politischen oder religiösen Schlagworten — kurzum alles, was die Quintessenz seines Wesens bildet, weist denselben Weg.][10]

Given which, the call made at the end of the nineteenth century by Friedrich Theodor Vischer,[11] renewed by Friedrich Meinecke in the aftermath of the Second World War,[12] that Sunday morning church services be replaced by an hour spent reading Goethe or other classical German authors, appears less strange than at a first glance it might.[13]

The remaining papers in this section examine two themes that arise from the eighteenth century, and explore the relation the life of the mind to the demands of society. In his paper, Karl Leydecker discusses the question of divorce as it appears in literary texts, not just German (Goethe's *Elective Affinities* or *Die Wahlverwandtschaften* of 1809 being a notable example), but in French and English literature, too. In so doing, Leydecker investigates how literature reflects social reality, while at the same time helping to shape the consciousness of a particular age, just as for Cassirer (as we have seen) the function of the symbolic forms lies in 'an entirely determinate formation, not exactly *of* the world, but rather making for the world' (*eine ganz bestimmte Gestaltung nicht sowohl der Welt, als vielmehr eine Gestaltung zur Welt*).

Now if his relationships to women constituted a significant influence on the personal and artistic development of Goethe,[14] in a way that has been given a psychoanalytic twist in the recent biography of Goethe by Nicholas Boyle,[15] so women played a formative role in the life and thought of a figure who, almost as insistently as Cassirer, makes reference to Goethe — Friedrich Nietzsche.[16] In her paper on Nietzsche's 'eccentricity', Barbara Naumann shows, using a word whose very etymology (*ek* + *kentron*, *kentron* meaning a peg or stationary point of a pair of compasses) is implicitly deconstructive, how Nietzsche's thought has eminently pragmatic (political, stylistic) implications. To put it another way, she demonstrates how that notoriously misunderstood Nietzschean concept, the *Übermensch*, stands in precisely the relationship to beauty and joy as the French philosopher Michel Onfray has recently explained:

> The *Übermensch* is a designation for the individual who knows the tragic nature of reality, because he has understood the mechanism of the eternal return of things under the sign of the same; as a consequence, liberated about the question of free will which he knows to be an illusion, he understands that there is no other solution than to consent to this tragic situation, to love it; from now on, he attains joy . . .

> [Le surhomme désigne l'individu qui sait la nature tragique du réel, parce qu'il a compris le mécanisme de l'éternel retour des choses sous le signe du même; en conséquence, affranchi sur la question du libre arbitre qu;il sait être une illusion, il comprend qu'il n'y a pas d'autre solution que de consentir à ce tragique, de l'aimer; dès lors, il accède à la joie . . .][17]

The second section gathers together papers that deal with aspects of twentieth-century thought and culture reflecting the persistence of the eighteenth-century classical outlook, with particular reference to the thought of Ernst Cassirer.

In *Memories, Dreams, Reflections* (*Erinnerungen, Träume, Gedanken*) (1961), — a work which, subsequent to the recent publication of his famous *Red Book*, has acquired fresh credibility — the analytical psychologist C. G. Jung summarized what he had gained from his lifelong engagement with Goethe's *Faust*: 'Respect for the eternal rights of man, recognition of "the ancient", and the continuity of culture and intellectual history' (*die Respektierung der ewigen Menschenrechte, die Anerkennung des Alten und die Kontinuität der Kultur und der Geistesgeschichte*).[18] This remark serves well to demonstrate the common ground between Cassirer and Jung, but the contribution prepared for this volume by its editor builds on previous work to argue for an even more extensive set of affinities between these two seminal thinkers of the twentieth century, and specifically in respect of their understanding of mythology, imagination, and the symbol.

Next, John Michael Krois examines Cassirer's concept of symbolism in relation to the notion of the 'basic phenomenon' or *Basisphämomen*, illuminating this difficult part of Cassirer's thought with reference to the ethical import of Cassirer's thinking. With rare exceptions, such as Bertrand Vergely's short but significant study, *Cassirer: La Politique du juste* (1998), this aspect of Cassirer's work tends to go unnoticed; yet, in his notes for the fourth volume of his *Philosophie der symbolischen Formen*, Cassirer points out that the call of the Delphic oracle, *gnothi seauton*, is really a call to action:

> Know your *work* and know 'yourself' *in* your work; know what you do, so you can do what you know. Give shape to what you do; give it form by starting from mere instinct, from tradition, from convention, from routine, from {experience} and {habituation} in order to arrive at 'self-conscious' action — a work in which you recognize yourself as the sole creator and actor.

> [Erkenne Dein Werk und erkenne 'dich selbst' *in* Dein Werk; *wisse*, was Du tust, damit du *tun* kannst, was Du weisst. *Gestalte* Dein Tun, bilde es aus dem blossen *Instinkt*, der Tradition, Konvention, der Routine, der *empeiria* and *tribē* um zum 'selbstbewussten' Tun — zu einem Werk, in den Du *Dich*, als seinen Schöpfer und Täter erkennst.][19]

In her contribution, Birgit Recki takes a close look at the cultural pessimism that regards technology as a disaster, arguing instead that the philosophy of symbolic forms provides a theoretical framework to understand how *homo symbolicus* is above all a tool-using animal. She uses Freud's wonderfully ironic comments on technology in his major work of *Kulturkritik*, *Civilization and its Discontents* (*Das Unbehagen in der Kultur*) (1930), to open up a discussion about the role of technology and its uses, rather than its abuses.

Finally, Isabella Woldt reminds us of the extent to which Cassirer's project of a philosophy of symbolic forms was part of a larger effort, undertaken by the members of the Kulturwissenschaftliche Bibliothek Warburg (or KBW) in Hamburg, and later the Warburg Institute in London, to explore the human endeavour to construct a cultural world through symbols. In particular, she discusses the eludication of 'symbolic world construction' offered by Aby Warburg's *Mnemosyne Atlas*, including his investigation of the archetypal images in Ovid's *Metamorphoses*. Her paper, like the preceding ones, underlines the point made by another inheritor of the literary tradition of German classicism, Thomas Mann — in his letter of Klaus Mann of 22 July 1939 — 'But in the end, to inherit something one has to understand it; inheritance is, after all, culture' (*Aber schließlich, zu erben muß man auch verstehen, erben, das ist am Ende Kultur*).[20]

Notes

[1] Friedrich Nietzsche, *The Gay Science*, ed. and trans. by Walter Kaufmann (New York: Vintage, 1974), p. 168; *Werke in drei Bänden*, ed. by Karl Schlechta (Munich: Hanser, 1966), vol. 2, p. 115.

[2] Ernst Cassirer, *The Philosophy of Symbolic Forms*, vol. 1, *Language*, trans. by Ralph Manheim (New Haven and London: Yale University Press, 1955), pp. 79–80; *Philosophie der symbolischen Formen*, vol. 1, *Die Sprache* [*Gesammelte Werke: Hamburger Ausgabe*, vol. 11] (Hamburg: Meiner, 2001), p. 9.

[3] Lessing, *Eine Duplik*, translated in Friedrich Nietzsche, *Basic Writings*, ed. and trans. by Walter Kaufmann (New York: Modern Library, 1968), p. 95; Lessing, *Sämtliche Schriften*, ed. by Karl Lachmann, 3rd edn, ed. by Franz Muncker, 23 vols (Stuttgart: Göschen, 1886–1924), vol. 13, p. 24.

[4] *The Birth of Tragedy*, §15, in Nietzsche, *Werke in drei Bänden*, vol. 1, p. 84.

[5] See 'Concerning Human Dignity', in *Fichte: Early Philosophical Writings*, trans. by Daniel Breazeale (Ithaca: Cornell University Press, 1988), pp. 83–86; Fichte, *Sämtliche Werke*, ed. by I. H. Fichte, 8 vols (Berlin: Veit, 1845-1846), vol. 1, pp. 412–16.

[6] Rüdiger Safranksi, *Schiller oder Die Erfindung des Deutschen Idealismus* (Munich and Vienna: Hanser, 2004).

[7] Martin Swales and Erika Swales, *Reading Goethe: A Critical Introduction to the Literary Work* (Rochester, NY, and Woodbridge: Camden House, 2002).

[8] Toni Cassirer, *Mein Leben mit Ernst Cassirer* [1981] (Hamburg: Meiner, 2003), pp. 87–88.

[9] Cassirer, *Mein Leben mit Ernst Cassirer*, p. 88.

[10] Cassirer, *Mein Leben mit Ernst Cassirer*, p. 88.

[11] Friedrich Theodor Vischer, 'Über allerhand Verlegenheiten bei Besetzung einer dogmatischen Lehrstelle in der jetzigen Zeit' (first published in the *Hallischen Jahrbüchern für deutsche Wissenschaft und Kunst*, 4 (1841), 257–627), in *Kritische Gänge*, vol. 1 (Tübingen: Fues, 1844), pp. 131–59.

[12] Friedrich Meinecke, *Die deutsche Katastrophe: Betrachtungen und Erinnerungen* (Wiesbaden: Brockhaus, 1946), S. 173–77.

[13] See Robert Herzstein, 'The Phenomenology of Freedom in the German Philosophical Tradition: Kantian Origins', *The Journal of Value Inquiry*, vol. 1, no. 1 (March 1967), 47–63.

[14] For a survey of Goethe's relations to women, see Astrid Seele, *Frauen um Goethe* (Reinbek bei Hamburg: Rowohlt, 1997).

[15] See Nicholas Boyle, *Goethe: The Poet and the Age*, vol. 2, *Revolution and Renunciation (1790–1803)* (Oxford: Clarendon Press, 2000). Boyle identifies Lili Schönemann as the 'ghost'

who 'all the while in and out of the great events, and the letters and conversations that told of them' was 'threading her way, never seen herself but unexpectedly half-recognized in many women — in Friederike Brun, in Dorothea Stock, in Christiana Vulpius [. . .], in another Christiana too, perhaps, the actress Becker-Neumann who in 1795 was 17, as the ghost had been in 1775, and as for Goethe she would always remain, the image of a promise unfulfilled' (p. 418). Recently, it has been argued that our view of Goethe's relation to Charlotte von Stein requires urgent revision, on the basis Goethe was in fact in love with Duchess Anna Amalia, mother of the prince of Sachsen-Weimar-Eisenach and Goethe's friend, Carl August (see Ettore Ghibellino, *J.W. Goethe und Anna Amalia: Eine verbotene Liebe* [Weimar: Denkena Verlag, 2003; 2nd edn, 2004]).

[16] For a survey of these relations, see Mario Leis, *Frauen um Nietzsche* (Reinbek bei Hamburg: Rowohlt, 2000). For a recent discussion of Nietzsche's indebtedness to Goethe, see the section entitled 'Goethe et Nietzsche' in a monograph by the distinguished (and recently deceased) French intellectual historian Pierre Hadot, in *N'oublie pas de vivre: Goethe et la tradition des exercices spirituels* (Paris: Albin Michel, 2008), pp. 256–67.

[17] Michel Onfray, *Le Crépuscule d'un idole: L'affabulation freudienne* (Paris: Grasset, 2010), p. 542.

[18] C. G. Jung, *Memories, Dreams, Reflections of C.G. Jung*, ed. by Aniela Jaffé (London: Collins/Routledge & Kegan Paul, 1963), p. 262; *Erinnerungen, Träume, Gedanken von C.G. Jung* (Olten und Freiburg im Breisgau: Walter, 1971), p. 239.

[19] Ernst Cassirer, 'On Basis Phenomena', in *The Philosophy of Symbolic Forms*, vol. 4, *The Metaphysics of Symbolic Forms*, ed. by John Michael Krois and Donald P. Verene, trans. by John Michael Krois (New Haven: Yale University Press, 1996), p. 186; 'Über Basisphänomene' (*c.* 1940), in *Zur Metaphysik der symbolischen Formen* [*Nachgelassene Manuskripte und Texte*, vol. 1], ed. by John Michael Krois *et al.* (Hamburg: Felix Meiner, 1995), p. 190. Thus Cassirer remains true to the totality of the original injunction inscribed above the temple of the oracle at Delphi: 'Know thyself — and thou shalt know all the mysteries of the gods and of the universe'.

[20] Thomas Mann, *Briefe, 1889–1955*, ed. by Erika Mann, 3 vols (Frankfurt am Main: Fischer, 1961–1965), vol. 2, p. 107.

R. H. STEPHENSON — AN APPRECIATION

Man ist nur vielseitig, wenn man zum Höchsten strebt, weil man muß (im Ernst),
und zum Geringern herabsteigt, wenn man will (zum Spaß).[1]

As anyone who has ever met Roger Stephenson will know, his roots lie in Liverpool, and he has never been slow to extol the spirit of his hometown, which he equates with that 'felt-thought' (*Gehalt*) that, according to Goethe and Schiller, animates all living culture with *joie de vivre*. After all, in one of his 'big dreams', Jung dreamed that he was in Liverpool, and he interpreted the name of the city as meaning it represented 'the pool of life';[2] and, even today, a ready wit and a good heart are what Scousers pride themselves on.[3] So perhaps it is no surprise that the high value placed by Liverpudlians on fusing tradition with innovation forms one of the characteristics of Roger Stephenson's work.

As an undergraduate at University College London he experienced two great encounters that shaped his life. The one was with Goethe, on his year abroad in the Saarland, 1966–1967, when he read the authors of the great German tradition — Thomas Mann, Kafka, Heine, Schopenhauer, Nietzsche, Schiller, and the Romantic poets, but pre-eminently Goethe. The other encounter was with Elizabeth M. Wilkinson — or 'the perfect teacher', as he describes her in the memoir he wrote for the British Academy.[4] Under her, he studied for a PhD on a topic close to his heart and mind, one he chose for himself: an investigation into what André Gide described as Goethe's *banalité supérieure*. As it turned out, the thesis proved to be both an historical and an analytic study,[5] and this deft combination of historical and theoretical breadth with meticulous close-reading has remained a hallmark of his work.

Similarly, the complex distinctions between rhetoric and poetry, and between poetry and aesthetic discourse (*schöner Vortrag*), that he found at work in Goethe and Schiller, have also served him as key analytical tools. Most Germanist colleagues are probably familiar with Roger Stephenson's work as a Goethe scholar: on the *Maximen und Reflexionen*, on the *Sprüche*, on the *weltanschauliche Gedichte*; indeed, on Goethe's 'Wisdom Literature', as he called it in his 1983 book of that name. At the same time, he has also written and lectured on many other authors and many other topics: on the Schlegels and Novalis, on Jean Paul and Kleist, on Kafka and Keller, even on La Rochefoucauld and Stendhal. His work has been valued well beyond the confines of *Germanistik*, so that he has been hailed, for instance, as one of the founding fathers of the new discipline of *Aphoristik*;[6] equally, his publications on the cultural significance of Goethe's science have attracted the attention of scientists and historians of ideas alike;[7] and, by the same token, his most recent work on the cultural theory of Weimar classicism in the light of Ernst Cassirer's theory of symbolism led to invitations to talk on the topic from Sheffield to Zurich, from London to Amsterdam and Yale, and many other centres of cultural study.[8] His promotion to a Titular Professorship in German in 1994, to an Appointed Chair of German Language and Literature a year later, and his translation to the William Jacks Chair of Modern Languages ('with particular reference to the Language and Literature of Germany') in 1998, were fitting recognition by Glasgow of this international reputation.

After his appointment as Junior Lecturer at the University of Glasgow in 1972, Scotland became Roger Stephenson's academic base, and one towards which he always felt a strong sense of loyalty, indeed gratitude. If during his career he has often left Glasgow to undertake teaching and research abroad (as, for example, as Fellow of the Society for the Humanities in Cornell in 1979, or to undertake a British-Council-sponsored Italian lecture tour in 1997; or as Visiting Professor at Zurich [2005] and Hamburg [2007]), his commitment to his friends and colleagues — and, especially, his students — at Glasgow has been matched only by his loyalty to what he sees as the liberating, truly empowering, effect of German *Bildung*. For, despite his openness to new ideas (encountering the work of Jacques Derrida in Yale in the early 1980s; or his enthusiasm for making explicit what is inevitably implicit in all foreign-language study, namely the intercultural dimension of its work),[9] Roger Stephenson remains convinced of the power of Weimar classicism to illuminate the historico-cultural context of our contemporary world.

This clear (and, as such, controversial) vision of what education (and scholarship) can, and should, be has shaped his whole career. His two terms as Head of Department at Glasgow (1990–1993; 1993–1997), like his (inaugural) tenure of the Headship of its School of Modern Languages and Cultures (2000–2003) were undertaken, albeit with a certain reluctance, primarily in order to place scholarly research at the very centre of academic activity, influencing directly both teaching and administration. The progress made in these areas during his tenure is perhaps most apparent in the history of Glasgow University's Centre for Intercultural Studies, which he founded in 1992. During his sixteen years as Director, the Centre held regular guest lectures during the academic year and a biannual international conference, in addition to the University's Annual Ernst Cassirer Lecture in Intercultural Relations, an initiative he launched in 2000. Much of the work produced in the Centre has appeared in print, for example, in the yearbook he co-founded and co-edited from 2000, *Cultural Studies and the Symbolic* (and the final issue of which is in the reader's hands). This work in the Department and the Centre culminated in the award by the AHRC in 2002 of a Large Research Grant (at the time, the largest awarded to a German unit), completed in 2007, and this study of Ernst Cassirer's theory of culture succeeded in its ambition of bringing to the attention of Germanist and non-Germanist scholars at home and abroad (in particular, in German-speaking Europe) the relevance, historical and contemporary, of Goethe's and Schiller's own cultural theory.

In the preface to his first book, Roger Stephenson spelt out the methodological principles that, though modified and developed over the years, have ever since guided his scholarly activity. Taking as his cue the methodological tenet of what Goethe (in his essay of 1798, *Erfahrung und Wissenschaft*) called 'self-rectifying common sense',[10] he drew 'on common intuitions concerning the nature of language, thought, and human action unless there is evidence — as opposed to mere opinion — to the contrary':

> Because I wish to enable the reader to follow critically [my] method of research and not simply inform [her/him] of its results, my argument has [. . .] the form of a successive interplay of historical evidence and (provisional) theorising. Historical evidence is first adduced as a test of the currently held theory, which is found to be inadequate; on the basis of this evidence possible hypotheses are constructed which, in turn, are disconfirmed by further evidence — until a theory emerges, that [. . .] is corroborated by all the historical evidence adduced. This theory, being the most probable available, is then tested (and further corroborated) by a close analysis of the texts.[11]

This volume includes a full bibliographical list of Roger Stephenson's publications, arranged in *reverse* chronological order to highlight his intellectual development, and illustrative of the depth and breadth of his conception of scholarly interests; as well as a list of papers given, not only as an indicator of the range of his academic activities, but more importantly as a reminder of how, as writer and public lecturer alike, his aim is always to persuade his audience of the life-enhancing — indeed, life-changing — power of aesthetic phenomena, once set in their proper historical (but not historicist) context. A poem (say, Goethe's 'Selige Sehnsucht'), he would tell generations of students — and anyone else who would listen — is 'like a tiny nuclear device: once set off by aesthetic perception, its power to resonate in, and shape, one's heart-and-mind is incalculable, and ever-lasting'. Roger Stephenson's work and career thus offers a testimony to his sense of personal debt to the rigours and delights of aesthetic education.

Notes

[1] *Maximen und Reflexionen*, ed. by Max Hecker, no. 1096; Goethe, *Werke* [Hamburger Ausgabe], ed. by Erich Trunz, 14 vols (Munich: Beck, 1982), vol. 13, p. 502.

[2] C. G. Jung, *Memories, Dreams, Reflections*, ed. by Aniela Jaffé (London: Collins; Routledge and Kegan Paul, 1963), p. 224.

[3] Compare with Christopher Hart's response, on visiting Liverpool in 2008 during its Year as European City of Culture: 'All that sentimental guff about Liverpool being somehow "special", and having "a great heart" and "the people" — my God, I was beginning to

think — it's all true' (*The Sunday Times*, 8 June 2008). See, too, 'Pool Party' by Jan Morris, *The Times*, 13 June 2008; and the entry on Liverpool in the fifteenth edition of the *Encyclopaedia Britannica*, where the people of that city are described as unlike any other in the United Kingdom, in evincing 'a unique blend of cosmopolitanism and parochialism' (pp. 1275–79 [p. 1275]).

[4] R. H. Stephenson, 'Elizabeth Mary Wilkinson, 1909–2001', *Proceedings of the British Academy*, 120 (2003), 471–89 (p. 483).

[5] 'Goethe's Transmutation of Commonplaces: an Historical and Rhetorico-Stylistic Inquiry into the Nature, Causes and Effects of his *Maximen und Reflexionen*', PhD thesis (University of London, February 1977).

[6] See his 'Goethe's Prose Style', *Publications of the English Goethe Society*, NS 66 (1997), 33–42.

[7] '"Binary Synthesis": Goethe's Aesthetic Intuition in Literature and Science', *Science in Context*, 18 (2005), 553–81.

[8] See '"Eine zarte Differenz": Cassirer and Goethe on the Symbol', in Cyrus Hamlin and John Michael Krois (eds), *Symbolic Forms and Cultural Studies* (New Haven: Yale University Press, 2004), pp. 157–84.

[9] 'The Proper Object of Cultural Study: Ernst Cassirer and the Aesthetic Theory of Weimar Classicism', in Paul Bishop and R. H. Stephenson (eds), *Cultural Studies and the Symbolic*, vol. 1 (Leeds: Northern Universities Press, 2003), pp. 82–114.

[10] Goethe, *Werke* [Hamburger Ausgabe], ed. by Erich Trunz, 14 vols (Munich: Beck, 1982), vol. 13, p. 25.

[11] *Goethe's Wisdom Literature: A Study in Aesthetic Transmutation* (Berne: Peter Lang, 1983), pp. 11 and 23. For more recent elaborations of this methodological doctrine, see Paul Bishop and R. H. Stephenson, *Friedrich Nietzsche and Weimar Classicism* (Rochester, NY: Camden House, 2005), pp. 183–84.

ON LESSING'S LIFE AND WORKS: BIOGRAPHICAL REFLECTIONS

By H. B. NISBET

Since the middle of the twentieth century, the need for a new and comprehensive biography of Lessing has repeatedly been voiced. I have attempted to fill this gap.[1] It is of course impossible, in the space of a short essay, to describe this work in detail. Instead, I shall try to highlight a few basic tendencies in Lessing's life and works which help to define his unique identity and confer a certain unity on his biography.

Lessing's career is not one of steady upward progress. The only ambition he admits to in his early years — his wish to become 'a German Molière'[2] — was fulfilled at the latest by 1767 with the publication of *Minna von Barnhelm*. But his repeated attempts to reform German literature came to an end two years later with the failure of the Hamburg National Theatre and the completion of the *Hamburg Dramaturgy*. Around the same time, he had to abandon his long-cherished wish to live as an independent writer, for he was compelled to withdraw, at considerable financial loss, from his plan to publish and market the works of German authors without recourse to the existing commercial network. From this point onwards, a note of disillusion with contemporary literary life and with the German public can be detected in his letters and conversations; he now prefers to occupy himself with the past (for example, with medieval philology and ecclesiastical history) and with the long-term future of humanity (as in the three main works of his final years). In addition, the last decade of his life is marked by recurrent depression and increasing ill health.

For all these reasons, it can scarcely be argued that Lessing ever aimed to shape his life in accordance with a consistent plan or goal-directed ambition. On the contrary, he habitually reacts to current circumstances with little reflection and with no attempt to steer them in a new direction. As he puts it on one occasion when his work and step-children prevent him leaving Wolfenbüttel: 'How often I wish I could all at once return to my old isolated existence; to be nothing, to wish for nothing but what the present moment brings with it.'[3] This tendency is reinforced by a firm conviction that life is determined above all by imponderables rather than by conscious intentions. As his brother reports, 'he never gave [...] good advice either, because much, indeed almost everything, depends on contingency, which cannot be predicted even approximately, and people have to take risks';[4] or in Lessing's own words: 'Don't we often have to act thoughtlessly if we want to make fortune do something for us?'[5] The same attitude is apparent in his scholarly activities. As his brother puts it:

> In his studies, he never gave precedence to any one discipline by reflection and choice, but saw them all as equally important and therefore relied entirely on chance and momentary impressions.[6]

For the same reason, he indulged assiduously in games of chance and lotteries in the second half of his life — despite the repeated discovery that they merely aggravated his chronic financial difficulties.

Lessing's dislike of firm plans for the future derives from a character trait which is evident from early in his life but becomes increasingly conspicuous in his later years, namely the need for change. He suffered greatly from boredom, as Friedrich Jacobi noticed:

> Lessing could not reconcile himself to the idea of a personal and absolutely infinite being in the unchanging enjoyment of its supreme perfection. He associated this idea with such an impression of *infinite boredom* that he felt pain and anxiety at the very thought of it.[7]

Thus he likewise replied, when an acquaintance welcomed the appearance of the green leaves in springtime: 'Oh, it has turned green so often before; I'd rather it turned red for a change.'[8] Even the awareness that he had grown fond of a particular place could make him wish to abandon it: as he said himself, 'it's no use staying for long in a place we find congenial'.[9] Thus someone who knew him well could tell him in his later years: 'Now I wish you a happy life — that is, a restless life. For restlessness is surely your element.'[10] There seems to be some kind of physiological need at work here. In Lessing's case, it generates a vital rhythm of constant alternation between permanence and change; for when he can no longer tolerate 'the same old monotony'[11] of a given situation, a compulsive urge to escape takes over, and if escape is impossible — as it often was in Wolfenbüttel — he relapses into depression.

This rhythm of conflicting impulses is scarcely compatible with that model of organic personal development that underlies the German *Bildungsroman* and numerous German biographies of the nineteenth and early twentieth centuries. But, in my view, the form of a biography should not in any case be determined by any literary model, but by the distinctive dynamics of the particular life depicted. Thus Lessing had no use for the ideal of *Bildung* in the sense of a self-contained and fully developed personality of the kind envisaged by Winckelmann and nearly all the leading figures of the classical age in Germany, including Wieland, Herder, Goethe, Schiller, and Wilhelm von Humboldt. Instead, he became increasingly convinced that the meaning of life is not to be found in some conclusive achievement or personal fulfilment, but in the ongoing process of activity itself. That this process, in which chance plays a dominant part, has an ultimate sense and continuity is guaranteed for Lessing by the presence of a guiding providence which directs everything for the best, a providence whose agency can, however, only be comprehended — if at all — with the benefit of hindsight. He clung to this belief throughout his life, despite his repeated experience that providence very rarely seemed to favour him.

Lessing's restless, impulsive nature also had negative consequences for both himself and his friends. Already in his schooldays his teachers noted 'that he sometimes has to be curbed if he is not to fritter away his energies'.[12] He was still inclined to dissipate his energies in later years: numerous projects were never completed and, even after printing had begun, he abruptly abandoned them on several occasions. His friends were sorely tried by his unannounced departures, missed deadlines, sudden changes of mind and fitful correspondence; Moses Mendelssohn declared 'that Lessing's *quite definitely* is scarcely worth as much as anyone else's *perhaps*'.[13] The fact that his friends continued to stick by him is testimony to his great personal charisma, not least in the eyes of women.

But Lessing's volatile nature had not only negative consequences. It is also responsible for the extraordinary variety of his interests, which bears comparison with that of Diderot, Voltaire, and Rousseau. It also accounts for the openness and versatility of his thought, for his distrust of dogmatic systems and his readiness to identify himself — if only provisionally — with the most unconventional and even heretical opinions. I shall shortly come back to the many unresolved contradictions to which this attitude gives rise in his writings. But I must first say something about the relationship between his life and his works.

★ ★ ★

Unlike Goethe's, Lessing's works are not 'fragments of a great confession'. His dramas do, admittedly, contain much criticism of contemporary affairs and many allusions to specific issues and personalities, by no means all of which have so far been identified. But there are also occasions on which tensions in his personal life are unexpectedly reflected in his works. One hitherto overlooked example may illustrate this point.

I have tried to show elsewhere how deeply the young Lessing was affected by the scandalous fate of his close friend and relative, Christlob Mylius.[14] In the year 1753, this erstwhile Bohemian and hack journalist, who had meanwhile gained some reputation as a scientist, managed to collect enough money, under the patronage of Albrecht von Haller, to undertake a voyage of exploration to America. But instead of proceeding directly to America, Mylius set off on a leisurely journey through North Germany, Holland, and England, enjoying to the full his new status as world traveller, until he had spent almost his entire allowance for two years in the space of one. Gravely ill and deeply in debt, he finally died in London after sending desperate pleas for more money to his sponsor Haller, who was already taking steps to denounce him as a swindler.

Soon after Mylius's death, Lessing dedicated to his memory an extensive selection of Mylius's publications with a preface consisting of six supposed letters to a mutual friend. Lessing's reactions in this preface are extraordinarily inconsistent: torn between grief and anger, sympathy and disapproval, he seems at one moment to excuse his friend as a victim of inadequate support and at another to unmask him as a rogue. On the one hand, he quotes in the opening letter the following lines from a (now lost) panegyric he had dedicated to his friend shortly before his departure: 'Whither, whither, with bloodied spurs / Does thirst for knowledge [*Wißbegier*] drive you, her hero, on?'[15] On the other hand, in the last of the six letters, which bears the date 20 June 1754, he draws attention to an early essay in which Mylius had made the satirical proposal that people with more money than sense might be persuaded to invest in world travels by 'knights errant, Don Quixotes and daredevils', who might — or might not — make discoveries of scientific value (LM, VI, 406–08). Lessing reprints this essay, prefaced by a vignette of a horned devil.[16]

We know that, in the mid-1750s, Lessing planned a drama on the Faust theme, and it is generally assumed that he attended a performance of the popular Faust play by Franz Schuch's company in Berlin on 14 June 1754[17] — that is, only six days before the date of the last letter in his preface to Mylius's works. And, in the first surviving draft of his own Faust-drama, he expressly names 'thirst for knowledge' (*Wißbegierde*) as the quality through which the devils plan to lead Faust astray (LM, III, 390). Two years later, Lessing set off with the Leipzig merchant Winckler on a journey to England, and although the journey was terminated in Amsterdam when the Seven Years War broke out, the itinerary it followed (as planned by Lessing) followed precisely the same circuitous route which Mylius had taken three years before.[18] It therefore seems that Lessing's tacit aim was to discover more about Mylius's fateful journey and to make his peace with his late friend's memory. It is also worth noting that he said of his Faust plan before his departure: 'I'm saving my work on the most terrible scenes for England [. . .], the home of *brooding despair*.'[19]

There is no need here to discuss the further development of Lessing's Faust plan in detail. It is enough to note that, in the 1770s, the planned drama ceased altogether to be a tragedy, for it was to be revealed at the end that the entire action was only a dream of the real Faust (LM, III, 389). In short, the contradiction between Faust's praiseworthy thirst for knowledge and his self-incurred destruction is not resolved, but simply eliminated — just as Lessing had not succeeded in explaining satisfactorily his old friend's transformation from a respected scientist into a self-destroying reprobate. The far-reaching consequences for German literature of Lessing's optimistic reinterpretation of the Faust legend are too well known to require further comment.

Other unresolved tensions in Lessing's inward life, which he rarely refers to explicitly, have left only occasional traces in his writings. They can, however, sometimes be inferred from his actions and casual remarks. Two such cases, both of which had decisive consequences for his future career, may serve as examples.

Early in 1775, Lessing received a letter from his fiancée Eva König, to whom he had not written for nine months, in which she informed him that, after almost three years of absence in Vienna, she was at last in a position to return to Brunswick and her home in Hamburg.[20] She now planned to revisit Lessing at the same time of year at which she had left him three years before, namely in the second half of February. Although Lessing replied that she should tell him when she expected to arrive in Brunswick,[21] he suddenly left for Leipzig in the middle of February without waiting for her answer. He went to Leipzig to visit the widowed Ernestine Reiske,[22] who — as he was fully aware — was passionately in love with him. After a week in Leipzig, he proceeded to Berlin; but Ernestine's ecstatic reaction leaves no doubt that Lessing had told her nothing about his engagement to Eva, and that she confidently hoped he would marry her.[23] Only the fortuitous circumstance that Eva had meanwhile fallen ill prevented her from arriving in Wolfenbüttel during Lessing's absence. Sensitive as she was, she had rightly concluded from his long silence and somewhat offhand letter that something was amiss. It would seem that the honest, anxious tone of her reply,[24] which contrasted favourably with Ernestine's unrestrained emotionality, released Lessing just in time from his uncertainty.

A similar ambivalence can be detected in Lessing's reactions to his journey to Italy. On the one hand, he constantly complains in his letters to Eva of heat, illness, and oppressive court ceremonial. Typical examples are his comment 'in truth, I myself have neither much pleasure nor utility from this journey',[25] or again, 'I heartily long to be back in Germany'.[26] But both before and after the time of these remarks, he writes much more positively of his Italian experiences to others. Already from Milan he writes to his brother: 'This foretaste [. . .] has completely revived my old idea of living and dying in Italy.'[27] On his return journey in Vienna, he told an acquaintance 'that Italy and especially Rome had appealed to him so extraordinarily that he

would probably undertake a second and longer trip there'.[28] And Maler
Müller, who moved to Italy soon after this time, later reported that Lessing,
who was meanwhile happily married, had 'most solemnly' assured him 'that
he would certainly conclude the last phase of his life with me, either in
Italy or elsewhere'.[29] In this instance, the tension between two incompatible
wishes on Lessing's part was not resolved, but overruled by external
circumstances.

★　★　★

I should like at this point to come back to those contradictions which are
so often encountered in Lessing's thought — for example, between the aesthetics of imitation in *Laokoon* and the aesthetics of effect in the *Hamburg
Dramaturgy*, between the affective ethics of his theory of tragedy and the
rationalistic ethics of *The Education of the Human Race*, or between his positive
treatment of Lutheran orthodoxy in the early 1770s and his simultaneous
preparations to publish Reimarus's attack on the Bible. In particular, I wish
to draw attention to the measures he took in the 1770s to justify such
contradictions and lend them epistemological legitimacy.

Already in his schooldays and as a student, Lessing familiarized himself with
the rationalism of Christian Wolff, but without subscribing to Wolff's system
as a whole. He was equally attracted to more open modes of thinking such as
the eclectic philosophy of Thomasius and others which survived alongside
rationalism in the early Enlightenment, and the scepticism of Pierre Bayle.
His own provisional lifestyle inclined him in any case to regard all truths as
provisional — that is, as relative. But in his early Wolfenbüttel years, he began
to seek theoretical justification for this belief in both philosophy and
theology. Thus he noted in his commonplace book (*Kollektaneenbuch*), with
apparent approval, a principle of Talmudic scholarship according to which
mutually incompatible interpretations of one and the same passage of
Scripture may be regarded as equally true, provided they do not contradict
any truths which are already established (LM, xv, 353–54). And around the
same time, he praises Leibniz's perspectivism in the following terms:

> In his investigation of truth, Leibniz never paid any heed to accepted opinion;
> but in the firm conviction that no opinion could be accepted unless it were true
> from a certain angle and in a certain sense, he was often considerate enough to
> turn and twist this opinion around until he succeeded in making that certain
> angle visible and that certain sense intelligible. (LM, xi, 470)

But the opposite is also the case: in the theological conflicts five years later,
it becomes clear to him that there is no infallible hermeneutics, no unchal-
lengeable method of establishing the truth of the biblical accounts, because

only a few passages in the entire New Testament give rise to the same concepts for everyone [. . .]. Which are the right concepts to which they *should* give rise? Who is to decide this? Hermeneutics? Everyone has his own hermeneutics. Which of them is true? Are they all true? Or is none of them true? And this thing, this wretched, irksome thing, is to be the test of inner truth? Then what would be its *own* test? (LM, XIII, 130–31)

It is clear from this and other similar statements that, by the 1770s, many principles of rationalism had lost their credibility not only for Kant, but also for Lessing. As Lessing's friend, Kästner, reports in a letter to Kant on his conversations with Lessing in 1777:

> In our conversations on current philosophy, he expressed the hope that things would soon have to change, because it had become so shallow that its shallowness could no longer sustain itself, even with people who did not wish to give the matter much thought.[30]

Likewise in theology, Lessing seems to have felt in his last years that he stood on the threshold of a new age. For example, he took seriously Girolamo Cardano's sixteenth-century prophecy that a significant change in Christianity was due to take place around 1800 (LM, XVI, 397–98; cf. LM, XV, 177–78). Maler Müller, whom Lessing had visited in 1777, later recalled a conversation on this topic:

> Lessing maintained that the present state of Christianity could not last for another half century, and that it was more sensible to demolish so rotten an edifice so that it would not cause as much damage as if it were left to collapse.[31]

In this connection, Lessing thought he was fully justified in publishing Reimarus's attack on Christianity. In short, both in philosophy and theology, he foresaw major developments in his later years and did his best to help them along. He applied his own vital impulses to his thought and found it preferable to accept inconsistencies, or even self-contradiction, rather than do anything that might impede the uninterrupted progress of the debate. He accordingly assembled a whole arsenal of rhetorical and poetic devices to call his own pronouncements into question as soon as they were uttered, declaring, for example, that the doctrine of a single God 'is both present and not present in the books of the Old Testament' (LM, XIII, 419), or that the books of the New Testament 'have illuminated human understanding [. . .] more than any other books, if only through the light which human understanding itself brought to bear on them' (LM, XIII, 429), or (quoting Augustine) that everything contained in *The Education of the Human Race* is 'in a certain respect true for the same reasons that it is in a certain respect false' (LM, XIII, 413). For similar reasons, it is also the case (as Wolfgang Kröger has shown) that Lessing's replies to his opponents in the quarrel over Reimarus's *Fragments* should not be interpreted as dogmatic assertions or personal confessions of faith: even his famous words on 'the broad and ugly ditch' which he cannot get across are designed rather to draw the consequences of his opponent Schumann's historically based faith than to express genuine spiritual agonizing on Lessing's part.[32]

In view of Lessing's ambiguous, often ironic and evasive replies to his critics, it is no wonder that his chief opponent Goeze demanded more than once that Lessing state 'his complete profession of faith' and explain with no excuses 'what kind of religion he himself recognises and accepts as true'.[33] It seems to be taken for granted in Lessing scholarship that Lessing never answered this question[34] — not least because he expressly declared in a letter to Elise Reimarus that he wished to avoid answering it.[35] But, even if he did not answer the question publicly, it can be shown that he did answer it privately. The editors of his works (for example, Franz Muncker and Arno Schilson) date the following fragment from Lessing's *Autobiographical Reflections and Ideas* [*Selbstbetrachtungen und Einfälle*], first published in 1799 by Georg Gustav Fülleborn from no longer surviving manuscripts, to the winter of 1777–78, and link it with Lessing's reply to Schumann (*On the Proof of the Spirit and of Power*).[36] But since the fragment in question expressly presents itself as a personal profession of faith and as the reply to a question from theological quarters, it is virtually certain that it is Lessing's reply of May or June 1778 to Goeze's demand. Here, then, is Lessing's personal declaration, slightly abridged, on his relation to Christianity (note how often he qualifies his statements):

> I believe it and consider it true, as well and as fully as one can believe and consider anything historical to be true. For I am absolutely unable to refute it with regard to the historical evidence on which it is based. I cannot counter the historical testimonies adduced in its favour with other testimonies, whether or not no such testimonies existed or all other testimonies were destroyed or deliberately refuted. [. . .]
>
> I should think that at least those theologians who reduce all Christian faith to what human beings find acceptable and who have no use for any supernatural intervention on the part of the Holy Spirit might be satisfied by this statement. But to reassure those others who still assume such intervention, I may add that I nevertheless consider this opinion of theirs to be more firmly based in Christian doctrine and handed down from the beginning of Christianity, and scarcely open to rebuttal by mere philosophical reasoning. I cannot deny the possibility of direct intervention by the Holy Spirit: and I shall certainly not knowingly do anything that might prevent this possibility from becoming reality.
>
> I must, of course, admit —
> [the fragment breaks off here]

(LM, XVI, 536)

Interpreting this statement — as so often with Lessing's late pronouncements — is like peeling the proverbial onion: it is surrounded by so many reservations that one never reaches a firm and conclusive centre. His aim on this occasion, as with all his attempts to counter dogmatic claims, is above all to avoid the least appearance of trying to persuade others to regard his own principles as anything more than provisional. And that, of course, is why he did not find it expedient to publish this statement.

★　★　★

This brings me to the last main topic of this essay, namely Lessing's positive belief in individual autonomy and in the inalienable right of the individual to self-determination. Already in one of his earliest philosophical utterances, the fragment *The Christianity of Reason*, he defines the fundamental law of human morality as follows: 'Act in accordance with your individual perfections' (LM, xiv, 178). The word 'individual' is particularly significant. For whereas the majority of eighteenth-century philosophers are chiefly concerned with what they describe as 'human nature' or 'man's essential character' — that is, with what is common to all human beings — Lessing is more concerned with what makes people different. He believes that each individual should be in a position to realize his individual aspirations, however modest, unpopular, unconventional, or heretical these may be — provided that they do not detract from the freedom of others to do likewise.

It has often been pointed out that, with this aim in mind, Lessing seeks to promote independent thought (*Selbstdenken*) on the part of his readers. In the century of the Enlightenment, this was, of course, far from unusual, because traditional attitudes were regularly called into question and new ones put forward for discussion. But, in Lessing's later writings, his argumentation becomes progressively refined inasmuch as his own views (as already noted) become increasingly difficult to pin down. Thus in *The Education of the Human Race*, for example, we encounter apparently unequivocal statements (as in paragraph 4) with which we either agree or disagree — only to discover, as we read further and more closely, that they are perhaps not Lessing's views at all, and that other views which he had earlier seemed to reject reappear in a new and apparently plausible form (as in paragraph 77). The effect of this is that the reader is prompted to question not only what he originally thought were Lessing's views, but his own views as well, until he finally concludes that, from different perspectives, some or all of those views which at first sight seemed incompatible might be at least *relatively* true.

In employing this strategy, Lessing's intention is not to sow universal doubt, but simply to prevent his own views, or those he puts up for discussion, hardening into dogmas of the kind on which intolerant and tyrannical groups and individuals have based their claims to authority since time immemorial. On the other hand, he attacks his opponents in the Reimarus controversy — notably Goeze and Ress — not so much because he considers their views as necessarily false, but because those who propound them are intolerant and try to compel others to adopt them. Lessing nevertheless continues to be accused from time to time of believing that the secular rationalism or deism he allegedly upholds is absolutely true, and of seeking to convert others — especially the adherents of revealed religion — to his belief.[37]

One of the best-known ideals of the Enlightenment is that of toleration, a word which is endlessly repeated and promoted by leading thinkers from John Locke's *Letters on Toleration* (1689–92) to Voltaire's *Traité sur la tolérance* (1763). Even Lessing's grandfather Theophilus Lessing had published a treatise in 1669 entitled *De religionum tolerantia*. And whenever toleration is mentioned in connection with the German Enlightenment, Lessing is invariably named as its most influential proponent. I was therefore surprised to discover recently, when I tried to determine the frequency of the word in Lessing's writings, that he seems to have used it only twice. Its first occurrence is in a footnote to his *Vindication of Lemnius* (*Rettung des Lemnius*) of 1753 (although this footnote does not appear in the version published by Lessing himself, but only in the posthumous edition published by his brother in 1784); the footnote simply points out that the sixteenth-century Reformers did not believe in toleration (LM, v, 40 and 45). The second occurrence is in the *Hamburg Dramaturgy*, in which Lessing criticizes the crusaders in Cronegk's tragedy *Olint and Sophronia* as intolerant (LM, IX, 210). In both cases, he is dealing with past ages of history (the Reformation and the Middle Ages) in which toleration was virtually unknown, and, in both cases, his aim is not so much to recommend toleration to his contemporaries as a positive value as to deplore its absence — that is, intolerance — in the past. Similarly, the adjective *tolerant* rarely appears in his writings, and when it does, it serves to emphasize the intolerance of the persons or attitudes he criticizes: for example, it is used by the Templar in *Nathan the Wise* when, in a rage, he condemns Nathan as a 'tolerant windbag' (*toleranten Schwätzer*).[38] To explain these facts, we must remember that in Lessing's day, the word 'tolerance' in religious contexts signified passive sufferance of so-called heretics.[39] For example, in the anonymous extract from Reimarus's clandestine treatise published by Lessing in 1774 under the title *On the Sufferance of Deists* (*Von Duldung der Deisten*), the word *Toleranz* is used several times as a synonym of *Duldung* (LM, XII, 256, 260–61, and 264): in other words, Reimarus does not expect orthodox Lutherans to abandon their belief in the absolute truth of their own dogmatics, but only to cease persecuting deists and other heretics. That, of course, was not enough for Lessing. Far from being incapable (as one theologian has recently claimed) of entertaining a pluralistic conception of tolerance or of recognizing 'a genuinely alien orientation',[40] Lessing repeatedly took the part of outsiders of every description and even took them into his house, as he did with the Jew Alexander Daveson on his release from prison and with the atheistic vagabond Könemann, without describing their views as erroneous or attempting to convert them to beliefs of his own.[41] In his long essay on the Lutheran pastor Adam Neuser who fled from Germany to Turkey as a result of Calvinist persecution and converted to Islam, Lessing likewise passes no negative judgement (LM, XII, 201–54). In short, he never pleads for toleration as understood in his day, because such toleration was in his eyes only a first step towards recognizing the right of every individual to free self-determination. In the same way, he could not bring himself to consign the arch-outsider of European literature, namely Faust, to eternal damnation, nor in the last resort to condemn his unfortunate youthful friend Christlob Mylius.

In recent years, Lessing has also fallen victim at times to postmodernism's sweeping criticisms of the Enlightenment. A typical example is Botho Strauß's acceptance speech on receiving the Lessing Prize of the city of Hamburg in 2001.[42] Of the Enlightenment in general, Strauß declares: 'We have no further need of the Enlightenment. We are enlightened to the point of internal breakdown [*Zerrüttung*].' And of Lessing himself, he says:

> What a sad, unjust fate for someone to survive only as the most politically correct of the German classical writers! One who can never be knocked down from his pedestal, who can never be reworked, reinterpreted, rediscovered or further developed.

In his deeply pessimistic judgement on our times, Strauß also invokes Francis Fukuyama's thesis of the 'end of history', which he claims has replaced the lost optimism of the Enlightenment in the western democracies. But history regularly buries its own undertakers, and it did so once more in this case. It is, in retrospect, highly ironic that, only five days after Strauß's speech was published on 6 September 2001, history again showed that it was far from finished. The western democracies were suddenly confronted with much more serious problems than coming to terms with their own supposedly final state — and these were problems which no one in the history of German literature had dealt with more memorably and constructively than Lessing.

★ ★ ★

To conclude: readers may ask whether I have any new insights to offer on Lessing's major works. There are indeed a number in my biography, but one example must suffice here. Lessing scholars seem hitherto to have overlooked the fact that not just two of his important works — namely *The Jews* and *Nathan the Wise* — contain a reference to Jews in their titles. The same is true of a third. In the 1730s, a Jewish cabbalist came from Eastern Europe to Germany and soon became known, especially in Masonic circles, for his magic arts, alchemy, and conjuration of spirits. His name was Samuel Jacob Falk.[43] Falk led an itinerant life and visited, among others, Count Jörgen Ludwig Albrecht von Rantzau on his estate in Brunswick territory, where he conjured up spirits, discovered hidden treasure, conducted alchemical experiments and caused explosions. When this reached the ears of the Brunswick authorities, Rantzau was ordered to expel him. Soon afterwards, Falk was arrested in Westphalia and narrowly escaped with his life, since sorcery was still a capital offence.[44] He fled to Holland and finally to England, where he again attained prominence in Masonic circles and became known as 'the Ba'al Shem [i.e. Lord of the divine Name] of London';[45] he also established contacts with Swedenborg and Cagliostro. In his later years — he died in 1782 — he was venerated in Masonic circles in Germany as one of the so-called 'unknown superiors' of international Freemasonry, or perhaps as the only one.[46]

It is inconceivable that Lessing and his Masonic friends in Brunswick were unaware of Falk and his reputation, and the title of Lessing's *Ernst and Falk: Dialogues for Freemasons* undoubtedly contains an allusion to the Ba'al Shem of London. But just as the 'true Freemasons' referred to in Lessing's dialogues act on a higher plane than the real contemporary Freemasons with their Templar legend and empty secrets, Lessing's Falk appears as an enlightened counterpart to the real Samuel Jacob Falk with his alchemical experiments and necromancy. With this in mind, Falk's collocutor, Ernst, voices his impatience in the dialogues with the 'crackpots' (*Querköpfe*) of Freemasonry who try to 'make gold' and 'conjure up spirits' (LM, XIII, 392). Does this not imply that Lessing likewise condemns the Jew Falk and others like him as 'crackpots'? Not in the least. In this case, too, he remains tolerant in the most positive present-day sense, even if he regards the philosopher's stone and necromancy as figments of the imagination. For in response to Ernst's ridicule of the alchemists and necromancers, Lessing's enlightened Falk comments 'that in all these fantasies I discern a striving for reality, and even from all these false directions one can still deduce where the the true path lies' (LM, XIII, 393).

Notes
    [1] Hugh Barr Nisbet, *Lessing: Eine Biographie* (Munich: Beck, 2008).
    [2] Lessing to Johann Gottfried Lessing, 28 April 1749.
    [3] Lessing to Elise Reimarus, 9 August 1778.
    [4] Karl Gotthelf Lessing, *Gotthold Ephraim Lessings Leben*, ed. by Otto F. Lachmann (Leipzig: Reclam [1888]), p. 127.

[5] Lessing to Nicolai and Mendelssohn, 29 March 1757.

[6] Richard Daunicht (ed.), *Lessing im Gespräch: Berichte und Urteile von Freunden und Zeitgenossen* (Munich: Fink, 1971), p. 593.

[7] Heinrich Scholz (ed.), *Die Hauptschriften zum Pantheismusstreit zwischen Jacobi und Mendelssohn* (Berlin: Reuther & Reichard, 1916), pp. 95–96.

[8] Daunicht, *Lessing im Gespräch*, p. 526.

[9] Lessing to J. A. Ebert, 28 December 1769.

[10] K. A. Schmid to Lessing, 7 May 1778.

[11] Lessing to Eva König, 27 June 1772.

[12] Daunicht, *Lessing im Gespräch*, p. 16.

[13] Daunicht, *Lessing im Gespräch*, p. 141.

[14] H. B. Nisbet, 'Lessings Umgang mit Außenseitern', in Jürgen Stenzel and Roman Lach (eds), *Lessings Skandale* (Tübingen: Niemeyer, 2005), pp. 79–100 (pp. 89–93).

[15] Gotthold Ephraim Lessing, *Sämtliche Schriften*, ed. by Karl Lachmann, 3rd edn, ed. by Franz Muncker, 23 vols (Stuttgart: G. J. Göschen, 1886–1924), VI, p. 393 (subsequent references in text appear as LM plus volume and page number).

[16] Christlob Mylius, *Vermischte Schriften*, ed. by Gotthold Ephraim Lessing (Berlin: Haude & Spener, 1754; reprint Frankfurt am Main: Athenäum, 1971), pp. 280–91.

[17] See, for example, Erich Schmidt, *Lessing: Geschichte seines Lebens und seiner Schriften*, 4th edn, 2 vols (Berlin: Weidmannsche Buchhandlung, 1923), I, p. 355; Gotthold Ephraim Lessing, *Werke und Briefe*, ed. by Wilfried Barner et al. (Frankfurt am Main: Deutscher Klassiker Verlag, 1985–2003), IV, p. 826; Monika Fick, *Lessing-Handbuch: Leben-Werk-Wirkung* (Stuttgart and Weimar, 2000), p. 177.

[18] See Lessing to Johann Gottfried Lessing, 3 August 1756.

[19] Lessing to George [sic] August von Breitenbauch, 12 December 1755.

[20] Eva König to Lessing, 28 December 1774.

[21] Lessing to Eva König, 10 January 1775.

[22] See Johann Arnold Ebert to Lessing, 10 February 1775.

[23] See Daunicht, *Lessing im Gespräch*, pp. 338–39, 343, 357; also Heinrich Schneider, *Lessing: Zwölf biographische Studien* (Berne: Francke, 1951), p. 133.

[24] Eva König to Lessing, 16 February 1775.

[25] Lessing to Eva König, 2 June 1775.

[26] Lessing to Eva König, 12 July 1775.

[27] Lessing to Karl Lessing, 7 May 1775.

[28] Edward Dvoretzky (ed.), *Lessing: Dokumente zur Wirkungsgeschichte 1755–1968*, 2 vols (Göppingen: Alfred Kümmerle, 1971), I, p. 56.

[29] Daunicht, *Lessing im Gespräch*, p. 427.

[30] Daunicht, *Lessing im Gespräch*, p. 432.

[31] Lessing, *Werke und Briefe*, XII, p. 591.

[32] See Wolfgang Kröger, *Das Publikum als Richter: Lessing und die 'kleineren Respondenten' im Fragmentenstreit* (Nendeln: KTO Press, 1979), pp. 31, 42–43, 117–18, and passim.

[33] Lessing, *Werke und Briefe*, IX, pp. 128 and 371–72.

[34] See, for example, Arno Schilson in Lessing, *Werke und Briefe*, IX, pp. 1081–82.

[35] Lessing to Elise Reimarus, 9 August 1778.

[36] See Franz Muncker in LM, XVI, 536, and Arno Schilson in Lessing, *Werke und Briefe*, X, p. 1007.

[37] See, for example, Hans Mayer, 'Der Weise Nathan und der Räuber Spiegelberg', in *Lessing: Nathan der Weise*, ed. by Klaus Bohnen (Darmstadt: Wissenschaftliche Buchgesellschaft, 1984), pp. 350–73 (pp. 363–67); Ritchie Robertson, '"Dies hohe Lied der Duldung"? The Ambiguities of Toleration in *Die Juden* and *Nathan der Weise*', *The Modern Language Review*, 93 (1998), 105–20 (esp. pp. 116–17); and Friedrich Weber, 'Über die Grenzen von Lessings Toleranzbegriff', *Wolfenbütteler Vortragsmanuskripte*, 4 (Wolfenbüttel: Lessing-Akademie, 2007), p. 5.

[38] LM, III, 127; see also Lessing to Karl Lessing, 20 March 1777.

[39] See Karl S. Guthke, *Lessings Horizonte: Grenzen und Grenzenlosigkeit der Toleranz* (Göttingen: Wallstein, 2003), pp. 10–11.

[40] Weber, 'Über die Grenzen von Lessings Toleranzbegriff', p. 5.

[41] Nisbet, 'Lessings Umgang mit Außenseitern', pp. 97–99.

[42] Botho Strauß, 'Der Erste, der Letzte: Warum uns der große Lessing nicht mehr helfen kann', *Die Zeit*, 6 September 2001, pp. 51–52.

[43] I am indebted to Jim Reed and Marsha Schuchard, who first drew my attention to Samuel Jacob Falk: see especially Marsha Schuchard, 'Dr Samuel Jacob Falk: A Sabbatian Adventurer in the Masonic Underground', in Matt D. Goldish and Richard H. Popkin (eds), *Jewish Messianism in the Early Modern World* (Dordrecht: Kluwer Academic, 2001), pp. 203–26.

[44] Michal Oron, 'Dr Samuel Falk and the Eibenschuetz-Emden Controversy', in Karl Erich Grözinger and Joseph Dan (eds), *Mysticism, Magic and Kabbalah in Ashkenazi Judaism* (Berlin and New York: de Gruyter, 1995), pp. 243–56 (p. 246).

[45] H. Adler, 'The Baal Shem of London', *Transactions of the Jewish Historical Society of England*, 5 (1908), 148–73.

[46] Marsha Schuchard, 'Yeats and the "Unknown Superiors": Swedenborg, Falk, and Cagliostro', in Marie Mulvey Roberts and Hugh Ormsby-Lennon (eds), *Secret Texts: The Literature of the Secret Societies* (New York: AMS Press, 1995), pp. 114–68 (pp. 140 and 142).

SCHILLER, HUMBOLDT AND THE WELFARE STATE

By T. J. REED

The German version of this paper was done for a symposium on Schiller and the Humboldt brothers, Wilhelm and Alexander, which had the sub-title 'The reality of the idealists'. Alexander was the great explorer and empirical scientist of late eighteenth- and early nineteenth-century Germany. His realities were very clear; he was admired and emulated, as a traveller and a scientific thinker, by Charles Darwin. Wilhelm was a gentleman scholar, a pioneer in linguistics, and in later life one of the team of liberals who reshaped the Prussian state after the shock defeat by Napoleon at the battle of Jena-Auerstedt in 1806. Specifically his responsibility was for education, and he virtually created the ethos of German grammar schools and universities as they were to be and to function from then down more or less to our own times. Earlier, in the 1790s, he had written an essay on the desirable limits to be set on state action. It was never published in his lifetime but appeared in 1851, and was then taken up by liberal thinkers, most famously by John Stuart Mill, who used an epigraph from the text and took up Humboldt's central arguments in the third chapter of his essay *On Liberty* of 1859.[1]

Applying the concept of the welfare state to eighteenth-century thinkers may seem at first sight anachronistic. But the roots of sociopolitical thinking stretch back a long way, and the arguments that Wilhelm von Humboldt puts forward in his essay *On the Limits of State Action* have essentials in common with the criticisms that have commonly been levelled in our day at the damaging effects of the welfare state — psychological effects on the individual in the first instance, which then have general social and economic consequences. What Schiller's position on these matters was — whether indeed he had a position on them at all — is perhaps for students of his work an even more unexpected question. He did, however, take a stand on them on one occasion, implicitly at least and very briefly in a very short text, but in a way that seems to fall right outside the frame of his philosophical system; which raises intriguing and quite radical questions about his system, and its place in his life and work.

I

First, a résumé of the central ideas of Humboldt's essay. At root he is working with an ideal of individual human activity which is jeopardized by state

intervention, however well intentioned. He sees the essential powers of the
human being — the energy of action which he says is the 'first and only
human virtue' ['erste und einzige Tugend des Menschen'] — as threatened
by such static phenomena as possessions, prosperity, ease and happiness; the
challenge to be active in the world and to shape it by one's own efforts is
opposed by the lazy acceptance of any of these things if you do not have first
to struggle for them, and it is the struggle itself that is valuable in its effect on
body and mind. If we are given everything we need, then our powers and our
energy will atrophy. His ideal is put in some much quoted words from the
text: 'The true purpose of man — not the one which shifting inclinations but
the one which eternally unchanging reason prescribes — is the highest and
most balanced development of his powers into a single entity' ['Der wahre
Zweck des Menschen — nicht der, welchen die wechselnde Neigung,
sondern welchen die ewig unveränderliche Vernunft ihm vorschreibt —
ist die höchste und proportionierlichste Bildung seiner Kräfte zu einem
Ganzen'].[2] 'True reason' ['die wahre Vernunft'], he goes on, can only wish
on the individual human being a condition in which he works on his environment 'in the measure of his needs and his inclination, constrained only by
the limits of his powers and his rights' ['nach dem Maße seines Bedürfnisses
und seiner Neigung, nur beschränkt durch die Grenzen seiner Kraft und
seines Rechts'] (p. 69). In this sense, 'the whole endeavour of the state to raise
the positive prosperity of the nation' and 'the care of the state for the popula-
tion of the country, the maintenance of its inhabitants' [das ganze {...}
Bemühen des Staats, den positiven Wohlstand der Nation zu erhöhen {...}
die Sorgfalt {des Staates} für die Bevölkerung des Landes, für den Unterhalt
der Einwohner'] (p. 71), is undesirable.[3] For in that case 'the superior power
of the state will inhibit the free play of individual powers' ['die überlegene
Macht des Staates das freie Spiel der Kräfte hemmen'] (p. 71); the final
consequence must then be a complete uniformity among citizens, which
is 'precisely the state's intention' ['gerade die Absicht der Staaten'] (p. 71).
Human beings, on the contrary, need variety if they are to develop as individuals: that is an argument against, among other things, a coherent state
education system, which Humboldt assumes will impose total uniformity.
Individual achievement is what matters above all, for 'surely nobody has sunk
so deep as to prefer prosperity and happiness to greatness' ['und gewiß ist
noch kein Mensch tief genug gesunken, um für sich selbst Wohlstand und
Glück der Größe vorzuziehen'] (p. 72). Anyone who wants to give people
mere happiness is reducing them to the status of machines and weakening
both the powers and the moral character of the nation (p. 72). The state's
task is wholly and solely to ensure the outward security of its citizens. For
everything else, they should be left to look after their own needs.

II

The criticism of these arguments is so obvious as to be a platitude. Humboldt's own limits are clear. 'Greatness' as a goal for human ambition is clearly the preserve of relatively few. Yet Humboldt wants to extend his absolute demand for activity indiscriminately, right down to the lowest level of society: 'Does not everyone feel contempt for the beggar who would rather spend a year being nourished in an institution than find, after much suffering, not a squandering hand but a sympathetic heart' ['Verachtet nicht jeder den Bettler, dem es lieber wäre, ein Jahr im Hospital bequem ernährt zu werden, als, nach mancher erduldeten Not, nicht auf eine hinwerfende Hand, aber auf ein teilnehmendes Herz zu stoßen'] (p. 94). That such a heart would eventually be found seems for Humboldt not a matter of doubt, and quite what he expects its owner would then do is unclear. Humboldt quite realizes that people may object he has been legislating only for 'the interesting individual favoured by nature and circumstances, and therefore rare' ['nur den sehr von der Natur und den Umständen begünstigten, interessanten und eben darum seltenen Menschen vor Augen gehabt zu haben'] (p. 120). But he hopes to show that he is 'in no way overlooking the broad masses' ['den freilich größeren Haufen keineswegs übersehe' (p. 120). In any case, it seems to him that, 'wherever the enquiry concerns human beings, it is ignoble not to proceed from the highest considerations' ['unedel, überall da, wo es der Mensch ist, welcher die Untersuchung beschäftigt, nicht von den höchsten Gesichtspunkten auszugehen'] (p. 120). He does not, however, in the further reaches of the essay actually treat the interests and potentialities of the broad masses. Socially and culturally, it is clear, he is conditioned, as most eighteenth-century German cultural critics were, by the sublime example of the Greeks, and — as is also normal among cultural critics in eighteenth-century Germany — he overlooks the fact that the Greeks, too, were a society divided between an elite and the broad masses.

It is worth noting that Humboldt seems not to have always thought this way. A short time before he wrote his essay on the limits of state action, he put on paper a contrary idea, a socially quite radical one. A diary entry for 10 August 1789 reads: 'Almost all vices arise from the false relation of poverty to wealth. In a country where a general prosperity reigned throughout, there would be fewer or no crimes. For that reason no part of the administering of the state is as important as that which looks after the physical needs of its subjects' ['Alle Laster entspringen beinah aus dem Mißverhältnis der Armut gegen den Reichtum. In einem Lande, worin durchaus ein allgemeiner Wohlstand herrschte, würde es wenig oder gar keine Verbrechen geben. Darum ist kein Teil der Staatsverwaltung so wichtig als der, welcher für die physischen Bedürfnisse der Untertanen sorgt'].[4] That view may be explained by what Humboldt in a letter of 7 December 1792 to Schiller called his 'attachment to the French Revolution' ['Anhänglichkeit an der Französischen Revolution']. In an essay of 1792 he had understood the revolution as a system which had as its purpose 'only the freedom, peace and happiness of every single individual' ['nur die Freiheit, die Ruhe und das Glück jedes einzelnen'] as against the old absolutist system which had been calculated to 'draw from the nation as many of its resources as possible to gratify the ambition and extravagance of one man' ['soviel Mittel als möglich aus der Nation zur Befriedigung des Ehrgeizes und der Verschwendungssucht eines Einzigen zu ziehen'].[5] The change from a system of such extreme and exclusive individualism to the post-revolutionary one was obviously a historical improvement. But now, one year further on, Humboldt obviously felt that on closer inspection the new system, too, had its faults and dangers, which were perhaps less gross but still harmful to the health of the nation.

As a further defence of Humboldt, or at least a relativizing of his position, one must also mention that, after publishing some extracts from his essay in Schiller's journal *Neue Thalia* in 1792, and after vain attempts to place the whole essay with the Leipzig publisher Göschen, he felt it to be out of date or at least in need of revision. He resolved to put off publishing it, so he writes to Schiller on 18 January 1793, 'for an *indefinite* period' ['auf *unbestimmte* Zeit'] (his emphasis). In a letter to K. G. von Brinkmann of 26 September 1792 he refers to his essay as a saga of earlier times, a *Sage der Vorzeit*.[6] Its eventual publication years after his death belonged to a different age, as did its reception by a different public.

III

Crucially, in its own time Humboldt's position had clear affinities with those of Goethe's and Schiller's classicism as it was beginning to take shape in the early 1790s. At the time Humboldt wrote his essay, he and Schiller already enjoyed a close intellectual friendship. According to a slightly later letter of Humboldt's, 4 August 1795, they practised 'collaborative thinking'. The positions we are interested in came out very concretely in major poetic works of Goethe's and Schiller's in these years. In various contexts the energy of individual action that Humboldt preached as the central thesis in his essay was shown in operation, with notions of a broader social solidarity scarcely having any part to play.

Thus in Schiller's *Lied von der Glocke* ('Song of the Bell') at the point where a fire has devastated the town and the townsman's dwelling has been burnt to the ground ['Leergebrannt / Ist die Stätte'] and he is left no choice but to abandon the place and seek his luck elsewhere: 'Just one glance / At the grave / Of his fortune / He sends back – / Then seizes cheerfully his staff and leaves'

['Einen Blick / Nach dem Grabe / Seiner Habe / Sendet noch der Mensch zurück — / Greift fröhlich dann zum Wanderstabe'] (vv. 218 ff.). He is consoled by the thought that at least none of his family have perished in the fire. Much the same motif occurs in Goethe's small-town epic poem *Hermann and Dorothea*, now elaborated more fully in a flashback from the narrative present. In the previous generation, Hermann's parents met and became engaged in the ruins of their burned-out town. Help was available, but only within the family and as a consequence of the engagement. Hermann's future father says:

> See, our house is demolished. Stay here and help me to build it,
> And I will help in return your father with his reconstruction.
>
> [Siehe, das Haus liegt nieder. Bleib hier und hilf mir es bauen,
> Und ich helfe dagegen auch deinem Vater an seinem.]
>
> (vv. 148ff.)

The principle is, do it yourself. The energy that Humboldt labelled 'energy of action' is what must drive the restoration of the burnt-out town. In the course of time, Hermann's father has somewhat lost sight of the principle from his active youth. In the narrative's present he only thinks in a philistine manner of accumulating possessions and money. He wants Hermann to find a well-off bride with a dowry, so that 'in baskets and boxes the useful gifts will come flowing' ['in Körben und Kasten die nützliche Gabe hereinkommt'] (vv. 168, 173). Only Hermann's mother praises her son, with his inappropriate choice of a bride from among a mass of refugees passing through the town: he too, in a time of war, is courting in a different way but the same old spirit 'among the ruins' ['über den Trümmern'].

Just as a sidelight, it is worth quoting what Frederick the Great wrote to the inhabitants of Greifenberg, a town that in 1785 had likewise burnt down, offering them an ex gratia payment and replying to their thanks with a statement of principle: 'It is my obligation to help my subjects when they have suffered a disaster, that is what I am there for' ['es ist meine Schuldigkeit, daß ich meinen verunglückten Untertanen wieder aufhelfe, dafür bin ich da'].[7] Frederick the Great, then, socially somewhat to the left of the liberal Wilhelm von Humboldt.

The striking thing about the literary treatments of disasters suffered by the lower classes is the insistence on their contentment with their lot — Humboldt's insistence, for example, that country people living close to nature, so that their lives are dominated by it, gladly accept its vagaries. 'The fruits that must be sewn and harvested, but annually return and only seldom disappoint their hopes, make them patient, trusting and thrifty' ['Die Frucht, die gesäet und geerntet werden muß, aber alljährlich wiederkehrt und nur selten die Hoffnung täuscht, macht geduldig, vertrauend und sparsam'].

They are 'sweetly bound to their fields and their hearth' ['süß an seinen Acker und seinen Herd gefesselt'], the peasant remains 'cheerfully subject to natural custom and law' ['der Sitte und dem Gesetz froh unterworfen'] — as cheerful, that is, as Schiller's ruined townsman was when he picked up his staff and marched away. Schiller's later drama *The Maid of Orleans* similarly has Joan of Arc's father cheerfully accepting country catastrophes:

> We can look calmly on at such destruction,
> For storm-proof stands the earth we cultivate.
> The flames may burn our villages to ashes,
> Our crops get trampled down by hooves of horses,
> With each new spring there will be new crops growing
> And our light huts will quickly rise again.
>
> [Wir können ruhig die Zerstörung schauen
> Denn sturmfest steht die Erde, die wir bauen.
> Die Flamme brenne unsre Dörfer nieder,
> Die Saat zerstampfe ihrer Rosse Tritt,
> Der neue Lenz bringt neue Saaten mit,
> Und schnell erstehn die leichten Hütten wieder.]
>
> (vv. 376ff.)

The mention of trampled crops unavoidably calls to mind a poem by the radical Gottfried August Bürger entitled 'The peasant to his lordly tyrant' ['Der Bauer an seinen durchlauchtigsten Tyrannen'], which includes the lines:

> The crops your hunting tramples down,
> What horse and hound and you consume,
> The bread, you prince, is mine.
>
> [Die Saat, so deine Jagd zertritt,
> Was Roß, und Hund, und du verschlingst,
> Das Brot, du Fürst, ist mein.]

In contrast, the passage from *The Maid of Orleans* makes it sound as if the sequence of disaster and recovery, however caused, is just one more fact of nature's annual cycle. Whether it really was so easy for the countryman to rebuild his 'light huts' may reasonably be doubted. It seems more likely that the troubles of the lowly are being taken too lightly, from the poet's relative elevation. To that extent a comment of Schiller's about the nobleman Humboldt, with his family castles, can be applied to Schiller himself. To his friend Körner Schiller wrote on 18 May 1794: 'Humboldt has the advantage over you of a certain ease, which one can more easily acquire in his circumstances than in ours' ['Er hat vor Dir sehr viel an einer gewissen Leichtigkeit voraus, die man sich in seinen Lebensverhältnissen leichter erwerben kann als in den unsrigen']. So much for lightness and ease at different levels of society.

At issue here is the dual meaning of the concept of 'humanitas', which was a declared central principle of Weimar classicism. On the one hand, it contained the idea of developing to the full the *active potential* of the individual, of spurring people on to a higher state of being and creative striving. That was an extension of the Enlightenment notion of betterment for all. On the other hand, it wanted people when they were on the receiving end to be socially *better treated* than in times when political oppression had not yet been tempered by Enlightenment criticism and gradual piecemeal reform. The snag was that the two strands could be in contradiction with one another, as in a letter of Goethe's of 8 June 1781 where he is responding to a forthcoming part of Herder's grand work, *Ideas Towards a Philosophy of History of Mankind* [*Ideen zur Philosophie der Geschichte der Menschheit*] Goethe writes: 'He will certainly have expounded splendidly the ideal dream of mankind that things one day will go better for them. And I must say myself that I believe it to be true that the principle of humanity will one day be victorious, only I fear that at the same time the world will become one great hospital and everyone will be everyone else's humane sick-attendant' ['Er wird gewiß den schönen Traumwunsch der Menschheit daß es dereinst besser mit ihr werden möge trefflich ausgeführt haben. Auch muß ich selbst sagen halt ich es für wahr, daß die Humanität endlich siegen wird, nur fürcht ich daß zu gleicher Zeit die Welt ein großes Hospital und einer des andern humaner Krankenwächter werden wird']. And indeed Herder does talk in just these terms, for example when he narrates the way in early Christianity the charitable giving and receiving of alms became established and taken for granted: 'On the one hand alms were praised and on the other hand pursued' — that is to say, by the needy recipients — 'as the true treasures of heaven' ['auf der einen Seite Almosen als die wahren Schätze des Himmelreichs angepriesen, auf der andern gesucht'], so that 'human society came to be considered as one great hospital and Christianity as the common charitable bank' ['die menschliche Gesellschaft nur als ein großes Hospital, und das Christentum als die gemeine Almosenkasse desselben betrachtet'].[8] 'The result in moral and political respects was a very undesirable condition' ['in Ansehung der Moral und Politik zuletzt ein sehr böser Zustand daraus erwachsen' (ibid.). For what got lost in the process was 'that noble pride, the child of independent dignity' ['jener edle Stolz, der Sohn unabhängiger Würde']. Christian love for one's neighbour had thus produced a growth of 'weeds' ['Unkraut']. You can see from the phrase 'one great hospital' which Goethe's letter and Herder's text have in common that they had been talking the problem over.

Into this mixed picture of a hesitant humane will to assist others, and the fear that their powers will thereby be undermined, there bursts in 1797 an epigram of Schiller's with the title 'Dignity of Man'. It is one of the great series of satirical epigrams *Xenia* jointly composed by himself and Goethe. Schiller is on internal evidence the more likely author of this one, and at very least he endorsed it by co-signing it. It reads:

> No more of that, I beg you. Give him some food, give him shelter,
>   Once you have covered bare need, dignity comes by itself.

> [Nichts mehr davon, ich bitt euch. Zu essen gebt ihm, zu wohnen,
>   Habt ihr die Blöße bedeckt, gibt sich die Würde von selbst.]

This cuts the Gordian knot of conflicting priorities in a sense diametrically opposite to Wilhelm von Humboldt's essay. Where for Humboldt the fulfilment of material conditions led to a decay of human dignity, Schiller is here making basic material sufficiency the necessary, indeed the sufficient condition of human dignity. Where for Humboldt material ease is at most the consequence of virtuous energetic activity, Schiller sees dignity already resulting as soon as naked material needs are met. What makes his statement so mysterious (for mysterious in the context of his work it certainly is) is that its immediate context is a group of epigrams which look to be otherwise very much in harmony with Humboldt's position. They are sceptical (to quote the title of one of them) about the 'Majesty of human nature' ['Majestas populi'], which it says is not to be found among 'the masses'. The best state, another says, can be recognized by the fact that nobody talks about it, much as nobody has anything to gossip about if a woman has a good reputation (cf. his epigram 'The best state' ['Der beste Staat']). From that we can conclude that the ideal is for the state to do as little as possible that could be talked about. But the epigram on human dignity is on quite different ground from those two; and it is on very different ground from the essays in aesthetic and moral philosophy which Schiller had been writing earlier in the 1790s. In the essay *On Grace and Dignity* [*Über Anmut und Würde*], for example, he defines dignity as 'the expression of a sublime mindset' ['Ausdruck einer erhabenen Gesinnung'], which is made necessary by the physical conditions of human nature, because the human individual is an animal being up to the point where the will kicks in. But at that point the legislation of Nature, of sensuous being (*Sinnlichkeit*), ceases and the legislation of Reason, of morality (*Sittlichkeit*), begins. It is then no question which has to have priority — the basely material has to yield place, it has to be sacrificed. In stark contrast to all this systematic high-mindedness, the epigram 'Dignity of man' operates on that more basic, if not base level — a more basic level of reflection and a basic level of recommended social practice. It is treating — one might say, at last — the conditions of bare survival which were the daily experience of the 'broad masses' which Humboldt mentioned fleetingly but then left out of account in his sketch of the state.

There exists, it is true, a slender textual bridge between Schiller's aesthetic writings and our epigram, a kind of halfway station on the way to his radically materialistic insight. In a letter of 11 November 1793 to the Duke of Schleswig-Holstein-Augustenburg — so, from the genetic context of his treatise *On the Aesthetic Education of Man* — Schiller writes:

> The human mind must first be liberated from the yoke of necessity before it can be led to rational freedom. And only in this sense does one have a right to regard the concern for the citizen's physical well-being as the first duty of the state. If physical well-being were not the condition under which Man can awaken to mature independence of mind, it would not by far deserve for its own sake so much attention and regard. Man is as yet very little if he has warm shelter and has eaten his fill, but he must have warm shelter and enough to eat his fill if a better nature is to stir within him.

> [Erst muß der Geist vom Joch der Notwendigkeit losgespannt werden, ehe man ihn zur Vernunftfreiheit führen kann. Und auch nur in diesem Sinn hat man Recht, die Sorge für das physische Wohl der Bürger als die erste Pflicht des Staats zu betrachten. Wäre das physische Wohl nicht die Bedingung, unter welcher allein der Mensch zur Mündigkeit seines Geistes erwachen kann; um seiner selbst willen würde es bey weitem nicht so viel Aufmerksamkeit und Achtung verdienen. Der Mensch ist noch sehr wenig, wenn er warm wohnt und sich satt gegessen hat, aber er muß warm wohnen und satt zu essen haben, wenn sich die beßre Natur in ihm regen soll.][9]

In this passage physical well-being is still explicitly only a precondition: human dignity, the dignity of reason, is so far merely in prospect. A dignity that is *already created* by the satisfaction of material need is not yet in sight. So far Schiller sees that satisfaction as a necessary but by no means yet a sufficient condition.

Just as striking as the materialist content of Schiller's epigram is its forthright, even brusque tone. In the situation it implies, the speaker is reacting to a lengthy debate which he is tired of because it has involved hair-splitting and excessive subtleties. He points impatiently to the basic facts of life which have been lost sight of. But who exactly is he addressing with his demand to cut the cackle? Presumably not Wilhelm von Humboldt: it is three years since Humboldt's essay was written, it has never been published, it is not in any way topical — unless one imagines that he and Schiller have been privately talking these matters over, of which there is no sign in their letters or reminiscences. Moreover, Schiller had raised no objections to Humboldt's essay back in 1792, when he had the complete text in his hands immediately after its composition, and published sections of it in his journal *Neue Thalia*. He had also helped Humboldt's attempt to publish it in full, recommending it to the Leipzig publisher Göschen by saying that it contained 'very fruitful political suggestions', was 'constructed on a good philosophical basis', and

would have no problems with the censor 'since the author keeps to generali-
ties' [sehr fruchtbare politische Winke {...} auf ein gutes philosophisches
Element'] — (perhaps a slip of the pen for 'Fundament'?) — '[gebaut {...}
der Verfasser im Allgemeinen geblieben']. And finally, of course, the epigram
is addressed, the German makes plain, to a plural audience: 'ich bitt' euch'.

I cannot offer particular nameable addressees, and I do not believe there
were any. Rather, Schiller is talking to philosophers generally, which means
that the epigram is one of a considerable group of poems in which he is
sceptical about philosophy as such. For example, numbers 371 to 389 of the
Xenia deal with the best-known philosophers or systems, mostly unnamed but
easily recognizable, and mostly in a critical or mocking tone. A profound
scepticism, not to say cynicism, is contained in the poem 'The Wise of the
World', originally entitled 'The Deeds of the Philosophers'. Both versions of
the title should be read ironically: what I have translated literally as 'The Wise
of the World' is the word 'Die Weltweisen', an old-fashioned term for
'philosophers'. It was already by the 1790s sufficiently dated to make the
spotlight fall on its two constituent words. That is to say, it already asks
implicitly whether any philosopher can offer a wisdom that comes up to the
demands of the real world. 'The Deeds of the Philosophers' can likewise be
read as querying whether they have achieved much, because the individual
stanzas show how pathetic their results have been. They have risen above the
ground of reality only to flop back down with commonplaces or tautologies:
'ten is not twelve', 'wetness makes things damp', 'brightness gives light'. And
all the time these grand conclusions are being arrived at, nature has to keep
the world running by dint of real basic impulses:

> *Doch weil, was ein Professor spricht,*
> *Nicht gleich zu allen dringet,*
> *So übt Natur die Mutterpflicht*
> *Und sorgt, daß nie die Kette bricht*
> *Und daß der Reif nie springet.*
> *Einstweilen, bis den Bau der Welt*
> *Philosophie zusammenhält,*
> *Erhält sie das Getriebe*
> *Durch Hunger und durch Liebe.*

[But since what a professor says / doesn't get through at once to everyone, /
it's the task of Nature to make sure the chain that links things doesn't break /
and the ring that contains them doesn't burst. / Until such time as philosophy
/ holds the world together, / Nature keeps things running / through hunger
and through love.]

These lines were incidentally a favourite quotation of the great realist
Sigmund Freud. He expressly classified all fundamental human drives under
the heading of either hunger or love.[10]

The lines again confront us with universal material factors that show up the shakiness of abstract constructions. In this 'jokey poem', as Schiller called it,[11] he had 'made fun of the principle of contradiction' ('ten is not twelve') — this in a letter to Goethe, where he goes on to say that philosophy always strikes him as 'ludicrous when it tries from its own resources to extend knowledge and legislate for the world without admitting its dependence on experience' ['immer lächerlich, wenn sie aus eigenem Mittel, ohne ihre Abhängigkeit von der Erfahrung zu gestehen, das Wissen erweitern und der Welt Gesetze geben will'].[12] This is of course itself a philosophical argument: an empiricist, anti-rationalist argument and hence exactly in line — not surprisingly, given Schiller's debts to Kant — with the central argument in Kant's *Critique of Pure Reason*, which discredits all empty speculation that goes beyond human experience as untenable because unreal. And this criticism could of course be applied in retrospect to Humboldt's social theorizing, for example where he appeals in those passages I quoted earlier to the authority of a question-begging 'unchanging reason' or 'true reason', and most especially when at a crucial point in his argument he openly admits that he does not have the empirical evidence to support his generalizations and roundly declares that it is not needed:

> Here would be the place to go through in detail the particular kinds of craft, agriculture, industry, commerce and everything else about which I am here speaking collectively, and to analyse from technical knowledge what advantages and disadvantages are provided by freedom and being left to act for oneself. The lack of just this technical knowledge prevents me from entering into such a discussion. Nor do I think it any longer necessary for the topic itself.

> [Hier wäre es nun der Ort, die einzelnen Arten der Gewerbe, Ackerbau, Industrie, Handel und alles übrige, wovon ich hier zusammengenommen rede, einzeln durchzugehen und mit Sachkenntnis auseinanderzusetzen, welche Nachteile und Vorteile Freiheit und Selbstüberlassung ihnen gewährt. Mangel eben dieser Sachkenntnis hindert mich, eine solche Erörterung einzugehen. Auch halte ich dieselbe für die Sache selbst nicht mehr notwendig.]
> (pp. 91–92)

Another poem of Schiller's, 'The Metaphysician', uses the same approach. It starts with a monologue by the title-figure, who like a roofer is up on a metaphorical tower high above humanity. This leads to the final question: 'The tower from which your gaze / Looks down so proud and grand, / What is it made of, on what does it stand?' ['Der Turm, von dem dein Blick so vornehm niederschauet, / *Wovon* ist er — *worauf* ist er erbauet?']. Once again, the loss of contact with reality is attacked, and once again with a strong Kantian flavour. For Kant repeatedly points out that the flaw in traditional rationalist metaphysics is that it lacks solid foundations. Laying *real* foundations for all future philosophy is his declared task, and as a central symbol for the extravagant claims of the old metaphysics he uses the tower of Babel.[13]

Significantly, all the poems I have been talking about are grouped in the mid-1790s, at a time when Schiller was proposing, as he wrote, to 'close his philosophical shop' and become a poet again after nearly ten years spent working in the realm of abstraction. In a letter to Goethe of 7 January 1795 he declares that the poet 'is the only true human being and the best of philosophers is only a caricature in comparison' [der einzig wahre Mensch und der beste Philosoph nur eine Karikatur gegen ihn].[14] This means, I think, that the impatient call in our epigram — 'No more of that' [Nichts mehr davon] — is addressed to himself as well, it is a piece of self-criticism. He, too, may have lost contact with the ground of reality in his high idealistic reflections. This would fit in, more broadly, with Schiller's doubts and inner conflicts over how real elevated values are. These doubts and conflicts create the dialectical tension and the essential interest of some of his best-known poems: in the paired poems 'The Words of Faith' and 'The Words of Illusion' he struggles to sustain the reality of the concepts of Freedom, Virtue, God, and Truth, from two radically different standpoints. Schiller is known as a philosophical poet, a philosopher-poet, his poetry is commonly labelled 'poetry of ideas' ['Gedankenlyrik']. But it is rarely a matter of firm beliefs being turned confidently into verse. What makes it a *poetry* of ideas, what gives it its lyrical element, is precisely the emotion of uncertainty, the oscillation of mood between confidence and doubt, or between two divergent or even opposed views of the same large theme as captured in different but related poems. So where one major statement, in the poem 'The Artists', celebrates the growth of abstract reason out of an origin in the perception of beautiful forms, another equally major statement, in the poem 'The Gods of Greece', laments the loss of beautiful forms through the growth of abstract reason.

And if we look even further back in Schiller's work than the 1790s, the poem 'Resignation' of 1786 contains the most relentless questioning of idealism: the believer in ideals cannot expect any ultimate reward, no cash payout, so to speak. You have a choice on earth between high-minded hope and frank enjoyment. If you do not opt for enjoyment, the fact that you hoped and believed will be — will *have been* — your only reward. Once more, it is a recognition of the reality base, almost a reduction to the reality base: ideals are a precarious superstructure. This of course also has what seems a completely confident idealistic opposite in the 'Ode to Joy'.

The insistence on material realities in the epigram 'Dignity of Man' may, however, have another, deeper motivation than this habitual oscillation in Schiller's poetic positions. This seems to me the most important thing to come out of the present enquiry because of the light it casts on the whole shape of Schiller's career and the relation of his thinking to his lived experience. The younger Schiller — at least up to the mid-1780s — was a radical social critic, class-conscious, with revolutionary impulses, and very much concerned with the concrete realities of life. His first three plays all have a mood and motifs of rebellion; and when in 1784 he theorizes about the theatre, he focuses on its palpable social influence as an arm of the Enlightenment. In the 'Ode to Joy' of 1786, the poem that Beethoven set parts of in the last movement of his Ninth Symphony, one of the best-known lines declares that under the influence of joy 'All humanity become brothers ['alle Menschen werden Brüder']. The original version, instead of this grand generalization, read 'Beggars become princes' brothers' ['Bettler werden Fürstenbrüder'] which is much more explicit about the social differences that need abolishing if equality is to be achieved.

But if we then look at two statements of the end of the 1780s, the poem 'The Artists', and Schiller's inaugural lecture as Professor of History at the University of Jena, what we find is the opposite of radical social criticism. They paint a picture of the present time as a harmonious fulfilment of historical processes that are moving mankind towards some ideal enlightened goal. Even Germany, which Schiller's early dramas showed was being tyrannized by hard-nosed princes and corrupt courts and in need of purification by the violence of a robber-band — even Germany is now a place where everything in the garden is lovely.

Both these statements were made in 1789. The date marks a clear turning-point, not because it is the year of the French Revolution — that only begins later in the year — but, on the contrary, as the moment when Schiller has begun to establish himself after his years of wanderings and crises. With his professorship of history (albeit unpaid) and his marriage into the minor nobility he gets a first foothold in society. That will surely have had an effect on the attitudes of a radical — I need not say what a professorial title does for (or to) people. The shift might be called a kind of 'realism', though in a somewhat cynical sense: it is a realism that leads away from the hard social realities as Schiller had earlier perceived and pilloried them. And as holder of a university position from now on he moves in the paths of high theory.[15] But then in the mid-1790s we suddenly get the erratic block of that epigram, where he impatiently sweeps away high abstraction and complexity and demands instead a recognition of human dignity that is a long way from — a long way below — all high theory. It is surely a reminder to himself of essentials, even a return to his more radical early thinking. It can be seen as making a pattern that points back to his rebellious Storm and Stress days but also onward to the materialist politics of the nineteenth century, the politics of food and need, what Heinrich Heine was to label 'the soup question', culminating in the lines from his satirical poem *Germany: A Winter's Tale*:

> There's bread enough grows here on earth
> to feed mankind with ease
>
> [Es wächst hienieden Brot genug
> Für alle Menschenkinder]

after which other, more advanced but equally material enjoyments are to follow for the people, bread being only the first necessity:

> and roses and myrtle, beauty and joy
> and (in the season) peas.
>
> [Und Rosen und Myrten, Schönheit und Lust,
> Und Zuckererbsen nicht minder.][16]

It looks onward to that other, grimmer diet of peas in Buchner's *Woyzeck*, which shows up the great gulf in the view of realities between the cocksure doctor's confidence that 'Man is free, in Man the individuality is transfigured into freedom' ['Der Mensch ist frei, in dem Menschen verklärt sich die Individualität zur Freiheit'] and the experience of the economically and physically helpless squaddie that 'nature comes at you' ['Wenn einem die Natur kommt'].[17] And it looks beyond the nineteenth century to Brecht and his line 'For creatures all need help from other creatures' ['Denn alle Kreatur braucht Hilf' von allen'].[18] So it is not just ironic when Thomas Mann in his *Essay on Schiller* of 1955 quotes the epigram 'Dignity of Man' and exclaims: 'That's surely socialist materialism, heaven help us!' ['Das ist ja sozialistischer Materialismus, Gott behüte!']. Schiller's isolated short text thus stands in a historical continuum of political thought. It holds on to basic reality in a time of idealism.[19]

Notes

[1] John Stuart Mill, *On Liberty; Representative Government; The Subjection of Women; Three Essays* (London: Oxford World's Classics, 1966), pp. 2 and 71–72.

[2] *Versuch, die Grenzen der Wirksamkeit des Staates zu bestimmen*, in *Gesammelte Werke*, ed. by Andreas Flitner and Klaus Giel, 5 vols (Darmstadt: Wissenschaftliche Buchgesellschaft, 1960), vol. 1, p. 64.

[3] Further references, in brackets in text, are to this German edition, cited in note 2.

[4] *Wilhelm von Humboldt. Sein Leben und Wirken dargestellt in Briefen, Tagebüchern und Dokumenten seiner Zeit*, ed. by Rudolf Freese (Berlin: Verlag der Nation, [n.d.]), p. 93.

[5] *Werke*, ed. cit., vol. 1, p. 35.

[6] Freese, pp. 165–66.

[7] *Gespräche Friedrichs des Großen*, ed. by Friedrich von Oppel-Bronikowski and Gustav Bertold Volz (Berlin: Reimar Hobbing, 1919), p. 306.

[8] Herder, *Werke*, vol. 6, ed. by Martin Bollacher (Frankfurt am Main: Deutscher Klassiker Verlag, 1989), p. 714.

[9] Schiller, *NA* [*Werke: Nationalausgabe*, ed. on behalf of the Goethe- und Schiller-Archiv, the Schiller-Nationalmuseum, and the Deutsche Akademie, 43 vols (Weimar: Böhlau, 1943–)], vol. 26, p. 299 (henceforth cited as *NA*).

[10] For example, 'We can classify all the organic drives operating in our psyche, in the words of the poet, as hunger or as love' ['Als "Hunger" oder als "Liebe" können wir nach den Worten des Dichters alle in unserer Seele wirkenden organischen Triebe klassifizieren'] ('Die psychogene Sehstörung in psychoanalytischer Auffassung' [1910]), in *Gesammelte Werke*, vol. 10 (Frankfurt am Main: Fischer, 1999), p. 153. I owe this reference to my friend and colleague Siegbert Prawer.

[11] In a letter to Körner of 21 December 1796 (*NA*, vol. 28, p. 137).

[12] 16 October 1795 (*NA*, vol. 28, p. 79).

[13] Cf. *Critique of Pure Reason* B 735; the original in *Kants Werke*, ed. by Ernst Cassirer, vol. 3 (Berlin: Bruno Cassirer, 1912–1922), p. 481. In 1784 Kant's friends struck a medal showing the Leaning Tower of Pisa and bearing the inscription 'perscrutatis fundamentis stabilitur veritas' [once the foundations have been thoroughly examined, truth is stabilized]; cf. Kant to Johann Schultz, 4 March 1784, in *Werke*, ed. cit., vol. 9, p. 249, and see Hans Vaihinger, 'Die Kant-Medaille mit dem schiefen Turm zu Pisa', *Kant-Studien*, 2 (1898), 109–15.

[14] Schiller, *NA*, vol. 27, p. 116.

[15] A telling detail: Schiller's 1784 lecture, originally called 'The effect of theatre on the people', had its title changed for republication in 1802 to 'The theatre considered as a moral institution'.

[16] Heine, *Deutschland: A Winter's Tale*, ed. and trans. by T. J. Reed (London: Angel Books, 1997), p. 31.

[17] Georg Büchner, *Sämtliche Werke und Briefe*, ed. by Werner H. Lehmann, vol. 2 (Hamburg: Christian Wegner, [n.d.]), p. 174.

[18] 'Von der Kindsmörderin Marie Farrar', in Brecht's *Hauspostille*.

[19] One further document, contemporary with Schiller's epigram, deserves to be noted. In 1794 Karl Philipp Moritz published a 'New ABC', subtitled 'Also an Introduction to Thinking for Children'. Its word under U is 'Ungleichheit' (Inequality), illustrated by plants of unequal growth, a hyssop and a cedar. The text reads: 'Poor and lowly people are made exactly like the rich and noble. The rich and noble cannot therefore be compared with the cedar, nor the lowly with the hyssop. Every person is in need of help. When the poor and lowly are ill, they need help. And when the rich and noble are weak and ill, they too need help. [...] No human being must despise another. For to be a human being is the highest dignity' (Moritz, *Werke*, ed. by Horst Günther, vol. 3 (Frankfurt am Main: Insel, 1981), pp. 381–82). This attempt of Moritz's to educate the very youngest is more directly political than Schiller's project of aesthetic education. Dignity is here not a goal that human beings must aspire to, but their definition. The idea that they all inherently need help locates an intermediate concept between Humboldt's extremes of liberal laissez-faire or incapacitating over-provision, namely mutual solidarity.

SYMBOLIZATION AND HIERARCHIZATION: REFLECTIONS ON TWO EARLY GOETHE POEMS

By Martin Swales

Ernst Cassirer's work on symbolic forms alerts us to extent to which — and the many ways in which — imaginative literature mediates, and in the process meditates on, human experience. As a result, that experience is invested with a sense of priority, of foreground and background, of central and peripheral, in a word, of hierarchy. By this token, to borrow a favourite phrase of Roger Stephenson's, literature makes sense of sense experience. This is nowhere more true in German literature than in the work — particularly the poetry — of the early Goethe. For him, as for the other writers of the Sturm und Drang generation, the animating impetus was impatience with convention, an urgent need to re-shape literary utterance and thereby to re-activate human perception. The great watchword of the Sturm und Drang was freedom, freedom to challenge the established significations and hierarchizations of both literature and life — not so much with the aspiration to replace one hierarchy by another but rather to understand hierarchization as a continuous process, one linked to the urgency and flow of life itself. Living, then, was perceived as a process of movement and flux, a dynamic shifting of priorities; and to that shifting, to that change in signification the literature of the time bears witness.[1]

★ ★ ★

I want briefly to explore these issues in two Goethe poems from the early 1770s. I begin, without apology, with a text that is probably too well known for its own good — 'Mailied':

> *Wie herrlich leuchtet*
> *Mir die Natur!*
> *Wie glänzt die Sonne!*
> *Wie lacht die Flur!*
>
> *Es dringen Blüten*
> *Aus jedem Zweig*
> *Und tausend Stimmen*
> *Aus dem Gesträuch*

Und Freud und Wonne
Aus jeder Brust.
O Erd, o Sonne!
O Glück, o Lust!

O Lieb, o Liebe!
So golden schön,
Wie Morgenwolken
Auf jenen Höhn!

Du segnest herrlich
Das frische Feld,
Im Blütendampfe
Die volle Welt.

O Mädchen, Mädchen,
Wie lieb ich dich!
Wie blickt dein Auge!
Wie liebst du mich!

So liebt die Lerche
Gesang und Luft,
Und Morgenblumen
Den Himmelsduft,

Wie ich dich liebe
Mit warmem Blut,
Die du mir Jugend
Und Freud und Mut

Zu neuen Liedern
Und Tänzen gibst.
Sei ewig glücklich,
Wie du mich liebst!

How splendid nature
Shines all for me!
The sun, it sparkles!
Fields laugh with glee!

From all the branches
The blossoms push,
A thousand voices
From every bush

And joy and rapture
From every breast.
O earth, o sunshine,
O bliss o zest,

O love, o love
So golden bright
As clouds of morning
Upon that height,

On fresh fields richly
Your blessings spill,
With haze of blossom
The world you fill!

O girl my darling
How I love you!
Your eyes, how shining!
How you love too!

So loves the skylark
Its song on high
And morning flowers
The fragrant sky

As I am burning
With love for you
Who give me courage
And youth anew,

Give joy, set singing
And dancing free;
Be ever happy
As you love me.[2]

It is a poem that speaks of and incarnates reciprocity. The repeated 'wie' signals that much because the word betokens both likeness, kinship on the one hand and experiential intensity on the other. Except that there is not really an 'on-the-one-hand, on-the-other' because the two meanings interlock in the sense that such fervour (as a student of mine once put it, the 'wow effect') seems to derive from and to confirm intimations of relatedness.[3] It is a poem that (as we might put it) resists all notions of separation and compartmentalization, such is the incantatory force of the cascading, 'wie's'. In the sentence that binds together stanzas two and three, the 'Blüten' of the vegetable world, the 'Stimmen' of the animal world, and the 'Freud und Wonne' of the human world all belong together as the delayed grammatical subjects of 'es dringen'. The final two lines of stanza three and the first line of stanza four are simply a list of nouns, prefaced by the exclamatory 'o'. The final noun 'Lieb' is repeated and becomes the subject of the sentence in stanza five which depicts abundant blessing being poured over a world that is alive with joy. Once love has been named, it never leaves the poem, and it recurs in each of the last four stanzas. Divisions, separations, distinctions are overcome as the sense of the poem moves back and forth across stanza divisions. Just as we moved, in stanzas two and three, along a chain of being that brings vegetable, animal, and human worlds into blissful alignment, so, too, in stanzas seven and eight that same alignment is reaffirmed in reverse order (we begin with the human sphere — 'Mädchen' — and then pass, via the 'Lerche' to 'Morgenblumen').[4] Except that the process does not stop there. Rather, again by means of the all-important 'wie', the natural sphere is linked to the human world. The sentence that conjoins stanzas seven, eight, and nine is, then, one that extends in almost tautological bliss from the human sphere to the world of animate nature, of inanimate nature, and then back to humans. The human self is part of, and not simply an onlooker at, the processes of which the poem speaks. Indeed, the poem itself, as a May Song, also becomes part of that process because (as the last stanza tells us) it is triggered by the love of the girl who gives 'Freud und Mut / Zu neuen Liedern'.

I do not want to belabour the poem — if for no other reason than that it is so splendidly immediate that one does not want to blunt the fizzing urgency that it has on the page. But there are, of course, points that would merit further consideration — the anthropomorphic force of the verb in 'Wie lacht die Flur' which links natural and human worlds; the force of the dative 'mir' in the opening two lines which fuses human sentience and the radiance that floods the landscape; the last two lines of the poem which use this love as the benchmark for all future happiness. I want to close with three remarks. One is that the poem does have, on the page, a clear strophic structure. While its import may entail the overriding of all divisions and separations (hence the importance of the enjambements), yet it does acknowledge them — in order to override them. In spite of its ecstatic feel, the poem does sustain a clarity of discursive statement. It is, in other words, decipherable rather than impenetrable. Yet, while respecting notions of coherence and poetic form, it is a revolutionary lyric. Revolutionary because it runs the risk of subverting hallowed notions (in 1770) of what it is that constitutes a poem. It challenges traditional notions of poetic diction (not least by its incorporation of dialect speech in the rhyme 'Zweig' and 'Gesträuch' — reminiscent of Gretchen's rhyming, in the Urfaust, of 'neige' with 'Schmerzensreiche'). And in that linguistic impudence it so dismantles stratificatory understanding of what constitutes a literary statement, of seemliness and decorum, that it runs the risk of banality. In this sense, it is a poem that takes risks. And, as a result, it plants emotional immediacy at the heart of literary statement; it re-hierarchizes the lyric possibility by making something that sounds like an outburst into a poem. Nature, as a property of both experience and of literature, is the supreme value.

Let me move forward a mere four years to consider 'An Belinden', one of the 'Lili' poems — and one that offers a clear intertextual debate with 'Mailied':

Warum ziehst du mich unwiderstehlich,
Ach, in jene Pracht?
War ich guter Junge nicht so selig
In der öden Nacht?

Heimlich in mein Zimmerchen verschlossen,
Lag im Mondenschein,
Ganz von seinem Schauerlicht umflossen,
Und ich dämmert ein;

Träumte da von vollen goldenen Stunden
Ungemischter Lust,
Hatte schon das liebe Bild empfunden
Tief in meiner Brust.

Bin ichs noch, den du bei so viel Lichtern
An dem Spieltisch hältst?
Oft so unerträglichen Gesichtern
Gegenüber stellst?

Reizender ist mir des Frühlings Blüte
Nun nicht auf der Flur;
Wo du, Engel, bist, ist Lieb und Güte,
Wo du bist, Natur.

Why do you draw me so irresistibly,
Alas, into that splendour?
Was I, such a good little boy, not so blissful
In the desolate night?

Secretly locked away in my little room,
Lying in the moonlight,
Utterly bathed in its eerie radiance,
And I drifted into sleep.

Dreamt there of full golden hours
Of unalloyed bliss,
I`d already had the lovely image
Enter deep into my heart.

Am I the same person, whom you, amidst so many lights,
Keep prisoner at the gaming table?
And whom you place opposite
Those often so detestable faces?

To me, the blossoms of spring
Are not more appealing in the meadow;
Where you, angel, are is love and goodness,
And where you are, there nature is.[5]

It is a poem of discomfort, discomfort that the experience of love has utterly changed the priorities of the self. One can hear the disquiet in the questions that dominate stanzas one and four, and in the paradoxes ('ach' is linked by assonance to 'Pracht' in line two, and the former self is described as being 'selig' in 'der öden Nacht'). It is important to register that the poem is grounded in a sense of temporal contrasts. Lines one and two of the first stanza are in the present, as are the last two stanzas of the poem. But lines three and four of stanza one and the whole of stanzas two and three are in the past. The memories take us back to a time that antedates the current, troubling relationship with the girl. The retrospective view is affectionate but also incredulous. The past self contrived to be happy in the empty nights; the dreamy, dozy condition was (it seems) as much joy as was to be had; and it was a joy that was made up of fantasies of 'ungemischter Lust', and not of the reality of a relationship. Yet that reality, that relationship, is disquieting. There is, to recall the paradox to which I have already drawn attention, splendour ('Pracht'), but it is an unwelcome one ('ach'). The fourth stanza spells out some of the anguish; and it derives from the fact that the girl inhabits a particular kind of social world — brightly lit, with gaming tables, full of 'unerträglichen Gesichtern'. This, then, is high society; the 'splendour' is a very worldly one of casinos, parties, soirées. It is a world in which the poet's self is anything but at home. Hence he cannot believe the change that love for this girl has wrought in him ('Bin ich's noch . . .?'). Yet it seems that there is no going back to the untried innocence of the former self, the 'guter Junge' in his little room (the diminutive 'Zimmerchen' is telling). That former home was a place of secret wish dreams ('heimlich'); but it was as unalloyed as it was untried. Now the world has got larger, as has the self. And no re-miniaturization is possible.

In this sense, then, 'An Belinden' is a poem of contrasts, contrasts between then and now, and, above all else, between the then self and the now self. Yet the poem moves beyond simple juxtaposition to find a kind of precarious resolution. The final stanza of the poem starts as though it were going simply to repudiate the disagreeable present. The first line reads:

Reizender ist mir des Frühlings Blüte (. . .).

That is to say: the poem seems to affirm the greater beauty and worth of the former life, a life lived close to nature (the 'Blüten' of 'Mailied') rather than in the midst of worldliness. But the sense does not stop there. The sentence continues into the next line which resolutely negates the opening statement —

Nun nicht auf der Flur (. . .).

In other words, there is, apparently, nothing 'unnatural' about the love that the poet feels for the sophisticated, worldly girl. Where she is — even, presumably in the bright lights of the gaming rooms — there nature is at work:

Wo du, Engel, bist ist Lieb und Güte,
Wo du bist, Natur.

The closing rhyme (*Flur / Natur*) makes an intertextual link with 'Mailied'. And we as readers register how far the poet's self has travelled from the meadows to the gaming tables. Yet both, we are told, are forms of nature. What is entailed here is a complex reflection on priorities, a taking back of simplicities that were so rapturously asserted. In 'Mailied' nature was the force that united all orders of being in a blissful, unquestioning totality. Now nature has changed her aspect; she is at work, it seems, in the love felt by a radically changed self for a radically different girl in a radically different world. 'An Belinden' shows us nature functioning in a sophisticated social context.

'An Belinden' is a more complex poem than 'Mailied'. It speaks complexly of a divided self who is endeavouring to come to term with unsettling experiences. The poem, and the experience it mediates and on which it reflects are expressive of an acutely felt shift in priorities and hierarchies. What was true no longer quite is. The experienced world and the self that does the experiencing have changed, changed decisively. The past is still close enough to be felt; the self remembers a former self; the poem remembers a former poem. Yet there can be no going back because the present has brought about a different set of priorities that are urgently and immediately felt. The emotional charge behind the twice-repeated 'so' is telling ('so viel Lichtern', 'so unerträglichen Gesichtern') — not least because it echoes and modifies the intensity of those early, untried fanatsies of love ('so selig'). Both the 'then' and the 'now' are linked by their sheer experiential authority. But now the love is different; the desire is different; the social world is different. Yet, troublingly, they are still related to nature. These are some of the psychological implications of the poem. And it also explores philosophical dilemmas. Above all, they derive from the conundrum that sophisticated social behaviour can exert an attraction that is embedded in the natural flux of human desire. Once again, the issue of hierarchy comes to the fore. Is society, that is, culture, a part of human nature? Is it superior to it, secondary to it, a more complex version of it? The cognitive drama is grounded in the mysterious processes of human knowing, a knowing that is both mental and physical, a property of both mind and body.

Both these poems are part of that astonishing birth of German as a truly literary language for which Goethe is largely responsible. Even now, reading them over two hundred years later, they have an extraordinary expressivity. Both poems display the clear formal control of a strophic structure which is underpinned by the strong rhyme scheme (abcb in 'Mailied', abab in 'An Belinden'). Yet that formal control strikes us as anything but an exercise in going through the (poetic) motions because of the sheer colloquial force of the language (the rapturous urgency and dialect rhyme in 'Mailied', the suppressed first-person pronouns of 'Lag im Monenschein', 'Träumte da', 'Hatte schon' in 'An Belinden'). The poems, then, feel like the record of a self trying to understand itself and the world around it.

Both poems come from the period of Goethe's life that is chronicled in *Dichtung und Wahrheit*. That period sees the birth of the artist from the spirit of experiential intensity. One form that intensity takes is, as it were, that which is felt on the pulses. Both our poems have urgently to do with what it feels like to be in love. But the poems also capture the cognitive force of love — the way the experience impinges on the forms, categories, and hierarchizations of human knowing. The processes of self-understanding change. What our poems show is the sense that the selfhood of the poet and the value structures by which he lives are dynamic, are in flux.[6] This process that begins in the early 1770s accompanies Goethe throughout his life: the self is in movement, as are the forms of its knowing. It never comes to rest because living is changing. *Dichtung und Wahrheit* is important not so much for the biographical facts that it gives us; similarly, our two poems are important not so much for the life story they tell (from Sesenheim to Frankfurt, from Friederike to Lili). What is important in both the autobiography and in the poems is the sense of the self in process, of its values and priorities as changing entities.

Goethe was enough the product of both the Enlightenment and of *Empfindsamkeit* to know that human self-understanding is not a given, not a fixity but is, rather, made, un-made and re-made in the ceaseless energy of the living process as knowing and being constantly interact. That does not in any sense imply a solipsistic hierarchy in which the subject is, as it were, monarch of all he or she surveys. On the contrary, it is the result of and a tribute to experiential contestation and challenge.

Notes

[1] See David Hill, 'Introduction' and '"Die schönsten Träume von Freiheit werden ja im Kerker geträumt": The Rhetoric of Freedom in the Sturm und Drang', in David Hill (ed.), *Literature of the Sturm und Drang* [*The Camden House History of German Literature*, vol. 6] (Rochester, NY: Camden House, 2003), pp. 1–44 and 159–84.

[2] The translation is to be found in Goethe, *Selected Poems*, trans. by John Whaley (London: Dent, 1998), p. 3.

[3] See Klaus Weimar, *Goethes Gedichte 1769–1775: Interpretationen zu einem Anfang* (Paderborn, Munich, Vienna, Zurich: F. Schöningh, 1982), pp. 32–39.

[4] See Dorothea Hölscher-Lohmeyer, 'Die Entwicklung des Goetheschen Naturdenkens im Spiegel seiner Lyrik', *Goethe Jahrbuch*, 99 (1982), 11–31; and Carl Pietzcker, 'Johann Wolfgang Goethe: Mailied', *Wirkendes Wort*, 19 (1969), 15–28.

[5] The translation of 'An Belinden', which makes no claims to poetic effect but aims only to be accurate, is by myself.

[6] That sense of flux is captured nowhere more vividly than in the late poem 'Um Mitternacht' which, in its second stanza ('Wenn ich dann ferner in des Lebens Weite / Zur Liebsten musste, musste, weil sie zog'), generates an intertextual reference to 'An Belinden', just as 'An Belinden' intertextually harks back to 'Mailied'.

WOMEN'S LIVES AFTER DIVORCE IN THE EUROPEAN NOVEL AROUND 1800

By KARL LEYDECKER

In Goethe's *Die Wahlverwandtschaften* (1809), the issue of women's lives after divorce is brought into sharp focus by the following passage:

> Charlotte asked after an old friend and was dismayed to hear that she was about to be divorced. 'It is very disagreeable', said Charlotte. 'We imagine our absent friends to be safe and well, we suppose a particular dear person to be quite catered for, and the next we hear her fate is precarious and she has been obliged to set off again on paths that may again be less than safe.'[1]

> [Charlotte {erkundigte sich} nach einer Jugendfreundin und mit einiger Befremdung vernahm, daß sie ehstens geschieden werden sollte. Es ist unerfreulich, sagte Charlotte, wenn man seine abwesenden Freunde irgend einmal geborgen, eine Freundin, die man liebt, versorgt glaubt; eh' man sich's versieht, muß man wieder hören, daß ihr Schicksal im Schwanken ist und daß sie erst wieder neue und vielleicht abermals unsichre Pfade des Lebens betreten soll.][2]

Charlotte's words indicate that she views marriage as an oasis of certainty where the woman is catered for, including materially, the word 'versorgt' having connotations of 'Versorgungsehe' or marriage that meets material needs, often used in contrast to the term 'Liebesehe', or marriage for love. For Charlotte, marriage is the normative structure, and divorce, though apparently under certain conditions inevitable, is, at least for a woman, unwelcome because it heralds uncertainty, both emotional and material. Indeed, Goethe's novel is haunted by this question of the consequences of divorce for Charlotte, so that repeatedly she and Eduard stand on the brink of divorce before backing away from that outcome.

The fate of women after divorce is a key issue not only for Goethe in this novel, but more broadly for German, French and English novelists, many of them women, who grappled with the issue of divorce in their novels in the late eighteenth and early nineteenth century. That there was a vogue for novels about divorce not only in the German states, but also in France and Britain, during this period is not widely appreciated, the common view until very recently being that divorce is not a prominent feature in the novel until the mid-nineteenth century.[3] There one thinks in England of the trigger of the Caroline Norton case in the 1830s and the eventual passage of the Matrimonial Causes Act in 1857, in Russia of Leo Tolstoy's *Anna Karenina*

(1877), in Germany of the novels of Theodor Fontane in the 1880s and 1890s, in America also from the 1880s the novels of William Dean Howells, whose *A Modern Instance* (1882) is reckoned to be the first American divorce novel, Henry James, and later Edith Wharton. In France meanwhile divorce was not permitted before 1884 except for the period from 1792–1816 in the aftermath of the French revolution, with Guy de Maupassant's *Bel-Ami* (1885) a prominent example of a novel featuring a divorce which appeared in the immediate aftermath of its legalization.

While divorce had been permitted in the Protestant German states since the reformation, a considerable liberalization occurred in the late eighteenth century, with Prussia's introduction of a new Civil Code in 1794 marking the high point of liberal divorce legislation in the German states until the 1970s.[4] Meanwhile in France there was a short window of great liberality between 1792 and 1803, during which time, as Pasco notes 'it took very little to break a marriage', there being an estimated 30,000 divorces in France in those years.[5] The important element in common between the Civil Code in Prussia and the revolutionary divorce law in France was that both permitted divorce by mutual consent or on the grounds of incompatibility as perceived by either partner. Moreover, even in England, where divorce could only be obtained on the grounds of adultery on the part of the wife by an Act of Parliament, an expensive and very public process which rendered divorce comparatively very rare by comparison, nevertheless in Allen Horstman's words 'after 1770 and again after 1790 [...] contemporaries discerned a "divorce epidemic" raging in England'.[6]

It is only very recently, however, that scholars have begun to explore the literary response to the reality or perception of the relative liberalization of divorce laws or practice in the late eighteenth century. Indeed, Pasco's observations with respect to France are equally valid for Germany and England: '[H]owever little the critics have been struck by divorce, it was the topic of much contemporary discussion. The extraordinary amount of commentary in literature [...] leaves no doubt that France was in the throes of disquiet over the issue' (p. 140).[7] While critics have recently begun to focus on the representation of divorce in the German and French novel of the time, there has not hitherto been any comparative study of literary representations of divorce in the novel in Germany, France and Britain during this period.[8] This chapter addresses that gap, focusing on the depiction in the novel of women's lives after divorce, a subject which preoccupied those writers, nearly all of them women, who tackled the issue of divorce in their novels. The chapter will begin with a discussion of German novels of divorce from the 1780s on, then look at a key novel from the French revolutionary period that depicts divorce, and finally compare and contrast depictions of divorce there with the treatment of divorce by English writers around 1800. It will be shown that the depiction of divorce in the English novel is strongly coloured by a consciousness of continental, and especially French, radicalism in divorce law and practice in the last decade of the eighteenth century, with the French model clearly an inspiration for Mary Wollstonecraft's advocacy of liberal divorce. In the work of conservative writers, by contrast, the French influence manifests itself in the form of a moral panic about the effects of liberal divorce laws, an important consequence being that in their works, in contrast to German and French novels of the period, the strong implication is that there can be no life for women after divorce. Indeed, this was a position which even Wollstonecraft, for all her advocacy of divorce for women, ultimately had great difficulty departing from.

DIVORCE IN THE LATE EIGHTEENTH-CENTURY GERMAN NOVEL

As early as the 1780s, German women novelists began tentatively to depict divorce and to explore what divorce meant for women. The first such example known to me is *Maria* (1784), by Meta Liebeskind (1765–?). Here the central character is divorced by her husband who wrongly suspects her of adultery. This appears to free the way for her to marry Eduard, with whom she was in love prior to her marriage and whom she would have married in the first place had it not been for villainous trickery of another character. But the problem is that for religious reasons Marie cannot contemplate a life after marriage, to the extent that she is persuaded by the tortuous arguments of a Pastor's wife that, since she was not in fact unfaithful to her husband, the divorce can never be regarded as legitimate in the eyes of God. So, instead of marrying Eduard, Marie illogically blames herself for the collapse of her marriage, putting it down to her excessive sentimentality. She then promptly dies of a mystery illness to which so many eighteenth-century fictional women succumb. *Maria* is thus a highly conservative novel which, while on the one hand implying the need for divorce to bring about the union of an ideally-suited couple, ultimately shies away from its own logic to foreground divorce as means of punishment for female adultery, the consequences of which are death.[9] The clear implication is that there can be no life after divorce for women.

If *Maria* represents the conservative end of the spectrum, *Julchen Grünthal* (1784) by Friederike Helene Unger (1741–1813) is fascinatingly ambivalent. One the one hand it presents divorce as a boon to the feckless husband wishing to free himself from a marriage in order to take another lover: the eponymous central character forms a relationship with her cousin's husband, who then divorces his wife for her, only later to abandon Julchen by eloping with the maid, leaving Julchen to flee to Russia with a Russian nobleman. Thus, a woman precipitating a divorce, even where she is not herself divorcing, leads to social ostracism, taking a woman beyond the pale of respectable society. More interesting, however, is the fate of the divorced wife, Julchen's cousin Karoline. The text breaks new ground in its depiction of her role in the divorce and her fate after divorce. For although she still loves her husband very much, she can see the writing on the wall for her marriage. Consequently it is she who initiates the discussion about divorce with her husband and it is she who performs the task of persuading her uncle, Julchen's father, to accept the divorce. Given Karoline's stance, he is compelled to do so, and because the divorce is by mutual consent it is rapidly approved by the courts. Yet even though Karoline does not fight tooth and nail to stay married, rather than have her die of the mystery illness that she promptly contracts, the text is able to envisage an independent life for her after divorce. Thus, in contrast to *Maria*, divorce is here presented as a legitimate and appropriate course for women where warranted by the poor behaviour of the husband, freeing her to lead an independent life or indeed, as occurs in the second volume of the novel, which was added when the third edition appeared in 1798, to enter into a second marriage contract.

Even more openly positive about divorce, and the possibilities of life after divorce for women, is Marianne Ehrmann's two-volume novel *Amalie* of 1788.[10] Amalie is forced into a marriage, her husband turns out to be a gambler and a violent man whose physical abuse of Amalie causes her to have a miscarriage, leading to an initial separation. Amalie, who is Catholic, refuses at the end of the first volume to contemplate the divorce urged by her Protestant friend Fanny. But at the beginning of the second volume, the escalating violence of the husband precipitates a separation ['Trennung'][11] — it is never confirmed explicitly that the final separation is in fact a legal divorce, and we learn some time later of the eventual death of the husband. Her friend prays that she will soon find a new and better husband, but it is significant that at the time of the divorce there is no such prospect. Initially Amalie retires to a convent and, upon hearing definitively that her husband is not going to return she at first rails against the chains that bind her to him still and deny her the possibility of a new love, shuts herself in and starves herself. But at the crisis point of her dangerous illness, she is saved by the intervention of a doctor. It is at this point that the novel radically departs from the abject female renunciation ['Entsagung'] that is the dominant paradigm of German fiction by women in the period: she journeys alone to Italy, dresses as a man in order to observe a brothel, becomes an actress, and teases hordes of unsuitable suitors by making them fall in love with her and then jilting them. This goes on for some 200 pages of narrative, the majority of the second volume. Inevitably her picaresque, carnivalesque progress is curtailed at the end of the novel, as she meets and marries a suitable man within the last twenty pages of the second volume, but the brevity of this episode serves only to highlight the expansiveness of the highly unusual description for the period of a woman's life of seemingly total freedom after divorce. Thus, German novels from the 1780s on are on occasion able to envisage life, rather than death or its equivalent — the cloistered life — for women after divorce. Invariably that life after divorce eventually ultimately results in remarriage (and then often only after the death of the original husband), which serves to indicate how transgressive was the depiction of women's single lives after divorce.[12] Moreover, sometimes, as in Ehrmann's *Amalie*, the remarriage does not occur straight away, opening up new narrative trajectories of self-realization outside marriage for women after divorce.

DIVORCE IN THE FRENCH NOVEL OF THE REVOLUTIONARY PERIOD: MADAME DE STAËL'S *DELPHINE*

Two French novels of the revolutionary period also tackle the question of divorce head on, with both taking the position that divorce should be legalized so as to bring about a new marital union. As its title implies, Louvet de Couvray's *Emilie de Varmont ou le divorce nécessaire et les amours du curé Sévin* (published in 1791, but set in 1782) argues for the necessity of divorce as well as the abolition of convents and the ending of celibacy for Catholic priests. The whole plot is constructed in order to emphasize the need for divorce, as Emilie, believing her husband dead, has fallen in love with another man, while her husband, believing Emilie dead, has bigamously married his first love whom he had been unable to marry originally due to her family arranging a marriage for her to another. When all is revealed at the climax of the novel, the characters anticipate the coming revolution when divorce will be legalized, which would allow Emilie and her husband to divorce and marry their respective ideal partners. Until that time, however, the only option is for Emilie and her husband's bigamous second wife to retire to a convent, presented here as so often in French fiction in the eighteenth century as a living death.[13] Thus, whereas Liebeskind's *Maria* had foregrounded the barriers to divorce arising from religious views, in this novel the legal barriers to divorce are foreground. At the same time, as in *Julchen Grünthal* there is a strong anti-Catholic overtone to the presentation of the divorce question.

If *Emilie de Varmont* anticipates the revolution's relaxation of divorce laws, Madame de Staël's novel *Delphine* of 1802 is set in 1790–1792 at the time of the introduction of divorce in France and, as both Pasco and Gengembre have recently argued, has the issue of divorce at its heart.[14] This enormously popular and controversial novel which was banned by Napoleon is interesting in its own right as perhaps *the* major novel of divorce in France during this period, setting out very deliberately to refute the conservative tract *Réflections sur le divorce* (1794) published by de Staël's mother, Suzanne Necker.[15] It is doubly interesting in this context in that it also prompted a strong reaction across the channel in England.

Delphine shares some characteristics of the novels discussed so far in that, like *Emilie de Varmont*, it advocates the legalization of divorce and, like *Julchen Grünthal*, it adopts an anti-Catholic stance. But, unlike *Julchen Grünthal*, the novel emphasizes the negative social effects of divorce on the innocent wife in two separate plot strands, thereby tempering its advocacy of divorce and foregrounding the moral dilemma which divorce throws up. In terms of the narrative, the first episode that foregrounds the divorce issue is the story of the subsidiary character Madame de Lebensei. Her divorce, and second marriage to M. de Lebensei, the representative of enlightened liberalism and spokesperson in the novel for the legalization of divorce, exemplifies both the novel's radical advocacy of women freeing themselves from unhappy marriages through the introduction of liberal divorce laws, and also the high social price that is exacted by Catholic French society for divorce. At eighteen, Mme de Lebensei had married M. de T., a colonialist who had exercised 'despotic tyranny' ['despotisme tyrannique'] over his slaves in America and subjected her to the same tyranny.[16] The language here makes explicit the connection between divorce and political revolution, Pasco noting that 'in *Delphine* divorce and revolution are linked symbiotically'.[17] Eventually she met and fell in love with M. de Lebensei and, being resident in Holland, initiated divorce proceedings against her husband under Dutch law. Although the husband disputed the divorce as a way of trying to get her to make over her fortune to him, it was eventually granted and she was able to marry Lebensei. The fact that her husband is presented in a very negative light and they have no children, common traits in novels which represent legitimate divorce by women, serves to render her decision to divorce him acceptable in the eyes of the reader, if not French society as represented in the novel. Mme de Lebensei's decision is not legitimized by reference to over-whelming passion but rather is represented as the product of Enlightenment rationality, Delphine referring to her as 'enlightened and rational rather than passionate' (p. 109) [éclairée, raisonnable plutôt qu'exaltée' (p. 282)]. Under-pinning her decision is a moral system which pervades the whole novel, that the pursuit of individual happiness is justified if, but only if, that individualism does not impinge on the happiness of another: 'I was convinced that, properly understood, morality and religion did not forbid me to marry Henri, since through that decision I was not troubling anyone's destiny, and since I had to account only to God for my happiness' (p. 115) ['J'étois convaincue que la morale et la religion bien entendues, ne me défendoient point d'épouser Henri, puisque je ne troublois, par cette résolution, la destinée de personne, et que je n'avois à rendre compte qu'à Dieu de mon bonheur' (p. 294)]. Nevertheless, the social consequences for the divorced woman are severe, amounting to total exclusion from society. The message is very clear that 'perfect happiness can never be the lot of a woman who contracts a bad marriage through her parents' error or her own' (p. 116) ['le bonheur parfait ne peut jamais être le partage d'une femme, à qui l'erreur de ses parents ou la sienne propre, ont fait contracter un mauvais mariage' (p. 296)]. On this view, the woman's life after divorce is necessarily a very circumscribed one, heavily dependent on her second partner with whom she must create a private world of fulfilment reminiscent of mid-Enlightenment bourgeois idylls: 'In sum, she must find in the object of her sacrifices the ever-living source of the varied pleasures of heart and reason, and the two of them must go through life leaning upon one another, loving one another, and doing good' (p. 117) ['Enfin, il faut trouver dans l'objet de nos sacrifices, la source toujours vive des jouissances variées du coeur et de la raison, et traverser la vie appuyés l'un sur l'autre, en s'aimant et faisant le bien' (p. 295)].

The Lebensei episode occurs relatively early in the novel and provides the ideological framework for the playing out of the divorce issue in the main plot, which turns for long periods on the question of whether the man Delphine loves, Léonce, who has been tricked into marrying another woman, will take advantage of the introduction of the divorce law in France in the course of the novel to divorce his wife to marry Delphine. It falls to M. de Lebensei, who is the spokesperson for Enlightenment rationality and strongly correlated with English good sense, to put the case for the legitimacy of divorce. He advocates divorce on the grounds of the right of the individual to pursue happiness, accepting that individual circumstances will dictate whether a particular divorce is legitimate or not: 'it is the individual situation that will decide whether divorce, sanctioned by law, can be accepted by the tribunal of public opinion and of our own hearts' (p. 305) ['Ce sont les circonstances particulières à chacun qui déterminent, si le divorce autorisé par la loi, peut être approuvé par le tribunal de l'opinion et de notre propre coeur' (p. 655)]. He goes on to criticize English divorce law for allowing divorce only on the grounds of adultery, for in his view 'infidelity breaks the contract, but the impossibility of loving strips life of the primary happiness nature intended; and when that impossibility truly exists, when it is confirmed by time, reflection, and the reasoning even of our friends and relatives, who will dare pronounce that such a marriage is indissoluble?' (p. 305) [L'infidélité rompt le contrat, mais l'impossibilité de s'aimer dépouille la vie du premier bonheur que lui avoit destiné la nature; et quand cette impossibilité existe réellement, quand le temps, la réflexion, la raison même de nos amis et de nos parents la confirment, qui osera prononcer qu'un tel mariage est indissoluble?' (p. 656)]. In a manner reminiscent of *Julchen Grünthal*, an opposition is set up between Catholicism on the one hand, and 'Nature, guided by Providence' (p. 305) ['la nature, guidée par la Providence' (p. 657)] on the other, with the Protestant countries (England, Holland, Switzerland and America are named) being held up as positive examples. Perhaps most radical of all is Lebensei's advocacy of divorce even where the marriage was not childless, for this went beyond the position adopted for example by the Prussian Civil Code. Lebensei concludes his argument by expressing the view that divorce will strengthen marriage: 'morals will become stricter, marriage will be respected more, and people will sense that all of these good things result from the possibility of finding happiness in duty' (p. 308) ['les mœurs deviendront plus austères, le mariage sera plus respecté, et l'on sentira que tous ces biens sont dus à la possibilité de trouver le bonheur dans le devoir' (p. 662)]. At the same time he makes a critical point that would certainly have resonated across the Channel as well as in France when he notes that: 'It is true that divorce will displease some people far more for being the result of a revolution they detest than for any other reason' (p. 308) ['Il est vrai que le divorce, paroissant à quelques personnes le résultat d'une révolution qu'elles détestent, leur déplaît sous ce rapport beaucoup plus que sous tous les autres' (p. 662)]. As we shall see, the association of divorce with revolution was very strong in the minds of those, be they conservative or radical, who focused on divorce in England in the 1790s and the first decade of the nineteenth century.

While in theory Delphine accepts Lebensei's justification of divorce, in practice she is unable to accept that her own happiness through marriage to Léonce should be achieved at the expense of Léonce's wife, Matilde, raising again the issue of the fate of women after divorce: 'Divorce would throw Matilde into deep despair, she would regard it as a crime, would never consider herself free, and would shut herself away in a cloister for the rest of her days' (p. 310) ['Le divorce jetteroit Matilde dans un profond désespoir, elle le regarderoit comme un crime, ne se considéreroit jamais comme libre, et s'enfermeroit dans un cloître pour le reste de ses jours' (p. 665)]. Delphine, and with her the text as a whole, adopts an ambivalent middle position between enlightenment liberalism and Catholic conservatism: 'happiness, I agree, should be considered the aim of Providence; but morality, the order given man to fulfil God's purpose on earth, often requires the sacrifice of an individual happiness to the general happiness' (p. 311) [c'est le bonheur, j'en conviens avec vous, qu'on doit considérer comme le but de la Providence; mais la morale, qui est l'ordre donné à l'homme de remplir les intentions de Dieu sur la terre, la morale exige souvent que le bonheur particulier soit immolé au bonheur général' (p. 667)]. Delphine's resolve is only reinforced by the revelation that Mathilde is pregnant, indicating that, while Lebensei's justification of divorce where a marriage was not childless was acceptable in theory and in French law at the time, in practice there was a very strong taboo against it (Charlotte's pregnancy being similarly employed as a narrative element at the end of the first volume of Goethe's *Die Wahlverwandtschaften* to raise a barrier to Eduard's determination to divorce). Moreover, even the subsequent deaths of Mathilde and her child do not lead to the marriage of

Delphine and Léonce. In ways that also parallel *Die Wahlverwandtschaften*, psychological barriers eventually replace legal and social ones to the union of the star-crossed couple, as Léonce acknowledges: 'Of all the torments, surely the most frightful, the most extraordinary is to find in our own hearts a feeling that separates us from the object of our tenderness, to harbor the obstacle in ourselves when all other obstacles have disappeared' (p. 442) ['de tous les supplices le plus affreux, le plus extraordinaire n'est-il pas de trouver dans son propre cœur un sentiment qui nous sépare de l'objet de notre tendresse? d'avoir en soi l'obstacle quand tous les autres ont disparu?' (p. 920)]. After many trials and tribulations, Delphine commits suicide as Léonce is about to be executed, so that both are dead at the end of the text, just as Eduard and Ottilie are at the end of *Die Wahlverwandtschaften*. *Delphine* is thus ultimately ambivalent about divorce, advocating it in theory, and demonstrating it in practice in the case of Mme de Lebensei, yet in the end ensuring that divorce is avoided in the main plot, ostensibly on the grounds of the assumed devastating social effects of divorce on the wife, but at a deeper level because of the psychological barriers to divorce that exist in the minds of the central characters and, one suspects, the author.

Divorce in the English Novel Around 1800

The passage of the revolutionary divorce law in France in 1792 had profound reverberations in England, not least because it coincided with an upsurge in petitions for divorce in England, and fuelled what Katherine Binhammer calls 'the sex panic of the 1790s'.[18] Divorce had certainly featured in English novels as far back as the 1750s, as for example in Sarah Fielding's *The History of the Countess of Dellwyn* (1759) which, in line with the legal reality of the time, presents divorce as a punishment for the adulterous wife (the central character is divorced by her husband on account of her adultery, flees to Paris, is thwarted in her desire to marry again when news of her divorce reaches Paris, and returns to England to lead her life as a social outcast). It is, however, around 1800 that the issue of divorce becomes prominent in the English novel, with the model of liberal divorce in France provoking very contrasting approaches to the issue by novelists on the other side of the channel.

Mary Wollstonecraft's *Maria, or The Wrongs of Woman* (1798) is a milestone in the history of representations of divorce in the novel. It is a broadside against prevailing marriage and divorce laws and their effects on women, and a manifesto for divorce reform. At the same time the question of whether divorce in practice leads only to misery for women or whether new possibilities of life after divorce can be envisaged is left open at the end of what is an unfinished novel. The novel opens with Maria imprisoned in an asylum by her libertine husband, a literal extension of the marital state of being 'in a trap, caged for life'.[19] In a famous phrase it is made explicit that Wollstonecraft's campaign in the novel for the legal reform of marriage and divorce is inspired by the revolution in France with its attendant liberalization of divorce, as Maria laments that 'marriage had bastilled me for life' (p. 76). In spite of the implication that there is no escape from marriage, Maria's benevolent uncle contemplates taking her away from her husband: 'For I am far from thinking that a woman, once married, ought to consider the engagement as indissoluble (especially if there be no children to reward her for sacrificing her feelings)' (p. 78). Maria is now pregnant, however, so that the presence of children (as so often in divorce novels of the period) is represented as a key obstacle even to separation, let alone divorce, a point reinforced in that later Maria says that it was the subsequent death of the child which 'dissolved the only tie which subsisted between me and my, what is termed, lawful husband' (p. 119). As had been the case in Ehrmann's *Amalie*, the appalling behaviour of the husband, who in this case tries to prostitute her, leads Maria to leave the marital home, but in trying to escape to the continent after the birth of her child, she is imprisoned and her child abducted. In the asylum she meets Darnford and becomes his lover. On her escape, her husband sues Darnford for adultery.

The particular importance of *Maria* as a novel of divorce is amplified in that it is the only literary representation of a criminal conversation or divorce trial in eighteenth-century literature known to me, and one which in its focus on the public interrogation of female sexuality prefigures the divorce court journalism and literary culture arising from it that flourished following the passage of the 1857 Matrimonial Causes Act, so fascinatingly explored by Barbara Leckie.[20] Maria, keen to secure a legal divorce so as to be able to marry Darnford to avoid 'the odium of society' (p. 116), decides to plead guilty. After the opening statement from her husband's lawyer, Maria's statement is read out, culminating in her demand: 'I claim then a divorce' (p. 120). Effectively Maria attempts to subvert the criminal conversation trail, by trying to turn it into a divorce case. Of particular interest are the terms in which the judge rejects her demand, for they highlight the extent to which, for Wollstonecraft, the divorce issue was framed by developments in divorce law in France: 'We did not want French principles in public or private life' (p. 121). Moreover, the conclusion of the judgment is framed in a way that established the parameters for future debates about divorce through the nineteenth century and beyond, namely the balance that should be struck between the interest of the State in upholding marriage on the one hand, and the rights of the individual to pursue personal happiness on the other (we saw above how *Delphine* had turned on this same question). The judge's final words are paradigmatic of the line of argument adopted by opponents of divorce: 'Too

many restrictions could not be thrown in the way of divorce, if we wish
to maintain the sanctity of marriage; and though they might bear a little hard
on a few, very few individuals, it was evidently for the good of the whole'
(p. 121). These sentiments would be echoed in classic conservative statements
in defence of the institution of marriage through the nineteenth century, as
for example in *Die Wahlverwandtschaften* where Mittler's famous encomium
on marriage includes a rejection of divorce couched in very similar terms:
'Marriage is the basis and the pinnacle of culture. [. . .] It must never be dissolved, for it brings so much happiness that in comparison any individual
unhappiness is of no significance' (p. 65) [Die Ehe ist der Anfang und
der Gipfel aller Kultur. [. . .] Unauflöslich muβ sie sein; denn sie bringt so
vieles Glück, daβ alles einzelne Unglück dagegen gar nicht zu rechnen ist'
(p. 349)].

The trial scene was the last chapter of *Maria* that Wollstonecraft completed.
Various brief notes of possible conclusions left by her were published when
the novel appeared posthumously. Two of these indicate that the outcome
of the trial was 'a separation from bed and board' (pp. 122 and 123) rather
than a divorce, which is consistent with the judge's indication in the trial
chapter that she might possibly obtain such a separation in another court. The
tersest of the summaries — all of which have roughly the same import — is
as follows: 'Divorced by her husband — Her lover unfaithful — Pregnancy
— Miscarriage — Suicide' (p. 123). This outcome conforms to a pattern
for the fate of the (guilty) woman after divorce which would become the
stock-in-trade of conservative English novelists in the early decades of the
nineteenth century, notably Jane Austen, whereby the divorced adulteress
inevitably has a bad time of it, typically descending into poverty, social exclusion, often sexual promiscuity or prostitution, and finally death. Two examples illustrate this fate. The first is Eliza in Austen's *Sense and Sensibility* (1811),
who is 'married against her inclination to [Colonel Brandon's] brother'.[21]
He 'treated her unkindly', she 'resigned herself at first' but then committed
adultery, and was divorced (p. 154). When Colonel Brandon returned from
the East Indies three years after hearing of this, he tried to find her:

> I could not trace her beyond her first seducer, and there was every reason
> to fear that she had removed from him only to sink deeper in a life of sin. [. . .]
> At last, however, after I had been six months in England, I *did* find her. Regard
> for a former servant of my own, who had since fallen into misfortune, carried
> me to visit him in a sponging-house, where he was confined for debt; and
> there, in the same house, under a similar confinement, was my unfortunate
> sister. So altered — so faded — worn down by acute suffering of every kind!
> (p. 155)

She was also in 'the last stage of a consumption' (p. 155) and died shortly
afterwards. The second is Maria Edgeworth's *Ennui* (1809), in which the

marriage of the central male character, the Earl of Glenhorn, contracted as a purely financial transaction, collapses early on in the narrative when his wife, whom he has treated less than well, runs away with another man, leading to a divorce. Some considerable time later, the Earl stumbles across his ex-wife's funeral, and learns what happened to her from a priest:

> She had, almost in her last moments, as he assured me, expressed her sense of, what she called, my generosity to her, and had shown deep contrition for her infidelity. She died in extreme poverty and wretchedness, with no human being who was, or even seemed, interested for her, but a maid-servant [. . .]. Crawley, it seems, had behaved brutally to his victim. After having long delayed to perform his promise of marrying her, he declared that he could never think of a woman who had been divorced in any other way than a mistress: she, poor weak creature, consented to live with him on any terms; but, as his passions and his interest soon turned to new objects, he cast her off without scruple, refusing to pay any of the tradesmen, who had supplied her while she bore his name.[22]

In both cases, there can be no respectable life after divorce for women, and before long literally no life at all. For these writers, the legal niceties of divorce do nothing to temper the dominant cultural paradigm of the fallen women, there being the same inevitability about the descent of the divorcée into poverty, illness and death that is exemplified in the fate of the fallen woman in William Hogarth's *A Harlot's Progress* (1732) and countless other eighteenth-century works.[23]

What these cases illustrate is the very reason why the liberalization of divorce laws was such an important issue for women. For as long as marriage remained the only real option for women, then only the possibility of full legal divorce that would allow women to remarry gave women any realistic chance of escaping the bastille of marriage.[24] It is thus not by chance that, as we saw earlier, even liberal texts such as Ehrmann's *Amalie* which depict the possibilities of divorce for women in a positive light and end happily eventually conclude with the remarriage of the divorced woman. Even then, in the English novel, remarriage after divorce is not always a panacea even in the works of progressive writers, as for example in the case of the younger William's wife in Elizabeth Inchbald's *Nature and Art* (1796) who marries the man with whom she commits adultery, but whose husband turns out to be a libertine, indicating that she is not destined to enjoy domestic bliss in her second marriage.

For all its critique of prevailing marriage laws, the sketched endings of *Maria* in which Maria is betrayed by her lover and commits suicide indicate that the novel was planned to end in conformity with the dominant paradigm in the English novel of this period of divorce as punishment. Perhaps aware that Maria's suicide risked an alignment of the novel with this conservative paradigm, in which there is no life after divorce for women, Wollstonecraft also drafted one page of a possible alternative ending. Having swallowed poison, Maria awaits her death, thinking of her supposedly dead child, but then the child is brought to her, she vomits, and the draft concludes with her words, 'I will live for my child!' (p. 124). Thus, with the two sets of endings of the novel Wollstonecraft left open the question of whether it was possible to envisage life after divorce for women under the social and legal conditions prevailing in England.

If Wollstonecraft's *Maria* positively embraces liberal ideas of divorce from revolutionary France, Maria Edgeworth's *Leonora* (1806), written quite consciously in reaction both to *Maria* and even more to de Staël's *Delphine* which appeared in January 1803 while Edgeworth was staying in Paris, and to both of which *Leonora* makes frequent allusion, is a sustained and explicitly British reaction to the perceived excesses of continental, especially French liberalism on the divorce question.[25] The novel focuses on the machinations of Lady Olivia, who separated from her husband as she was no longer in love with him, but unable to divorce him due to the 'tyranny of English laws' (p. 11) went abroad, took a lover there, and on her return to England (having left in France the child from her marriage) tries to steal the husband of the representative of English domestic virtue, Leonora. What is striking is the extent to which Edgeworth demonizes French attitudes to marriage and divorce, which are heavily caricatured. Although she succeeds in getting Leonora's husband to leave her temporarily, an act made all the more wrong in that Leonora is pregnant and gives birth to a son during his absence (p. 120), Lady Olivia's plans are eventually foiled, and she has to flee to the continent once again, reinforcing the point that in Edgeworth's textual world, as in most English novels of the period, life after divorce for women is not conceivable in England.

Nor does *Leonora* confine itself to illustrating the folly of divorce through its representation of Lady Olivia's behaviour, attitudes and fate. It also contains specific observations on the operation of liberal divorce laws in France, through the mechanism of Olivia's correspondent Gabrielle in Paris passing on the latest divorce news from there. Particularly telling is the fact that the liberalization of divorce is recognized as a danger to women even by the decadent Gabrielle, who notes that: 'This system of divorce, though convenient, is not always advantageous to women' (p. 41). This is exemplified by the news that Olivia receives from Gabrielle about a mutual acquaintance in France: 'Did I tell you that Mad. G—— is a second time divorced? But this time it is her husband's doing, not hers. This handsome husband has spent all the immense fortune she brought him, and now procures a divorce for *incompatibility of temper*, and is going to marry another lady, richer than Mad. G——, and as great a fool' (p. 41). The contrasting right–minded response to the divorce regime in France is provided by General B—— in correspondence with Leonora's husband, notably in letter XX in which he reinforces the message that divorce is bad for women: 'What can women expect from it but contempt? Next to polygamy, it would prove the most certain method of destroying the domestic happiness of the sex, as well as their influence and respectability in society' (p. 45). This brings us full circle to Charlotte's fears in *Die Wahlverwandtschaften* about the uncertainty that divorce bring to women. In *Leonora*, divorce threatens women's domestic peace and prosperity, challenging what is presented as the healthy English natural order, with the divorcée demonized as a foreign threat from a decadent, revolutionary continent that must be repulsed. *Leonora* thus stands at the opposite pole to Wollstonecraft's *Maria*, as conservative as the latter was revolutionary, but with both specifically reacting to the French experiment with liberal divorce laws between 1792 and 1803.

This comparison of the representation of divorce in novels by German, French and English novelists around 1800 reveals that divorce became an important literary topic for women writers across Europe during this period. While many novelists, notably in England, adopted a conservative stance, depicting divorce as punishment for wifely adultery and depicting the miserable demise of women after divorce, the most important divorce novels of the period such as those by Ehrmann, de Staël and Wollstonecraft are distinguished by their exploration of the possibility of divorce, and life after divorce, for innocent wives. These texts begin to challenge the paradigm of the suffering wife and tentatively to raise the possibility of divorce as a means to the pursuit of happiness for women. They constitute an attempt by women to secure for themselves the same opportunities that were becoming possible for men, Lawrence Stone noting for this period in the English context 'the shift of the function of Parliamentary divorce from the protection of property to the pursuit of happiness, defined as getting rid of an adulterous wife in order to remarry'.[26] While Wollstonecraft in particular sought to challenge patriarchal marriage and divorce laws head on, and *Delphine*, too, contains important reflection on the legal issues surrounding divorce, one surprising finding of this study is the comparative lack of focus on the legal aspects of, and barriers to, divorce. Indeed, divorce appears to be relatively accessible not only in Germany, but also in England, even though divorce in England was in practice much rarer than the novels of the period would appear to suggest. What also emerges is the generally cautious and ambivalent approach to the subject of divorce even where there are apparently few barriers to divorce, a notable tendency being the substitution of psychological barriers for legal ones, often in the shape of a strong taboo on divorce where the marriage has produced children, as in *Delphine* and *Die Wahlverwandtschaften*. That caution would only increase after 1800 as divorce came to be strongly correlated with (French) revolution, not only in France but in English discussions of divorce not only in the novels of the period but also in parliament.[27] Thus, by the first decade of the nineteenth century, a European-wide reaction to the brief period of literary as well as legal experimentation with divorce was underway, resulting in representations of divorce becoming relatively infrequent in Britain, France and Germany from around 1815 until the 1840s in the German states, the 1850s in England and the 1880s in France.

Notes

[1] Johann Wolfgang von Goethe, *Elective Affinities* (Oxford: Oxford University Press, 1994), p. 67.

[2] Johann Wolfgang Goethe, *Die Wahlverwandtschaften*, in *Sämtliche Werke nach Epochen seines Schaffens*, ed. by Karl Richter *et al.*, 21 vols (Munich: Hanser, 1987), vol. 9, p. 351.

[3] Anne Humpherys, for example, in an otherwise excellent chapter on the early Victorian divorce novel takes it as read that 'since divorce was practically impossible before the mid-nineteenth century, only a handful of novels talked about it in the first half of the century', the earliest novel she writes about being Charlotte Bury's *The Divorced* (1837), 'Breaking Apart: The Early Victorian Divorce Novel', in *Victorian Women Writers and the Woman Question*, ed. by Nicola Diane Thompson (Cambridge: Cambridge University Press, 1999), pp. 42–59 (p. 42).

[4] On the Prussian Civil Code (Allgemeines Landrecht), see Dirk Blasius, *Ehescheidungen in Deutschland im 19. und 20. Jahrhundert* (Frankfurt am Main: Fischer, 1992), pp. 27–33.

[5] Allan H. Pasco, *Revolutionary Love in Eighteenth- and Early Nineteenth-Century France* (Farnham: Ashgate, 2009), p. 131. After 1803, divorce was made much more difficult to obtain, and abolished completely in 1816.

[6] Allen Horstman, *Victorian Divorce* (London and Sydney: Crook Helm, 1985), p. 15. Horstman's table of parliamentary divorces before 1800 lists 126 divorces between the first case in 1672 and 1799, but, of these, 32 were between 1771 and 1779, and 41 between 1790 and 1799 (pp. 16–18), meaning that well over half of all divorces granted in England over 130 years were granted in those two decades. Lawrence Stone notes that 'the 12 petitions for divorce received in 1799 (10 of which were successful) were the highest number ever handled in a single year, before or after' (*Road to Divorce: England 1530–1997* [Oxford: Oxford University Press, 1990], p. 325). Stone also notes that 'beginning in 1770, there was a dramatic explosion of crim. con. cases which peaked in the thirty years from 1790' (p. 255), further adding to the sense of marital crisis during this period.

[7] Pasco, *Revolutionary Love in Eighteenth- and Early Nineteenth-Century France*, p. 140.

[8] On the representation of divorce in German novels by women at this time, see Karl Leydecker, 'Divorcing Women: Divorce and the Rise of the Women's Novel in Germany, 1784–1848', in Karl Leydecker and Nicholas White (eds), *After Intimacy: The Culture of Divorce in the West Since 1789* (Frankfurt am Main: Lang, 2007), pp. 11–29, and Maya Gerig, *Jenseits von Tugend und Empfindsamkeit: Gesellschaftspolitik im Frauenroman um 1800* (Cologne: Böhlau, 2008), especially pp. 120–46.

[9] Gerig discusses *Maria* together with Therese Huber's *Luise* (1796) as examples of divorce texts where divorce is represented as punishment (*Jenseits von Tugend und Empfindsamkeit*, pp. 134–41).

[10] On divorce in *Amalie*, see also Ruth P. Dawson, *The Contested Quill: Literature by Women in Germany, 1770–1800* (London: Associated University Presses, 2002), pp. 245–58 (especially pp. 250–52).

[11] *Amalie: Eine wahre Geschichte in Briefen, von der Verfasserin der Philosophie eines Weibs*, 2 vols ([Bern: Hortin], 1788), reprint edn. by Maya Widmer and Doris Stump (Stuttgart and Vienna: Paul Haupt, 1995), p. 237.

[12] A later novel, Julie Berger's *Ida und Claire oder Die Freundinnen aus den Ruinen* (Bremen: Joh. Heinr. Müller, 1807), which depicts a woman who divorces twice, similarly ultimately ends with her eventually marrying happily. See Gerig, *Jenseits von Tugend und Empfindsamkeit*, p. 144.

[13] Denis Diderot's *La Religieuse* [The Nun], first published posthumously in 1796, is perhaps the most famous depiction in French eighteenth-century literature of the convent as a living death.

[14] Pasco, *Revolutionary Love in Eighteenth- and Early Nineteenth-Century France*, pp. 139–46; Gérard Gengembre, '*Delphine*, ou la Révolution Française: un roman du divorce', *Cahiers Staëliens*, 56 (2005), 105–12.

[15] On the relationship between *Delphine* and Suzanne Necker's treatise, see Janet Whatley, 'Dissoluble Marriage, Paradise Lost: Suzanne Necker's *Réflections sur le divorce*', *Dalhousie French Studies*, 56 (2001), 144–53.

[16] Germaine de Staël, *Delphine*, translated with an introduction by Avriel H. Goldberger (DeKalb, Illinois: Northern Illinois University Press, 1995), p. 112; Madame de Staël, *Delphine*, ed. by Simone Balayé and Lucia Omacini (Geneva: Droz, 1987), p. 287. Subsequent references to the translation and the original are given by page number in the text.

[17] Pasco, *Revolutionary Love in Eighteenth- and Early Nineteenth-Century France*, p. 146.

[18] Katherine Binhammer, 'The Sex Panic of the 1790s', *Journal of the History of Sexuality*, 6.3 (1996), 409–34.

[19] Mary Wollstonecraft, *Maria, or The Wrongs of Woman* (New York: Dover, 2005), p. 66.

[20] See Barbara Leckie, '"One of the Greatest Social Revolutions of Our Time": The Matrimonial Causes Act, Divorce Court Journalism, and the Victorian Novel', in Leydecker and White (eds), *After Intimacy, pp. 31–56*; and *Culture and Adultery: The Novel, the Newspaper, and the Law* (Philadelphia: University of Pennsylvania Press, 1999).

[21] Jane Austen, *Sense and Sensibility* (Oxford: Oxford University Press, 2004), p. 153. Subsequent references are given by page number in the text.

[22] Maria Edgeworth, *Castle Rackrent and Ennui* (London: Penguin, 1992), p. 314.

[23] The death is, of course, not always literal in the texts of the period that feature divorce, for the fate of Maria Rushworth after her adultery and divorce from Mr Rushworth in *Mansfield Park* is not literally death, but a metaphorical death buried in the countryside, a situation 'which could allow no second spring of hope or character', her life after divorce reading like the English equivalent of the cloistered life, a kind of living death, which might have been the fate of a character in similar circumstances in eighteenth-century French literature: 'It ended in Mrs. Norris's resolving to quit Mansfield and devote herself to her unfortunate Maria, and in an establishment being formed for them in another country, remote and private, where, shut up together with little society, on one side no affection, on the other no judgment, it may be reasonably supposed that their tempers became their mutual punishment', Jane Austen, *Mansfield Park* (Harmondsworth: Penguin, 1985), p. 450.

[24] The currency of this issue during the period is indicated by the fact that between 1771 and 1809 there were four attempts by conservatives to pass legislation in England to prevent the divorced wife from marrying her lover. See Stone, *Road to Divorce: England 1530–1997*, pp. 335–39.

[25] On the importance of *Delphine* and *Maria* for the genesis of *Leonora*, see Marilyn Butler, 'Introductory Note', in *The Novels and Selected Works of Maria Edgeworth*, ed. by Marilyn Butler and Mitzi Myers, 12 vols (London: Pickering and Chatto, 1999), vol. 3, pp. vii–xxvi (pp. ix–xiii). The specific allusions to each novel are listed in the endnotes, pp. 332–46, Butler noting that 'Edgeworth associates the two novels together' (p. 332, note 3). References to *Leonora* are given by page number in the text.

[26] Stone, *Road to Divorce: England 1530–1997*, p. 329.

[27] See Stone, *Road to Divorce: England 1530–1997*, p. 332.

TRANSFERENCE OF ART, TRANSFERENCE OF VIOLENCE: ON NIETZSCHE'S 'ECCENTRICITY'

By Barbara Naumann

According to Nietzsche, thought, like cultural forms and institutions, is subject to formative powers which must be thought of as violent. The same applies to the development of the expressive forms of the individual and his thought, and it is particularly true when speaking about the aesthetic orientation of thought and life. Thought, including the thought of the beautiful, which is always seen by Nietzsche in relation to the body of whoever is thinking, has, because of this bodily relation, to come to terms with the traces of burdens, of suffering, and not least of violence. This is why Nietzsche speaks of the eccentric position of his ego with respect to his thought.

In the following article I wish to investigate how Niezsche's positioning of his philosophy as an 'eccentric' philosophy conforms to a perspective that is aware of the transference of violence in all philosophical thought. Particularly in his statements on the relation of aesthetics, bodiliness, and perspectivism, Nietzsche delinates the traces of this violence that inhabits thought. For this reason I would like to examine the connection between bodiliness, aesthetics, and thought in Nietzsche.

The entire philosophy of Nietzsche engages in a fundamental way with the question of violence — not only inasmuch as it treats violence as a theme, but in the sense that it exposes violence as a constitutive and unavoidable moment of existence and philosophical thought. Even philosophy itself, one could almost say, is, in Nietzsche's view, a transference of violence, and Nietzsche's philosophy tries to make visible this violent aspect of thought in a systematic way. In all phases of his work Nietzsche explained how the impulse behind philosophical thought sprang from a coming-to-terms with violence. Or even how the impulse itself marks the emergence of violence.

In Nietzsche's philosophy it is possible to determine distinct phases and corresponding variants of the codification of violence. True, one can only speak of 'codification' here in a specific sense: the expression should not be understood as a process of encoding, that one could, with access to a defined code, then decode and thus turn philosophy into a kind of direct, undisguised statement. Put briefly, Nietzsche's philosophy dispenses with any such kind of 'key'. Rather, in his thought it is a question of *processes* of expression, of transformations, translations, transferences. Nietzsche's philosophy stands under the very sign of the transference of power, its traces and its formative power in thought. The young Nietzsche was interested in the beautiful work of art, in whose origin he recognized an act of violence, as a product of such transferences; later, Nietzsche recognized the effectiveness of these processes even for the contours of the self, the 'I say' and the 'I do'. Each deed, each action, is marked by the veiling and transference of the violent aspects at the origin of thought.

The origin is not 'something' in the sense of a deed or a phenomenon, but rather, in Nietzsche's view, a stimulus, a movement, that gives rise to a process of transference, which is characterized by violent aspects. To this extent transference itself must be thought of as a structured form of violence. In Nietzsche's early writings, what is violent receives the mark of the Dionysian. It is not already comprehensible in its raw state of being, but rather in its veiling through expression or language, in a 'mask'. In his early writings Nietzsche equates the process of veiling with the masking of Dionysos. As an aesthetic form this veiling is equated with art and with artistic creativity; as such it is assigned to the Apollonian, yet still bears the traces of violence:

> For me the *Doric* state and Doric art are explicable only as a permanent military encampment of the Apollonian. Only incessant resistance to the titanic-barbaric nature of the Dionysian could account for the long survival of an art so defiantly prim and so encompassed with bulwarks, a training so warlike and rigorous, and a political structure so cruel and relentless.

> *Ich vermag den dorischen Staat und die dorische Kunst mir nur als ein fortgesetztes Kriegslager des Apollinischen zu erklären: Nur in einem unausgesetzten Widerstreben gegen das titanisch-barbarische Wesen des Dionysischen konnte eine so trotzig-spröde, mit Bollwerken umschlossene Kunst, eine so kriegsgemäße und herbe Erziehung, ein so grausames und rücksichtsloses Staatswesen von längerer Dauer sein.*[1]

THE TRANSFERENCE OF VIOLENCE IN THE SPHERE OF THE BIRTH OF TRAGEDY

In his early writings Nietzsche finds for the process of the transformation of violence above all the metaphors of *the veil* and *the mask*. They tend to mean the same as the arts which produces forms, in which the Dionysian, or what is violent and lacks expression, can be perceived and can thereby be endured.

Here the violence of the Dionysian, namely pain, blood, and ecstasy, are foregrounded. The violent aspects of Dionysos are always veiled by a mask; the masked nature of Dionysos can be understood as an early indication of the process of transference. In itself expressionless, caught up in ecstasy and pain, the Dionysian strives for representation and, in order to do this, it needs another, a secondary principle. In *The Birth of Tragedy* (*Die Geburt der Tragödie*) Nietzsche turns to the examples of fine art and architecture in the form of the temple. But it is above all texts, namely the tragedies of Sophocles and — in his scenes of violence — Euripides, that Nietzsche's argument has in mind.[2] In summary, one could say that Nietzsche recognizes the trace of bodiliness and violence in every beautiful representation, in architecture as in music, with its power to overwhelm us emotionally, in Greek drama as well as in all kinds of 'spiritual' forms and institutions.

Rhetoric of Violence

Transference and translation form in Nietzsche's view the specific modes of change and development in general and of the birth of language in particular. In the genesis of linguistic images this violence cannot be directly recognized, but it reveals itself as a trace, which compels the replacement of an immediate sensory stimulus by a sign and leads to the mode of transference and translation.[3] In these modes of transference and translation, rhetoric is at work; it does not simply follow the trace of original violence, but is itself an agent of this violence, that has found its own forms of representation in thought and in language. The rhetoric of language also produces a rhetoric of things, whose metaphorical nature points to the violent aspects of thought. In this sense, even architecture can, for example, be a rhetoric of violence:

> The most powerful human beings have always inspired architects; the architect has always been under the spell of power. His buildings are supposed to render pride visible, and the victory over gravity, the will to power. Architecture is a kind of eloquence of power in forms — now persuading, even flattering, now only commanding.

> *Die mächtigsten Menschen haben immer die Architekten inspiriert; der Architekt war stets unter der Suggestion der Macht. Im Bauwerk soll sich der Stolz, der Sieg über die Schwere, der Wille zur Macht versichtbaren; Architektur ist eine Art Macht. Beredsamkeit in Formen, bald überredend, selbst schmeichelnd, bald bloß befehlend.*[4]

One is, according to Nietzsche, compelled to thought; thought is a reaction to an original stimulus, which produces and accompanies its articulation. This is why thought is also characterized by a constant coming-to-terms with violence. Thought has to become rhetorical, in order to be effective. Even in the laws of rhetoric and grammar the violent key-forms of though reveal themselves. Hence one can speak of a 'rhetoric of violence' in Nietzsche in a dual sense — as a subjective and as an objective genitive. In Nietzsche's late texts, such as in his *Nachlass* of the 1880s, the 'will to power' appears as a central figure in his thought. This metaphor illustrates the desire to assert itself of the individual, the striving of the individual for recognition and survival, the striving of all given cultural forms to assert themselves and achieve dominance. Even if the will has social Darwinist implications, it nevertheless reflects in a more general sense the striving of life and its capacity to assert itself. In these later texts we find, hardly surprisingly, an excess of metaphors of violence and power.

Hence there is much talk of the artist as a 'creature of power' (*Krafttier*), as a 'superman' (*Übermensch*), we learn to 'philosophize with a hammer'.[5] Within the framework of the interpretation of violent aspects of life Nietzsche thinks of the strong individual, who has insight into the non-individual powers of formation, who translates them individually and brings them to representation. Nietzsche illuminates a way of thinking, according to which in the 'will to power' does not act alone in life as an individual capacity for self-assertion, but rather appears as the capacity of the acting subject to undertake interpretation of the world and of events in relation to itself. In this sense 'violence' governs everything that can be observed and interpreted in vital movements, including social and individual-psychological ones. The will represents an energy that takes as its goal, not wanting to *survive*, but rather to dominate, to impose its own form on its environment, to transfer what is its own as a model onto others.[6] The will shows itself to be violent particularly wherever it is not recognized as such. This is above all the case in particular cultural and philosophical forms, such as Christianity or Platonic thought. Just as Freud will later do in his *Civilization and its Discontents* (*Das Unbehagen in der Kultur*), Nietzsche criticizes the Christian ethics of pity and its moralism; from the perspective of the will to power they reveal themselves as the violence of the weak, whilst Platonic Idealism represents for Nietzsche a philosophy that could only constitute itself through a repression of the body and of its finitude.

Knowledge and Eccentricity

For Nietzsche there exists a 'basic condition of all life' (*Grundbedingung des Lebens*) that is of such fundamental significance that he considers it the precondition *par excellence* of all philosophical thought.[7] This basic condition is perspectivism. According to Nietzsche, perspectivism must always be a matter for reflection and it must always be won anew for philosophical thought. Yet it is not just in connection with philosophical questions of epistemology that Nietzsche tried out constantly changing perspectives and made the change of perspective his preferred instrument to question the positions of Platonism and Christian morality. His autobiographical reflections, or the repositionings of his writings — carried out *ex post* in, for example, the prefaces to the new editions of his works, and above all in *Ecce Homo* — also stand under the sign of dynamically changing and reversible perspectives. As an author who, as a young man, composed several biographical sketches and who, throughout his life, continually expanded, changed, or revised these self-images, Nietzsche was as familiar with the mobility and changeability of intellectual designs as he was with their dependence on the circumstances of life.

In Nietzsche's early writings the physiological determination of thought plays a central role. The body in various states of pleasure or suffering, the use of one's eyes or problems with them, one's food, digestion, and sleep, the fatigue of one's hand when writing, headaches — all these bodily phenomena, particularly painful ones, are read by Nietzsche as moments that determine not just the history of the individual, but cultural and aesthetic history as a whole. For, he insists, history, just like thinking about history, becomes symptomatalogical, i.e., formed by physiological factors or problems. Nietzsche's philosophy seeks to uncover the bodily impulses that make writing and thinking possible, that promotes or inhibits them. These are all aspects that belong to the perspectivization of thinking and writing, and thus also determine the reception of philosophy and art. That a philosopher with such views was considered by his age (and well beyond it) as a representative of extreme positions, and that the agility and reversibility of his positions is perceived above all as an *eccentric* stance, comes as no surprise.

Nor is it surprising that Nietzsche himself describes eccentricity as a consequence of his thought, as its 'second nature', and felt the perspectival balancing act between, on the one hand, attentiveness to life and to the body, and, on the other, intellectual distance to be the driving force behind his philosophy.[8] In December 1887 Nietzsche wrote in a letter to Carl Fuchs:

> In Germany there are strong complaints about my 'eccentricities.' But since people do not know where my centre is, they will find it hard to know for certain where and when I have till now been 'eccentric' — for example, being a classical philologist; this was being *outside* my centre (which, fortunately, does not mean that I was a bad classical philologist). Likewise today it seems to me an eccentricity that I should have been a Wagnerite.

> *In Deutschland beschwert man sich über meine 'Excentricitäten'. Aber da man nicht weiß, wo mein Centrum ist, wird man schwerlich darüber die Wahrheit treffen, wo und wann ich bisher "excentrisch" gewesen bin. Zum Beispiel, dass ich Philologe war — damit war ich außerhalb meines Centrums (womit, glücklicher Weise, durchaus nicht gesagt, ist, dass ich ein schlechter Philologe war). Insgleichen: heute scheint es mir eine Excentrizität, dass ich Wagnerianer gewesen bin.*[9]

Wherever the philosopher assumes a central point, and wherever the eccentric position of his thought can be correspondingly located, is subject to changes in perspective and in interpretation. The self that comments on itself cannot, as a matter of principle, avoid taking an eccentric standpoint. From an external perspective what appears as eccentric, as deserving criticism, perhaps as disconcerting, are the various centres of life and thought that had already taken shape in Nietzsche's biography.

But it is not only Nietzsche's philosophy as a whole that stands in an eccentric relation to the rest of contemporary thought. It is a consequence of this philosophy, and at the same time its reflexive and psychological foundation, that the ego should be understood in terms of the dynamic of tension between emotional engagement and distancing, between bodily experience and conceptual meditation — and thus has an eccentric perspective of the ego on itself as its necessary foundation. This is why eccentricity is one of the essential aspects characterizing Nietzsche's critique of the subject. Nietzsche's texts work through metaphors of the suffering body, of the extreme points of view to which it gives rise, and of eccentricity in numerous contexts. In the preface to *Human, All Too Human* (*Menschliches, Allzumenschliches*) there is talk of the 'great liberation' (*große Loslösung*) and the 'rebellious, arbitrary, volcanically erupting desire for travel, strange places, estrangements, coldness' (*aufrührerisches, willkürliches, vulkanisch stossendes Verlangen nach Wanderschaft, Fremde, Entfremdung, Erkältung, Ernüchterung, Vereisung*).[10] The eccentric image finds its culmination in the metaphor of the 'free spirits' (*freie Geister*), to whom *Human, All Too Human* is, after all, dedicated. The discourses and songs of Zarathustra are saturated with the great solitude of thinking a new thought, and towards the end of his intellectual life, in *Ecce Homo*, Nietzsche uses, alongside the pathos of passion, above all the pathos of singularity, distance, and isolation, in order to give a perspective to his review of his entire work. 'The ice is near' (*Das Eis ist nahe*), one reads there, 'the solitude tremendous — but how calmly all things lie in the light! How freely one breathes! How much one feels *beneath* oneself! Philosophy, as I have so far understood and lived it, means living voluntarily among ice and high mountains' (*die Einsamkeit ist ungeheuer — aber wie ruhig alle Dinge im Licht liegen! wie frei man athmet! wie Viel man unter sich fühlt! — Philosophie, wie ich sie bisher verstanden und gelebt habe, ist das freiwillige Leben in Eis und Hochgebirge*).[11] Eccentricity is so important for Nietzsche's thought, because it describes a perspective on the body, on things, on the world, on objects of thought, and thus suggests a certain relationship of the self to itself. 'I and Me are always two different persons' (*Ich und Mich sind immer zwei verschiedene Personen*), so runs a note written in 1882.[12] Nietzsche thus situates eccentricity in the very unity of the person. This is an insight of immense consequence for Nietzsche's thought, because it means that the presentation of philosophy also has to do with the rhetoric and aesthetics of self-representation. Hence the ego appears as an effect of various ways of writing that take their eccentric starting-point in the subject — in a subject whose thought is structured by bodiliness and by emotions.

NIETZSCHE'S ECCENTRICITY AND THE ART OF STYLE

With regard to Nietzsche's perspectival critique of the subject, one point of reference springs almost immediately to mind. Who else but René Descartes, the thinker of the 'I think', who, as Nietzsche says, conceded authority 'to reason alone' (*der Vernunft allein*); but 'reason is merely an instrument, and Descartes was superficial' (*aber die Vernunft ist nur ein Werkzeug, und Descartes war oberflächlich*)?[13] Nietzsche considers it to be a 'bold assumption' (*verwegene Behauptung*) to take 'I think' for an immediate certainty. Rather, Nietzsche sees in it nothing other than a logically ungroundable assumption and at the same time an effect of rhetorical and grammatical 'habit' (*Gewohnheit*), according to which 'I' emerges as the condition of the predicate 'to think'.[14] To the row of 'daring assertions' (*verwegene Behauptungen*) that are unproven and turn the cogito into the starting-point of thought, there also belong, 'for example, that it is *I* who think, that there must necessarily be something that thinks, that thinking is an activity and operation on the part of a being who is thought of as a cause, that there is an "ego", and, finally, that it is already determined what is to be designated by thinking — that I *know* what thinking is' (*zum Beispiel, dass ich es bin, der denkt, dass überhaupt ein Etwas es sein muss, das denkt, dass Denken eine Thätigkeit und Wirkung seitens eines Wesens ist, welches als Ursache gedacht wird, dass es ein "Ich" giebt, endlich, dass es bereits fest steht, was mit Denken zu bezeichnen ist, — dass ich weiss, was Denken ist*).[15]

At the origin of this thinking ego, but repressed by rationalism, stands — as at the origin of language — violence. Nietzsche criticizes the suppression of the influential role of physiology and of sensualism precisely in relation to the rational concept, at the centre of which lies the categorical separation of thinking from the body, of *res cogitans* from *res extensa*. Only the overshadowing and the 'forgetting' of the physiological, so Nietzsche argues in his famous essay 'On Truth and Falsity in Their Extra-Moral Sense' (*Ueber Wahrheit und Lüge im aussermoralischen Sinne*) of 1873, permits the revaluation of linguistic images and signs into (rational) concepts. For concepts are translations of what are originally nerve-stimuli into images and linguistic sounds. But the Cartesian cogito ignores this genesis of concepts and meaning from the senses.

So the development of language and rhetoric is the continual process of the transference and rewriting of violent circumstances that lie at their origins. The human being, for Nietzsche, 'as a "*rational*" being submits his actions to the sway of abstractions; he no longer suffers himself to be carried away by sudden impressions, concrete sensations; he first generalizes all these impressions into paler, cooler ideas, in order to attach to them the ship of his life and actions' (*stellt jetzt sein Handeln als vernünftiges Wesen unter die Herrschaft der Abstractionen: er leidet es nicht mehr, durch die plötzlichen Eindrücke, durch die Anschauungen fortgerissen zu werden, er verallgemeinert alle diese Eindrücke erst zu entfärbteren, kühleren Begriffen, um an sie das Fahrzeug seines Lebens und Handelns anzuknüpfen*).[16] 'Consciousness is the last and latest development of the organic' (*Die Bewusstheit ist die letzte und späteste Entwicklung des Organischen*), so Nietzsche pursues this thought in *The Gay Science*, and because of this 'the task of *incorporating* knowledge and making it instinctive is only beginning to dawn on the human eye and is not yet clearly discernible' (*neue und eben erst dem menschlichen Auge aufdämmernde Aufgabe, das Wissen sich einzuverleiben und instinctiv zu machen*).[17] But because philosophy as metaphysics, so it seemed to Nietzsche, represents a conceptual structure that has 'forgotten' its own genealogical, physiological, and violent origins (and consequently no longer possesses any feel for the onrush and driving-power of immediate and original sensory impressions), its statements must remain inadequate.

The sphere of sensory perception, of *aisthesis*, concerns above all the arts. At any rate, Nietzsche admits that, in the arts, the traces of bodily experience are not erased or forgotten, but 'masked', placed in forms and represented. Already the young Nietzsche regards the arts not only in an 'aestheticist' and decadent sense, for their own sake. Rather he hopes from the powers that oppose each other in art for a renewal of science and philosophy. This, at any rate, is Nietzsche's starting-point in his writings associated with *The Birth of Tragedy*, in which he insists on looking at 'science in the perspective of the artist' (*die Wissenschaft unter der Optik des Künstlers*).[18] The painful, orgiastic, excessive, and violent aspect of the Dionysian is related in its dynamic to the measure of beautiful representation; the latter even requires the Dionysian as its source of impulses. Already in this respect the arts — due to their specific way of dealing with the senses — bear the central burden of the new perspectivization of (tragic) philosophy.

The arts that have found a fruitful way of dealing with the 'forgetting' of the aesthetic and physiological features of thought and experience become the vanishing-point of philosophy. In *Beyond Good and Evil* and in *On the Genealogy of Morals* Nietzsche will then — once again with regard to Descartes — formulate the critique of the limitations of the cogito, the 'I think', as a critique of the grammar of subject and predicate. He rejects the assumption of a thinking 'something', of a *res cogitans*, of a subject behind thinking and unmasks the assumed doer behind the deed as 'a fiction added' (*Hinzugedichtetes*), as an effect of the grammatical subject-object-relation. Nietzsche's insight that science and philosophy follow a false understanding of the 'doer' and the subject, because they are still acting 'under the misleading influence of language' (*unter der Verführung de Sprache*),[19] opens up to philosophical critique the perspectives of linguistic reflection, of one's way of writing, and of style. In one go Nietzsche's philosophy opens itself to linguistic reflection as well as to poetic and linguistic creativity. It develops a poetic way of writing, revalues the relation of concept and metaphor, and restores dignity to the metaphor within philosophical argumentation. The most significant testimony to this strategy is the text of *Zarathustra* with its insistence on the role of rhetoric. Even in his early writings on the metaphysics of art

Nietzsche's sensibility to the rhythm of music and language points to the connection between aesthetic and linguistic theory: the rhythm, the physiological expression of a musical movement, leaves behind its trace in Apollonian representation and lends it 'formative power' (*bildnerische Kraft*). The various comments scattered across numerous works on the question of composition and style point in the same direction: the question of philosophical truth is always bound up with sensuousness, the *aisthesis* of the linguistic form.[20] 'The more abstract the truth is that you would teach, the more you have to seduce the senses to it' (*Je abstrakter die Wahrheit ist, die du lehren willst, umso mehr musst du noch die Sinne zu ihr verführen*), is how Nietzsche aphoristically summarizes this connection in *Beyond Good and Evil*.[21] Precisely because 'good style' is, for Nietzsche, not simply a question of sentence construction and rhythm, but bears bodily, gestural traces and thus acquires the potential to act as a stimulus on the sensory apparatus of the reader, he is able to have an effect similar to the arts: his way of philosophical writing, formed down to the very last stylistic detail, follows the traces of the bodily origin of thought; it avoids buying its abstractions at the cost of forgetting and recognizes the part played by 'poetry' ('*Dichtung*'), or fictionalization, in laying the metaphysical foundations of thought. Nietzsche asks his audience not to put its ears away in a drawer (*seine Ohren dabei in's Schubfach legen*) when reading him.[22] 'Good style' communicates an 'inner state' and expresses it 'through gestures' (*über die Gebärden*), for 'all the laws about long periods are concerned with the art of gestures' (*alles Gesetze der Periode sind Kunst der Gebärde*).[23]

In the context of nineteenth-century philosophy such a position must no doubt have appeared eccentric. But its insistence on a multiplicity of perspectives and on eccentricity lends the fragmented thought of Nietzsche an aspect of unity, even if this unity has many names — or even *none*. The letter from Nietzsche to Fuchs, cited above, continues as follows: 'To be sure, one's inmost being gradually disciplines one back to unity; that passion, to which no name can be put for a long time, rescues us from all digressions and dispersions, that *task* of which one is the involuntary missionary' (*Allmählich diszipliniert Einen freilich das Innewendigste zur Einheit zurück; jene Leidenschaft, für die man lange keinen Namen hat, rettet uns aus allen Digressionen und Dispersionen, jene Aufgabe, deren unfreiwilliger Missionär man ist*).[24] The possible reversibility of every different way of looking at things philosophically finds its counterpart in the free — yet not disorderly or unrestrained — activity of the artist or the writer, who precisely obeys 'thousandfold laws' when he experiences the 'moments of "inspiration"' (*Augenblicke der 'Inspiration'*).[25] To these 'thousandfold laws' belong the traces of the violent surges of the senses, of pain, of destruction, in short: the entire Dionysian complex.

In this way Nietzsche defined a way of philosophical writing that takes into account the trace of violence in thought, inasmuch as it avoids the conventional opposition of aesthetic and moral perspectivization of the world.

Nietzsche's style, with its rhythmic periods and its vocal sonorities, can thus appear as an aesthetic phenomenon, because he leaves the greatest possible space for *aisthesis* in its original sense.

Translated by Paul Bishop

Notes

[1] Nietzsche, *The Birth of Tragedy*, §4; in *Basic Writings of Nietzsche*, ed. and trans. by Walter Kaufmann (New York: The Modern Library, 1968), p. 47; Friedrich Nietzsche, *Sämtliche Werke: Kritische Studienausgabe*, ed. by Giorgio Colli and Mazzino Montinari, 15 vols (Berlin and New York; Munich: Walter de Gruyter; Deutscher Taschenbuch Verlag, 1967–1977 and 1988), vol. 1, p. 41 (henceforth referred to as *KSA*, followed by a volume and page reference).

[2] See David Wellbery, 'Form und Funktion der Tragödie nach Nietzsche', in Bettine Menke and Christoph Menke (eds), *Tragödie – Trauerspiel – Spektakel* (Berlin: Theater der Zeit, 2007), pp. 199–212. On the theme of transference, see also Wellbery's lecture at the University of Zurich, June 2007, entitled 'Übertragung und Medialität in Nietzsches *Geburt der Tragödie*'.

[3] See Jacques Derrida, *Grammatalogie* [*De la grammatologie*] (Frankfurt am Main: Suhrkamp, 1974), pp. 221–22. See, too, his essay 'Gewalt und Metaphysik: Essay über das Denken von Emmanual Levinas', in Jacques Derrida, *Die Schrift und die Differenz* [*L'écriture et la différence*] (Frankfurt am Main: Suhrkamp, 1972), p. 150.

[4] Nietzsche, *Twilight of the Idols*, 'Skirmishes of an Untimely Man', §11 (*The Portable Nietzsche*, ed. and trans. by Walter Kaufmann (New York: Viking Penguin, 1954), pp. 520–21; *KSA*, vol. 6, p. 118).

[5] As a result this discourse is frequently interpreted as an expression of decadence and as evidence of a proto-Fascistic way of thinking on Nietzsche's part.

[6] This is an important topic in the hard sciences, where contemporary biology, for example, is discussing whether the striving to pass one's own genes on to the next generation is a characteristic of life. For further discussion, see Manfred Eigen, *Stufen zum Leben: Die frühe Evolution im Visier der Molekularbiologie*, 3rd edn (Munich: Piper, 1993), as well as Gudrun Brockmann, Matthias Glaubrecht and Elke Dittmann, 'Genetische Variabilität und Anpassungsfähigkeit: Interdisziplinäres Zentrum der Humboldt-Universität zu Berlin', *Humboldt-Spektrum*, 15.1 (2008), 14–22.

[7] *Beyond Good and Evil*, Preface (*Basic Writings*, p. 193); *KSA*, vol. 5, p. 12.

[8] Günther Figal acknowledges the 'tension between keeping one's distance and being caught up in life' and the resulting eccentric position of his thought as a chief characteristic of Nietzschean philosophy (see Figal, *Nietzsche: Eine philosophische Einführung* [Stuttgart: Reclam, 1999], p. 33).

[9] Friedrich Nietzsche, *Selected Letters*, ed. and trans. by Christopher Middleton (Chicago and London: The University of Chicago Press, 1969), p. 280; cited in *KSA*, vol. 15, p. 168.

[10] *Human, All Too Human*, Preface, §3 (*Human, All Too Human*, trans. by R. J. Hollingdale (Cambridge: Cambridge University Press, 1986), p. 7; *KSA*, vol. 2, p. 16.

[11] *Ecce Homo*, Preface, §3 (*Basic Writings*, p. 674; *KSA*, vol. 6, p. 258).

[12] *KSA*, vol. 10, 3[1], §352, p. 96.

[13] *Beyond Good and Evil*, §191 (*Basic Writings*, p. 294; *KSA*, vol. 5, p. 113).

[14] *Beyond Good and Evil*, §17 (*Basic Writings*, p. 214; *KSA*, vol. 5, pp. 30–31).

[15] *Beyond Good and Evil*, §16 (*Basic Writings*, p. 213; *KSA*, vol. 5, p. 30).

[16] 'On Truth and Lying in Their Extra-Moral Sense', trans. by Maximilian A. Mügge, in Friedrich Nietzsche, *Philosophical Writings*, ed. by Reinhold Grimm and Caroline Molina y Vedia (New York: Continuum, 1995), pp. 87–99 (p. 92); *KSA*, vol. 1, p. 881.

[17] *The Gay Science*, §11 (*The Gay Science*, ed. and trans. by Walter Kaufmann (New York: Vintage, 1994), pp. 84–85; *KSA*, vol. 3, pp. 382–83.

[18] *The Birth of Tragedy*, 'Attempt at a Self-Criticism', §2 (*Basic Writings*, p. 19; *KSA*, vol. 1, p. 14).

[19] *On the Genealogy of Morals*, I, §13 (*Basic Writings*, p. 481; *KSA*, vol. 5, p. 279).

[20] For the aesthetic foundations of *The Birth of Tragedy* and later writings of Nietzsche, see Paul Bishop and R. H. Stephenson, *Friedrich Nietzsche and Weimar Classicism* (Rochester, NY: Camden House, 2004), esp. 'Introduction', p. 4, and the chapter entitled '*Die Geburt der Tragödie* and Weimar Classicism' (pp. 24–62). These authors characterize *The Birth of Tragedy* as 'a work dedicated to aesthetics' (p. 24) and pursue the path from Nietzsche's foundational aesthetic moment in *The Birth of Tragedy*, the 'moment' and 'appearance' (*Schein*), that leads from Goethe's and Schiller's aesthetics to Nietzsche's work.

[21] *Beyond Good and Evil*, §128 (*Basic Writings*, p. 277; *KSA*, vol. 5, p. 95).

[22] *Beyond Good and Evil*, §247 (*Basic Writings*, p. 372; *KSA*, vol. 5, p. 190).

[23] *Ecce Homo*, 'Why I Write Such Good Books', §4 (*Basic Writings*, p. 721; *KSA*, vol. 6, p. 304).

[24] Nietzsche, *Selected Letters*, p. 281; cited *KSA*, vol. 15, p. 168.

[25] *Beyond Good and Evil*, §188 (*Basic Writings*, p. 290; *KSA*, vol. 5, p. 108).

CASSIRER AND JUNG ON MYTHOLOGY, IMAGINATION, AND THE SYMBOL

By Paul Bishop

In a previous paper, I argued that an examination of their discussion of language points to an important affinity between the philosophy of symbolic forms of Ernst Cassirer and the analytical psychology of C. G. Jung.[1] In this paper, I wish to develop my discussion of Cassirer and Jung, and examine their concepts of mythology, imagination, and the symbol. For reasons of space, my discussion will focus largely, although not exclusively, on two major works, Cassirer's *The Philosophy of Symbolic Forms* [*Philosophie der symbolischen Formen*] (1923–1931), and Jung's *Psychology of the Unconscious* (the English translation of *Wandlungen und Symbole der Libido*) (1911–1912).[2]

In *Wandlungen und Symbole der Libido*, arguably his most important work, Jung distinguishes between two kinds of thinking, which he calls 'directed' and 'non-directed' or 'fantasy thinking'. Such a distinction is by no means new, forming as it does an important strand in twentieth-century thinking on language. As well as recalling the distinction made by Lucien Lévy-Bruhl (1857–1939) between rational, objective thought and the mystical, prelogical mentality,[3] it also anticipates the distinction made by Claude Lévi-Strauss (1908–) between the thinking of the modern theorist and the thinking in mythical terms (*bricolage*) of primitive societies,[4] and, in its suspicion of the language of 'directed thinking', it can also been seen as an early attempt at a critique of 'logocentrism'.[5] Let us remind ourselves of what Jung says about these two kinds of thinking.

On the one hand, there is 'directed' thinking, which he describes as 'reality thinking' (*ein Wirklichkeitsdenken*) (PU, §15), or as 'thinking with directed attention' (*Denken mit gerichteter Aufmerksamkeit*) (PU, §16), and which he more or less identifies with language (PU, §17). On the other, there is 'dream', 'fantasy', or 'associative' thinking (PU, §28, §27), which thinking recalls Kant's description of what he termed 'aesthetic judgement'. For in his Third Critique, Kant wrote that, in the aesthetic judgement of beauty, the imagination and the understanding were in a state of 'free play'; and that aesthetic judgements were characterized by 'purposefulness without purpose'.[6] Moreover, Jung himself quite explicitly allies 'non-directed thinking' with the aesthetic when he writes as follows:

Antiquity preferred a mode of thought which was more closely related to a fantastic type. Except for a sensitive perspicuity towards works of art, not attained since then, we seek in vain for that precise and concrete manner of thinking characteristic of modern science [*Neben einer seitdem nie mehr erreichten sinnlichen Anschaulichkeit des Kunstwerkes suchen wir in der Antike vergebens nach jener präzisen und konkreten Denkweise moderner Natur- und Geisteswissenschaft*]. [. . .] This fantastical activity of the ancient mind created artistically *par excellence* [*Diese phantastische Tätigkeit des antiken Geistes schaffte künstlerisch par excellence*]. (PU, §§31–32)

In this passage, we find Jung not only identifying 'non-directed thinking' with aesthetic perception, but also suggesting that aesthetic perception might be a way to unify both 'directed' and 'non-directed' thinking. Art, then, represents both the opposite of 'directed' thinking, and the synthesis of these two kinds of thinking.

What 'the antique spirit' creates, in Jung's view, is not science, but mythology (*Wir sehen den antiken Geist nicht Wissenschaft schaffen, sondern Mythologie*) (PU, §31), and this explains, for Jung, 'the bewildering changes, the kaleidoscopic transformations and the new syncretistic groupings, and the continued rejuvenation of the myths in the Greek sphere of culture': 'Here, we move in a world of phantasies, which, little concerned with the outer course of things, flows from an inner source, and, constantly changing, creates now plastic, now shadowy shapes [*bald plastische, but schemenhafte Gestalten*]' (PU, §32). Further on, Jung declares his view of the central importance in human development:

> The religious myth meets us here as one of the greatest and most significant human institutions which, despite misleading symbols, nevertheless gives man assurance and strength, so that he may not be overwhelmed by the monsters of the universe. The symbol, considered from the standpoint of actual truth, is misleading, indeed, but it is *psychologically true*, because it was and is the bridge to all the greatest achievements of humanity. (PU, §353)

From this statement, it is clear that what, for Jung, is most important about mythology is its symbolic function. Before examining more closely this function, we should note that, for Cassirer, it is its symbolic function that wins for mythology a place in the philosophy of symbolic forms: 'Language, myth, and theoretical knowledge are all taken as fundamental forms of the objective spirit, whose being it must be possible to disclose and understand purely as such, independently of the question of its "becoming"' (PSF, III, 49).

In terms of Cassirer's analysis, there is a close link between language and mythology, *qua* symbolic forms, and, in terms of method, he borrows a teleological leaf from Kant's Third Critique: 'The content of these [universal linguistic and religious] concepts and the principle which determines their structures become fully intelligible only if besides their abstract *logical* meaning we consider their *teleological* meaning' (PSF, I, 287–88). In volume I, Cassirer states the relationship between language and myth in a way which shows the limitations of language as follows:

> Like myth, language starts from the basic experience and basic form of personal activity; however, it does not, like mythology, weave the world in infinite variations around this one central point, but gives it a new form in which it confronts the mere subjectivity of sensation and feeling [*der bloßen Subjektivität des Empfindens und des Fühlens*]. (PSF, I, 288)

And in volume 3, having devoted an entire volume to *Mythical Thought*, Cassirer summarizes the significance of mythology in a passage that moves from the question of 'expression', an field to which he recognized Ludwig Klages as a major contributor,[7] via a description of the function of myth, to an allusion to Goethe's poem 'Allerdings. Dem Physiker' (1820):

> In dealing with the problems and the phenomenology of pure experience of expression, we can entrust ourselves to the leadership and orientation neither of conceptual knowledge nor of language. For both of these are primarily in the service of theoretical objectivization: they build up the world of the logos as a thought and spoken logos. Thus in respect to expression, they take a centrifugal rather than a centripetal direction. Myth, however, places us in the living center of this sphere, for its particularity consists precisely in showing us a mode of world formation which is independent of all modes of mere objectivization. It does not recognize the dividing line between real and unreal, between reality and appearance, which theoretical objectivization draws and must draw. All its structure moves on a single plane of being, which is wholly adequate to it. Here there is neither kernel nor shell [*weder Kern noch Schale*] (PSF, III, 164)

Yet, for all their differences, language and myth were, Cassirer argued, intimately related inasmuch as they represented different kinds of 'symbolic form': '[L]anguage and myth each reveal a "modality", which is specific to it and in a sense lends a common tonality to all its individual structures. If we hold fast to this insight into the "polydimensionality" of the cultural world, the question of the relation between concept [*Begriff*] and intuition [*Anschauung*] immediately takes on a far greater complexity' (PSF, III, 13).

In terms of intellectual history, Cassirer sees his account of myth in terms of a tradition that reaches back, via Johann Jakob Bachofen (1815–1887), to Johann Gottfried Herder (1744–1803):

> For it, myth, insofar as it is seen and understood in a truly comprehensive manner, provides the magic key that unlocks the world of history. Herder was fully aware of this. He was the first to promulgate the doctrine that mythic-religious narratives are not to be taken merely as poetic stories, but that they are to be conceived and used as the 'oldest *documents* of the human race' [see *Älteste Urkunde des Menschengeschlechts*, 1774–1776]. A sharp intellectual

foundation for this method and its ingenious application had to wait, however, for the philosophy of history as developed in the works of Bachofen. The center of Bachofen's comprehensive view consists of his interpretation of myth as an original intellectual form of historical knowledge. (PSF, IV, 88)

Similarly, Jung's identification of fantasy with mythology harks back to an earlier debate on the nature of mythology. For to Karl Philipp Moritz (1756–1793) in his *Götterlehre oder Mythologische Dichtungen der Alten* [*Doctrine of the Gods, or Mythological Poetic Works of the Ancients*] (1795), mythology was the 'language of fantasy':

> The mythological art-works of the writers of antiquity must be looked at as a *language of fantasy*: understood as such, they form a world of their own, and are truly lifted out of the relationship with real things.
>
> [Die mythologischen Dichtungen der Alten müssen als eine *Sprache der Phantasie* betrachtet werden: als eine solche aufgefaßt, bilden sie gleichsam eine Welt für sich, und sind aus dem Zusammenhange der wirklichen Dinge herausgehoben.][8]

By contrast, Friedrich Wilhelm Joseph von Schelling (1775–1854), to whose *Philosophie der Mythologie* (1842) both Jung (PU, §50, n. 37) and, more extensively, Cassirer (PSF, II, 3–10, 12, 15) referred, argued over a half a century after Moritz that mythology was based, not on fantasy, but on historical reality:

> The mythological process thus has not merely religious, but *general* significance, for it is the general process that repeats itself in it; correspondingly the truth, which mythology has in the process, a truth which excludes nothing, is universal. One cannot deny, as is usually done, that mythology has a *historical* reality, for the process through which it arises is itself a true story, a real occurrence.
>
> [*Der mythologische Proceß hat also nicht bloß religiöse, er hat allgemeine Bedeutung, denn es ist der allgemeine Proceß, der sich in ihm wiederholt; demgemäß ist auch die Wahrheit, welche die Mythologie im Proceß hat, eine nichts ausschließende, universelle. Man kann der Mythologie nicht, wie gewöhnlich, die* historische *Wahrheit absprechen, denn der Proceß, durch den sie entsteht, ist selbst eine wahre Geschichte, ein wirklicher Vorgang.*][9]

Subsequently, this view was taken up by Bronislaw Malinowski in his *Myth in Primitive Psychology* (1926), where he claimed that myth, far from being 'an explanation put forward to satisfy scientific curiosity', was rather 'the re-arising of a primordial reality in narrative form'.[10]

In this debate, Jung supports both sides, identifying mythology with fantasy, as we have seen, yet also insisting on the (pre)historical reality which is inscribed in the archetypes: 'The unconscious is the unwritten history of mankind from time unrecorded' (*Das Unbewußte ist die ungeschriebene Geschichte des Menschen seit unvordenklichen Zeiten*) (CW, 11, §280). And in 'The Psychology of the Child Archetype' (1940), Jung claimed: 'Myths are original revelations of the preconscious psyche, involuntary statements about unconscious beginnings. [. . .] Myths [. . .] have a vital meaning. Not merely do they represent, they *are* the psychic life of the primitive tribe' (CW, 9/i, §261). Both positions are tenable for Jung because, for him, the psyche itself is the basis of reality: 'Psychic existence is the only category of existence of which we have *immediate* knowledge, since nothing can be known unless it first appears as a psychic image [*psychisches Bild*]. Only psychic existence is immediately verifiable. To the extent that the world does not assume the form of a psychic image [*die Form eines psychischen Bildes*], it is virtually non-existent' (CW, 11, §769). Thus what emerges from Jung's discussion of language in the early pages of *Wandlungen und Symbole der Libido* is the suggestion that there exist certain recurring ideas or archaic images, which Jung later calls 'archetypes'.

Is there a link between the archetypes and what Jung calls 'fantasy thinking'? And is there an affinity here with what Cassirer has to say in *The Philosophy of Symbolic Forms* about the role of the imagination and the 'symbolic' function of mythology?

IMAGINATION

The background to what Cassirer and Jung say about the imagination is to be found in Kant's discussion of this faculty in the First Critique.[11] In that work, Kant makes a distinction between the productive and reproductive powers of the imagination, arguing that 'only the *productive synthesis of the imagination* can take place *a priori*; for the *reproductive* synthesis rests on the conditions of experience' (*Es kann aber nur die* produktive Synthesis der Einheit der Einbildungskraft *a priori stattfinden; denn die reproduktive beruht auf Bedingungen der Erfahrung*) (A 118). Such synthesis is, Kant explains, the effect of the imagination and, more precisely, of 'a blind though indispensable function of the soul, without which we would have no cognition at all, but of which we are seldom even conscious' (*einer blinden, obgleich unentbehrlichen Funktion der Seele, ohne die wir überall gar keine Erkenntnis haben würden, der wir uns aber selten nur einmal bewußt sind*) (A 78/B 103). Furthermore, according to Kant, the imagination in its productive modality has a transcendental function: 'The imagination is therefore also a faculty of synthesis *a priori*, on account of which we give it the name of productive imagination, and, insofar as its aim in regard to all the manifold of appearance is nothing further than the necessary unity in their synthesis, this can be called the transcendental function of the imagination' (*Die Einbildungskraft ist also auch ein Vermögen einer Synthesis a priori, weswegen wir ihr den Namen der produktiven Einbildungskraft geben, und, sofern sie in Ansehung alles Mannigfaltigen der Erscheinung nichts weiter, als die notwendige Einheit in der Synthesis derselben zu ihrer Absicht hat, kann diese die transzendentale Funktion der Einbildungskraft genannt werden)* (A 123). As a result, Kant attributes a constitutive role to imagination in the construction of experience: 'Both extremes, namely sensibility and understanding, must necessarily be connected by means of this transcendental function of the imagination, since otherwise the former would to be sure yield appearances but no objects of an empirical cognition, hence there would be no experience' (*Beide äußerste Enden, nämlich Sinnlichkeit und Verstand, müssen vermittelst dieser transzendentalen Funktion der Einbildungskraft notwendig zusammenhängen; weil jene sonst zwar Erscheinungen, aber keine Gegenstände eines empirischen Erkenntnisses, mithin keine Erfahrung geben würden)* (A 124).

The transcendental function of the imagination unites the forms of the understanding (the categories) and sensuous intuitions in the 'schematism', which combines the universality of a concept with the particularity of the content of that concept: 'This mediating representation must be pure (without anything empirical) and yet *intellectual* on the one hand and *sensible* [*sinnlich*] on the other. Such a representation is the *transcendental schema*' (A 138/B 177). According to Kant, the ability to subsume the particular under the universal is the faculty of judgement (*Urteilskraft*), whereas the crucial role of the schematism relies on the activity of the imagination, and, in terms that might well have appealed to Jung, Kant described the schematism as 'a hidden art in the depths of the human soul, whose true operations we can divine from nature and lay unveiled before our eyes only with difficulty' (*eine verborgene Kunst in den Tiefen der menschlichen Seele, deren wahre Handgriffe wir der Natur schwerlich jemals abraten, und sie unverdeckt vor Augen legen werden*) (A 141/B 181).

In *Kant and the Problem of Metaphysics* [*Kant und das Problem der Metaphysik*] (1929), Heidegger argued that, in the years between the first (1781) and second (1787) editions of the First Critique, Kant came to downplay the role of the imagination: 'Not only did imagination fill him with alarm, but in the meantime he had also come more and more under the influence of pure reason as such'.[12] But if, for Heidegger, Kant belonged to those who have 'forgotten Being', both Cassirer and Jung undertake the more precise task of attempting to rehabilitate the function of the imagination. For Cassirer, it is a central philosophical breakthrough that 'those three original sources of knowledge which according to the Critique of Pure Reason make all experience possible — sensation, imagination, and understanding [B 127, A 115] — prove, when viewed from the standpoint of the problem of symbolism, to be interrelated and linked to one another in a new way' (PSF, III, 48). Moreover, for Charles Hendel, Kant's notion of the schematism is central to understanding the philosophy of symbolic forms: 'The schema's the thing that caught the imagination of Cassirer. He interpreted the whole subsequent post-Kantian philosophy in Germany by reference to it. And his own philosophy of symbolic forms was a development of this new concept of form' ('Introduction', PSF, 1, 14), and Cassirer discusses the schema in detail on two occasions (PSF, 1, 200; PSF, III, 162).

To understand better Jung's concept of 'fantasy thinking' or *Phantasieren*, we need to turn to his second *magnum opus*, *Psychologische Typen* [*Psychological Types*], published almost ten years after *Wandlungen und Symbole der Libido* in 1921. In a glossary of 'Definitions' appended to this work, Jung devotes an entry to 'Fantasy' (*Phantasie*). Here, Jung distinguishes between *Phantasie* in terms of an activity and *Phantasie* in terms of a product (CW, 6, §711). As an activity, *Phantasie* is equated with 'imaginative activity' (*imaginative Tätigkeit*). In his entry, Jung defines this activity in negative terms as 'the reproductive or creative activity of the mind in general. It is not a special faculty, since it can come into play in all the basic forms of psychic activity, whether thinking, feeling, sensation, or intuition' (CW, 6, §722). In attributing to the imagination both a productive and a reproductive capacity, Jung is following Kant's discussion of the imagination in the First Critique. By the same token, Jung, elsewhere in *Psychologische Typen*, not only expresses the power of the fantasy in more positive terms than in his 'Definition', but similarly in Kantian terms:

> Only through the specific vital activity of the psyche does the sense-impression attain that intensity, and the idea that effective force, which are the two indispensable constituents of living reality. This autonomous activity of the psyche, which can be explained neither as a reflex action to sensory stimuli nor as the executive organ of eternal ideas, is, like every vital process, a continually creative act. The psyche creates reality every day [*Diese Eigentätigkeit der Psyche, die sich weder als reflektorische Reaktion auf den Sinnesreiz, noch als Exekutivorgan ewiger Ideen erklären läßt, ist, wie jeder Lebensprozeß, ein beständiger Schöpferakt. Die Psyche erschafft täglich die Wirklichkeit*]. The only expression I can use for this activity is *fantasy*. Fantasy is just as much feeling as thinking; as much intuition as sensation. There is no psychic function that, through fantasy, is not inextricably bound up with the other psychic functions. Sometimes it appears in primordial form, sometimes it is the ultimate and boldest product of all our faculties combined. Fantasy, therefore, seems to me the clearest expression of the specific activity of the psyche. It is, pre-eminently, the creative activity from which the answers to all answerable questions come; it is the mother of all possibilities, where, like all psychological opposites, the inner and outer worlds are joined together in living union. Fantasy it was and ever is which fashions the bridge between the irreconcilable claims of subject and object, introversion and extraversion. In fantasy alone both mechanisms are united. (CW, 6, §§77–78)[13]

In this passage, which shows Jung, as always, straining against the Kantian leash that prevents him from running through the fields of Romanticism, there are two further echoes of Kant's thought. Following his discussion of the imagination in the First Critique, Kant returned to this faculty in his discussion of aesthetics and teleology in the Third Critique. There, Kant spoke of the need to bridge the realms of the sensible (the object) and the supersensible (the subject): 'Albeit, then, between the realm of the natural concept, as the sensible, and the realm of the concept of freedom, as the supersensible, there is a great gulf fixed [. . .] still the latter is meant to influence the former — that is to say, the concept of freedom is *meant* to actualize in the sensible world the end proposed by its laws' (*Ob nun zwar eine unübersehbare Kluft zwischen dem Gebiete des Naturbegriffs, als dem Sinnlichen, und dem Gebiete des Freiheitsbegriffs, als dem Übersinnlichen, befestigt ist, [. . .] so soll doch diese auf jene einen Einfluß haben, nämlich der Freiheitsbegriff soll den durch seine Gesetze aufgegebenen Zweck in der Sinnenwelt wirklich machen*). Consequently, Kant argued, 'there must, therefore, be a ground of the *unity* of the supersensible that lies at the basis of nature, with what the concept of freedom contains in a practical way' (*also muß es doch einen Grund der* Einheit *des Übersinnlichen, welches der Natur zum Grunde liegt, mit dem, was der Freiheitsbegriff praktisch enthält, geben*), and this unity, he claimed, is to be found in the faculty of judgement.[14] More specifically, one such form of judgement is the aesthetic judgement. And aesthetic judgements, Kant wrote, entail a free play of the faculties (specifically, those of the imagination and the understanding in the case of the beautiful, and the imagination and reason in the case of the sublime): 'The cognitive powers brought into play by this representation are here engaged in a free play, since no definite concept restricts them to a particular rule of cognition' (*Die Erkenntniskräfte, die durch diese Vorstellung ins Spiel gesetzt werden, sind hiebei in einem freien Spiele, weil kein bestimmter Begriff sie auf eine besondere Erkenntnisregel einschränkt*).[15] Although Jung at no point in his writings discusses Kant's Third Critique in any detail, he does, in *Psychologische Typen*, devote a substantial chapter to Schiller's aesthetics, which are largely conceived on a Kantian basis.[16] For Kant, this free play of the imagination (*die Freiheit der Einbildungskraft*) is achieved in the case of 'free beauty' (*pulchritudo vaga*), and he cites the 'fantasy' (in the musical sense) as an example (Book I, §16).

IMAGE

In the First Critique, Kant writes that 'the imagination is to bring the manifold of intuition into an *image*' (*die Einbildungskraft soll nämlich das Mannigfaltige der Anschauung in ein* Bild *bringen*) (A 121). In the Third Critique, Kant returns to this point, in the context of the distinction between the *intellectus archetypus* (an intuitive understanding) and the *intellectus ectypus* (a discursive understand-ing, i.e., our own), when he describes this latter kind of understanding as 'an intellect which is in need of images' (*ein der Bilder bedürftiger Verstand*).[17] In *An Essay on Man* (1944), Cassirer calls this passage 'one of the most important and most difficult in Kant's critical works', claiming that 'it indicates a problem crucial to any anthropological philosophy'.[18] In his subsequent remarks, Cassirer goes on to show how this passage lies, too, at the core of his own philosophy of symbolic forms:

> Instead of saying that the human intellect is an intellect which is 'in need of images' we should rather say that it is in need of symbols. Human knowledge is by its very nature symbolic knowledge. It is this feature which characterizes both its strength and its limitations. And for symbolic thought it is indispensable to make a sharp distinction between real and possible, between actual and ideal things. A symbol has no actual existence as a part of the physical world; it has a 'meaning'. (*Essay*, p. 57)

Thus we find in Cassirer the argument that, to an increasingly complex degree as human culture develops, we come to use, not just images, but symbols. For Cassirer, the distinction that Kant makes between the image, as 'a product of the empirical faculty of productive imagination', and the schema, as 'a product and as it were a monogram of pure *a priori* imagination, through which and in accordance with which the images first become possible' (B 181/A 142), is central to this argument. What matters to Cassirer is the schema, rather than the image, for 'the schema of a pure concept of the understanding [. . .] is something that can never be brought to an image at all' (B 181/A 142); in other words, the schema is prior to the images, which 'must be connected with the concept, to which they are in themselves never fully congruent, always only by means of the schema they designate' (B 181/A 142).

In the case of Jung, by contrast, we find that the concept of the 'image' (*Bild*) is, right from the very start, moving toward the notion of the symbol. (Indeed, the confusion about whether an archetype is, in the Kantian/ Cassirerian sense, an 'image' or a 'schema', bedevils his entire theory of the archetypes and their symbolic function, and explains his use of the distinction between the archetype and the archetype *an sich*.) In one of his 'Definitions' in *Psychologische Typen*, Jung makes it clear that when he speaks of the image (*Bild*), he is not using the term in the Kantian sense, but in an aesthetic, albeit quasi-pathological, sense:

> When I speak of 'image' in this book, I do not mean the psychic reflection of an external object, but a concept derived from poetic usage [*nicht das psychische Abbild des äußeren Objektes, sondern vielmehr eine Anschauung, die dem poetischen Sprachgebrauch entstammt*], namely, a figure of fancy or *fantasy-image* [*Phantasie-bild*], which is related only indirectly to the perception of an external object.

This image depends much more on unconscious fantasy activity, and as the product of such activity it appears more or less abruptly in consciousness, somewhat in the manner of a vision or hallucination, but without possessing the morbid traits that are found in a clinical picture. (CW, 6, §743)

The impact of such an image corresponds to what Cassirer, following Klages, calls 'the purely expressive phenomenon' (PSF, III, 103). In other words, the image corresponds to what Jung calls a *phantasm* (*das Phantasmata*), which he defines as 'a complex of ideas [*Vorstellungskomplex*] that is distinguished from other such complexes by the fact that it has no objective referent' (CW, 6, §711). What Jung is emphasizing here is the freedom, or autonomy, of *das Phantasmata*: 'Although it may originally be based on memory-images of actual experiences, its content refers to no external reality; it is merely the output of creative psychic activity, a manifestation or product of a combination of energized psychic elements' (*Obschon eine Phantasie ursprünglich auf Erinnerungsbildern wirklich stattgefundener Erlebnisse beruhen kann, so entspricht doch ihr Inhalt keiner äußeren Realität, sondern ist wesentlich nur der Ausfluß der schöpferischen Geistestätigkeit, eine Betätigung oder ein Produkt der Kombination energiebesetzter psychische Elemente*) (CW, 6, §711). In this respect, fantasies in the Jungian sense share that autonomy manifested by the beautiful in Kant's account of aesthetic experience.

In *Psychological Types*, Jung goes on to complicate his definition of fantasy by distinguishing further between active and passive fantasy. Of these two kinds, passive fantasy is, in Jung's account, the poor relation. In accordance with Jung's complementaristic approach to the psyche, such fantasies are the product of its compensatory function. According to Jung, they appear as a result of a relative dissociation of the psyche; have their origin in an unconscious process that is antithetical to consciousness; and frequently bear a morbid stamp or show some sign of abnormality (CW, 6, §§712–14). As an example of passive fantasy, Jung cites St Paul's vision as recorded in the Acts of the Apostles (9: 3–9): 'Paul's conversion to Christianity signified an acceptance of the hitherto unconscious standpoint and a repression of the hitherto anti-Christian one, which then made itself felt in his hysterical attacks' (CW, 6, §714). By contrast, active fantasies represent for Jung something much more important:

Active fantasies are the product of intuition, i.e., they are evoked by an attitude directed to the perception of unconscious contents, as a result of which the libido immediately invests all the elements emerging from the unconscious and, by association with parallel material, brings them into clear focus in visual form [*Aktive Phantasien sind veranlaßt durch Intuition, d.h. durch eine auf Wahrnehmung unbewußter Inhalte gerichtete Einstellung, wobei die Libido alle aus dem Unbewußten auftauchenden Elemente sofort besetzt und durch Assoziation paralleler Materialien zur Höhe der Klarheit und Anschaulichkeit bringt*]. [. . .] It is not necessarily a question of a dissociated psychic state, but rather of a positive participation of consciousness. [. . .] Active fantasy is one of the highest forms of psychic activity. For here the conscious and the unconscious product of the subject flow together into a common product in which both are united. Such a fantasy can be the highest expression of the unity of a man's *individuality*, and it may even create that individuality by giving perfect expression to its unity [*Die aktive Form der Phantasie gehört oft zu den höchsten menschlichen Geistestätigkeiten. Denn in ihr fließt die bewußte und die unbewußte Persönlichkeit des Subjektes in ein gemeinsames und vereinigendes Produkt zusammen. Eine derart gestaltete Phantasie kann der höchste Ausdruck der Einheit einer Individualität sein und diese letztere eben gerade durch den vollkommenen Ausdruck ihrer Einheit auch erzeugen*]. (CW, 6, §§712–14)]

And in a brief remark, in parenthesis, which is omitted from the English *Collected Works*, Jung situates his discussion on fantasy directly within the Kantian and Schillerian tradition to which, as we have seen, he is implicitly working: 'Vgl. dazu Schillers Begriff der "ästhetischen Stimmung"' ('Compare with Schiller's concept of the "aesthetic mood"'). Turning back to Jung's earlier, extensive discussion of Schiller's *On the Aesthetic Education of Man* (*Über die ästhetische Erziehung des Menschen*) (1795), we find that Jung refers to Schiller's identification, in Letter 21, of the aesthetic mode with beauty: 'Schiller makes the "aesthetic mood" practically identical with "beauty", which of its own accord precipitates our sentiments into this mood' (CW, 6, §206). Moreover, Schiller, too, defined an object's aesthetic character in terms of its relation to 'the totality of our various faculties' (*das Ganze unserer verschiedenen Kräfte*) (CW, 6, §206)[19] (a definition with which Jung, because of his misunderstanding of Schiller's use of the term *ästhetisch*, has problems);[20] and, even more important, thanks to Schiller Jung develops a clear understanding of what a symbol is: 'The symbol unites antithetical elements within its nature; hence it also unites the antithesis between real and unreal, because on the one hand it is a psychic reality (on account of its efficacy), while on the other it corresponds to no physical reality. It is *reality* and *appearance* at once' (*Das Symbol vereinigt in seiner Natur das Gegensätzliche; so vereinigt es auch den Gegensatz real-irreal, indem es zwar einerseits eine psychologische Realität oder Wirklichkeit (seiner* Wirksamkeit *wegen) ist, anderseits aber keiner physischen Realität entspricht. Es ist eine Tatsache und doch ein* Schein) (CW, 6, §211). The concept of the symbol becomes not only central to Jung's discussion of how to interpret fantasies, both active and passive, but the site of his greatest, and most important affinity with Cassirer's philosophy of symbolic forms.

SYMBOL

To attempt to summarize all Cassirer's statements about symbolic form would be to over-simplify the complexity of the argument of *The Philosophy of Symbolic Forms*. It might, however, be useful to highlight those features that most clearly interlock with Jung's understanding of the symbol. In terms of intellectual antecedents, two thinkers in particular stand as predecessors of the philosophy of symbolic forms. First, inasmuch as 'the universal symbolic function' can be understood in terms of 'a system of signs' (cf. PSF, III, 45), then the Leibnizian 'characteristic' — which 'refers not directly to things themselves but to their representatives' (PSF, III, 46) — provides an example from the seventeenth century of how 'the concept of the symbol has become the actual focus of the intellectual world':

> [H]ere the guiding lines of metaphysics and of general epistemology run together; here the problems of general logic are linked with those of the special theoretical sciences. [. . .] Just as for Leibniz the concept of the symbol formed as it were the *vinculum substantiale* between his metaphysics and his logic, so in modern scientific theory it constitutes the *vinculum substantiale* between logic and mathematics — and further, between logic and exact science. Everywhere it proves to be the strict intellectual bond which cannot be severed without destroying the essential content along with the form of exact knowledge. (PSF, III, 46)

Second, and chronologically closer to Cassirer, there is the notion of 'organ projection' developed by Ernst Kapp (1808–1896) in his *Grundlinien einer Philosophie der Technik* (1877), where it refers to 'the fact that all primitive tools are primarily an extension of the action which man exerts on things with his own organs or limbs' (PSF, II, 215). This notion, Cassirer argues, can be applied to a much wider field of cultural achievement:

> The fundamental argument of the philosophy of Symbolic Forms has shown that the concept which Kapp designates as 'organ projection' holds a meaning which extends far beyond the technical mastery and knowledge of nature. While the philosophy of technology deals with the immediate and mediated bodily organs by which man gives the outside world its determinate form and imprint, the philosophy of Symbolic Forms is concerned with the totality of spiritual expressive functions. It regards them not as copies of being but as trends and modes of formation, as 'organs' less of mastery than of signification. And here again the operation of these organs takes at first a wholly unconscious form. Language, myth, art — each produces from itself its own world of forms which can be understood only as expressions of the spontaneity of the spirit. (PSF, II, 216–27)

If the philosophy of symbolic forms also extends the Kantian schematism from rational to all cultural activity, then we can see why Cassirer claims that '[i]t is in the basic symbolic function and its various directions that the spiritual consciousness and the sensory consciousness are first truly differentiated' (PSF, I, 107), and why it is in the concept of the symbol that he has attempted 'to encompass the totality of those phenomena in which the sensuous is in any way filled with meaning, in which a sensuous content, while preserving the mode of its existence and facticity, represents a particularization and embodiment, a manifestation and incarnation of a meaning' (PSF, III, 93). On Cassirer's account, it is in the ability to create 'meaning' that the real significance of the symbolic form lies:

> [T]he essential and characteristic achievement of all symbolic form — whether of language, myth, or pure cognition — does not lie simply in receiving given material impressions (which in themselves possess a fixed and definite character, a given quality and structure) and then grafting onto them, as though from outside, another form originating in the independent energy of consciousness. The characteristic achievement of the spirit begins much earlier than this. On sharper analysis even the apparently 'given' proves to have passed through certain acts of linguistic, mythical, or logical-theoretical apperception. Only what is *made* in these acts 'is'; even in its seemingly simple and immediate nature, what is thus made proves to be conditioned and determined by some primary meaning-given function. And it is this primary, not the secondary, formation which contains the true secret of all symbolic form, which must forever arouse new philosophical amazement. (PSF, II, 95)

The ability of the symbolic form to represent, by means of a concrete object, something beyond that concrete object, is what Cassirer refers to as its 'symbolic pregnance':

> By symbolic pregnance we mean the way in which a perception as a sensory experience contains at the same time a certain nonintuitive meaning which it immediately and concretely represents. Here we are not dealing with bare perceptive data, on which some sort of apperceptive acts are later grafted, through which they are interpreted, judged, transformed. Rather it is the perception itself which by virtue of its own immanent organization, takes on a kind of spiritual articulation — which, being ordered in itself, also belongs to a determinate order of meaning. In its full actuality, its living totality, it is at the same time a life 'in' meaning. It is not only subsequently received into this sphere but is, one might say, born into it. It is this ideal interwovenness, this relatedness of the single perceptive phenomenon, given here and now, to a characteristic total meaning that the term 'pregnance' is meant to designate. (PSF, III, 202)[21]

Hence symbolic form is responsible for our present state of consciousness — 'The symbolic process is like a single stream of life and thought which flows through consciousness, and which by this flowing movement produces the diversity and cohesion, the richness, the continuity, and constancy, of consciousness' (PSF, III, 202) — but also for developing the consciousness of the future. For, as Cassirer puts it, '*the symbol hastens ahead of reality, showing it the way and clearing its path*': 'Symbolic representation is no mere looking back on this reality as something finished, but becomes a factor and motif in its unfolding. It is this form of symbolic vision that specifically distinguishes the cultural, historical will from the mere will to live, mere vital instinct' (PSF, III, 182; my italics).

For Jung, as for Cassirer, it is the forward-looking nature of the symbol that matters most. Following Freud in the *Traumdeutung*,[22] Jung distinguishes between 'manifest' and 'latent' meanings in fantasies, but, for Jung, Freud's method is a 'reductive' one (CW, 6, §716).[23] Such a method, he explains, is appropriate for understanding fantasies *semiotically*, but not *symbolically* (CW, 6, §788). And symbols, he insists, have to be distinguished from *signs* and *allegories* (CW, 6, §815). Yet such fantasies as St Paul's vision, or, for that matter, St Peter's vision (Acts 10: 9–17; 11: 4–18), demand more than a reductive reading, which regards these fantasies '*semiotically, as a sign or symptom* of an underlying process' (*semiotisch, als Zeichen oder als Symptom eines grundlegenden Vorganges*) (for example, as expressions of Peter's hunger, or Paul's repressed envy) (CW, 6, §788). For Jung, a semiotic interpretation is a 'causal' reading, to which he opposes the 'constructive' or 'purposive' reading (CW, 6, §§701–04).[24] Only such a style of reading, he claims, is able to interpret the symbol: 'Purposively interpreted, the fantasy seems like a *symbol*, seeking to characterize a definite goal with the help of the material at hand, or trace out a line of future psychological development' (*Der finalen Erklärung dagegen erscheint die Phantasie als ein Symbol, welches mit Hilfe der vorhandenen Materialien ein bestimmtes Ziel oder vielmehr eine gewisse zukünftige psychologische Entwicklungslinie zu kennzeichnen oder zu erfassen sucht*) (CW, 6, §720).

The contrast between Freud and Jung in their approach to signs and symbols highlights their different modes of interpretation, particularly with regard to language. For Freud, language functions as a semiotic system, and it is just such a system that can be used to decode dreams, reversing the mechanisms of 'condensation' and 'displacement' by which the 'dream-work' operates. For Jung, language is connected with directed thinking, whereas it is 'fantasy thinking' and 'fantasies' that pose the real problems of interpretation, demanding an awareness of the symbolic, and hence aesthetic, dimensions of unconscious products. What Jung emphasizes is the autonomy of fantasy and its value as an expression of creativity:

> Because active fantasy is the chief mark of the artistic mentality, the artist is not just a *reproducer* of appearances but a creator and educator, for his works have the value of symbols that adumbrate lines of future development [*Weil die aktive Phantasie das hauptsächliche Merkmal der künstlerischen Geistestätigkeit ist, so ist der Künstler nicht bloß ein Darsteller, sondern ein Schöpfer und darum ein Erzieher, denn seine Werke haben den Wert von Symbolen, welche künftige Entwicklungslinien vorzeichnen*]. [...] For as every physical state, from the energic standpoint, is a dynamic system, so from the same standpoint a psychic content is a dynamic system manifesting itself in consciousness. We could say that fantasy in the sense of a phantasm is a definite sum of libido that cannot appear in consciousness in any other way than in the form of an image. A phantasm is an *idée-force*. (CW, 6 §720 and §722)

With the idea of autonomous contents in the psyche, one of Jung's earliest ideas finds reformulation in terms of an argument framed in terms of Kant's view of the imagination and Schiller's view of the symbol. What in 1905 Jung called 'the impotence of consciousness in face of the tremendous automatism driving up from the unconscious' (*die Ohnmacht des Bewußtseins gegenüber der Gewalt des aus dem Unbewußten auftauchenden Automatismus*)[25] is more positively expressed in *Mysterium coniunctionis* when he writes that 'the archetype is autonomous and the only question is whether a man is gripped by it or not' (*der Archetypus ist autonom, und die Frage ist nur, ob der Mensch von dessen Fülle ergriffen ist oder nicht*) (CW, 14, §746).

Although such statements foreground the power of the unconscious, Jung's psychology is far from being a celebration of the irrational. Instead, he places the emphasis on the integration of such unconscious contents with the conscious mind. In his essay entitled 'On Psychic Energy' (begun in 1912 and completed in 1928), Jung explains what he means by his claim in *Wandlungen und Symbole der Libido* that the symbol 'was and is the bridge to all the greatest achievements of humanity' (see above). Based on his energic conception of the mind, according to which 'the psyche [is] a *relatively* closed system' (CW, 8, §10), Jung argues that '[t]he psychological mechanism that transforms energy is the symbol' (CW, 8, §88). According to Jung, 'aside from all the other sorrows and hardships of human life the primitive is tormented by superstitions, fears and compulsions', but 'mankind was freed from these fears by a continual process of symbol-formation that leads to culture' (CW, 8, §§94–95). (Both Cassirer and Jung suggestively evoke the world as it appears to the primitive mind.)[26] In his volume on *Mythical Thought*, Cassirer writes that '[t]he transition to agriculture, to a regulated tilling of the fields, represents a crucial turning point in the development of the vegetation myths and cults' (PSF, II, 201). It is precisely this turning-point that Jung, thanks to his conception of the symbolic, seeks to explain. With reference to the spring ceremony performed by the Wachandi tribe in Australia,[27] Jung seeks to show how the bushmen's ritual illustrates what, in *Wandlungen und Symbole*, he called the 'canalization of libido' (*die Überleitung von Libido, die Verlagerung von Libido*) (PU, §236; cf. CW, 8, §79), whereby 'the transformation of instinctual energy is achieved by its canalization into an *analogue of the object of instinct*' (*die Umwandlung der Triebenergie geschieht durch Überleitung auf ein Analogon des Triebobjektes*) (CW, 8, §83):

> The psychological mechanism that transforms energy is the symbol. I mean by this a real symbol and not a sign. The Wachandi's hole in the earth is not a sign for the genitals of a woman, but a symbol that stands for the idea of the earth woman who is to be made fruitful. To mistake it for a human woman would be to interpret the symbol semiotically, and this would fatally disturb the value of the ceremony. It is for this reason that none of the dancers may look at a

woman. The mechanism would be destroyed by a semiotic interpretation —
[. . .] the semiotic interpretation becomes meaningless when it is applied exclusively and schematically — when, in short, it ignores the real nature of the
symbol and debases it to a mere sign. [. . .] So we have every reason to value
symbol-formation and to render homage to the symbol as an inestimable means
of utilizing the mere instinctual flow of energy for effective work. A waterfall
is certainly more beautiful than a power-station, but dire necessity [*dira
necessitas*] teaches us to value electric light and electrified industry more highly
than the superb wastefulness of a waterfall that delights us for a quarter of an
hour on a holiday walk. (CW, 8, §88 and §90)[28]

Central to this and other 'magical ceremonies', Jung claims, is the fact that
'the newly invested object acquires a working potential in relation to the
psyche', adding: 'Because of its value it has a determining and stimulating
effect on the imagination [*Durch seinen Wert wirkt es determinierend und vorstel-
lungsbildend*], so that for a long time the mind is fascinated and possessed by it'
(CW, 8, §89). Citing as further examples the buffalo-dances of the Taos
Pueblo Indians, the revenge ceremony of the Aruntas of Australia, and the
role of magic in general and of alchemy in particular in the development
of modern science (CW, 8, §86 and §90), Jung describes both the different
forms of symbolism — '[i]n abstract form, symbols are religious ideas; in the
form of action, they are rites or ceremonies' — and their twofold function,
not only as 'the manifestation and expression of excess libido', but also as
'stepping-stones to new activities, which must be called cultural in order to
distinguish them from the instinctual functions that run their regular course
according to natural law' (CW, 8, §91).[29]

In addition to such symbolism on the level of anthropological ceremony
and myth, symbols in the Jungian sense can also be found in the realm of
high art. In two highly problematic essays, 'On the Relation of Analytical
Psychology to Poetry' (first delivered as a lecture and then published in 1922)
and 'Psychology and Poetry' (published in 1930), Jung explored the function
of the symbol in art with reference to Friedrich Schiller, Goethe's *Faust*,
Nietzsche's *Zarathustra*, as well as such popular cultural texts as those of
Rider Haggard and Conan Doyle. Although Jung does not use the precise
term 'symbolic pregnance', he uses a similar idea when, speaking of works of
art that are 'openly symbolic', he writes:

Their pregnant language cries out at us that they mean more than they say. We
can put our finger on the symbol at once, even though we may not be able to
unriddle its meaning to our entire satisfaction. A symbol remains a perpetual
challenge to our thoughts and feelings. That probably explains why a symbolic
work is so stimulating, why it grips us intensely, but also why it seldom affords
us a purely aesthetic enjoyment. [. . .] A symbol is the intimation of a meaning
beyond the level of our present powers of comprehension. (CW, 8, §119)

Because, however, such works of art are not 'purely' or 'merely' aesthetic, Jung should not be read as denying that the essence of the symbol and its function lie in its *aesthetic* nature.[30] As is well known, Jung dubbed certain recurring symbolic forms 'archetypes', and his discussion of these forms shows how deep the affinity with Cassirer on this point is.

In the 'purely expressive phenomenon', Cassirer writes, we are 'at the centre of that symbolic relation in which the psychic appears related to the bodily and the bodily to the psychic' (PSF, III, 103); and in 'the images of the mythical fantasy', he writes, we find that, 'as in the development of all symbolic forms, light and shadow go together': 'The light manifests itself only in the shadow it casts: the purely "intelligible" has the sensuous as its antithesis, but this antithesis is at the same time its necessary correlate' (PSF, II, 245). It is this fusion of the sensory and the intelligible that marks out, for Cassirer, the symbolic form. Language, for example, is said to show itself 'to be *at once* a sensuous and an intellectual form of expression' (PSF, I, 319); and in the 'phenomenological analysis' of the 'individual symbolic forms', we are said to see again and again 'how inseparably the purely "intellectual" contents are interwoven with the "vital" ones' (PSF, IV, 41).

It is just such a combination of the sensuous and the intelligible, or, to put it another way, a combination of matter and spirit, that lies at the root of Jung's notion of the psychoid unconscious, first proposed in 1946 (in 'On the Nature of the Psyche'). With this concept, Jung tries to articulate the idea that the psychological and the physiological, the realm of the psyche and the realm of the organic world, are inextricably linked, representing opposite ends of a single continuum: 'Just as, in its lower reaches, the psyche loses itself in the organic-material substrate, so in its upper reaches it resolves itself into a "spiritual" form about which we know as little as we do about the functional basis of instinct' (CW, 8, §380). Further on, Jung introduces the archetype into this model, suggesting that certain symbols embrace both 'mind' and 'body':

> Since psyche and matter are contained in one and the same world, and moreover are in continuous contact with one another and ultimately rest on irrepresentable, transcendental factors, it is not only possible but fairly probable, even, that psyche and matter are two different aspects of one and the same thing. [. . .] Just as the 'psychic infra-red', the biological instinctual psyche, gradually passes over into the physiology of the organism and thus merges with its chemical and physical conditions, so the 'psychic ultra-violet', the archetype, describes a field which exhibits none of the peculiarities of the physiological and yet, in the last analysis, can no longer be regarded as psychic, although it manifests itself psychically. (CW, 8, §418 and §420)

Or as Jung put it in 'The Psychology of the Child Archetype' (1940), '"at bottom" the psyche is simply "world"' (*'Zuunterst' ist daher Psyche überhaupt*

'*Welt*') (CW, 9/i, §291). If Jung is hampered by that inability to express him-self clearly that Anthony Storr has noted,[31] then it is not for want of trying.[32] Using another image to describe the relationship of spirit to matter, he writes: 'Our present knowledge does not allow us to do much more than compare the relation of the psychic to the material with two cones, whose apices, meeting in a point without extension — a real zero-point — touch and do not touch' (CW, 8, §418). For all his apparent lack of sophistication, Jung's geometrical image recalls the argument in the *Aesthetic Letters*, where Schiller wonders how Beauty can link the two opposite conditions of feeling (*Empfinden*, associated with the body) and thinking (*Denken*, associated with the mind) when, between these two, there is no middle term (Letter 18, §2). In the language of Schiller's terminology of the drives, what can unite the material drive (*Stofftrieb*) with the formal drive (*Formtrieb*)? The third term here turns out to be the aesthetic state, the zero-point (*Null*) of human exis-tence (Letter 21, §4). In the next Letter, Schiller continues: 'If, then, in *one* respect the aesthetic mode of the psyche is to be regarded as *Nought* — once, that is, we have an eye to particular and definite effects — it is in another respect to be looked upon as a state of *Supreme Reality*, once we have due regard to the absence of all limitation and to the sum total of the powers which are conjointly active within it' (*Wenn also die ästhetische Stimmung des Gemüts in einer Rücksicht als* Null *betrachtet werden muß, sobald man nämlich sein Augenmerk auf einzelne und bestimmte Wirkungen richtet, so ist sie in anderer Rücksicht wieder als ein Zustand der* höchsten Realität *anzusehen, insofern man dabei auf die Abwesenheit aller Schranken und auf die Summe der Kräfte achtet, die in derselben gemeinschaftlich tätig sind*) (Letter 21, §1).

Conclusion

It is thus no exaggeration to say that Schiller's aesthetic education, Jung's psychological education, and Cassirer's philosophy of symbolic forms converge on the concept of the symbol. For the language used by Schiller, Cassirer, and Jung, the symbol represents the site where 'the opposites are united', and is dubbed by Schiller *lebende Gestalt* — living form.[33] And for Schiller, this living form, the symbol, is 'a concept serving to designate all the aesthetic qualities of phenomena and, in a word, what in the widest sense of the term we call *beauty*' (*ein Begriff, der allen ästhetischen Beschaffenheiten der Erscheinungen und mit einem Worte dem, was man in weitester Bedeutung* Schönheit *nennt, zur Bezeichnung dient*) (CW, 6, §171).[34] In volume 2 of *The Philosophy of Symbolic Forms*, Cassirer writes that '[m]easured by empirical, realistic criteria, the aesthetic world becomes a world of appearance; but in severing its bond with immediate reality, with the material existence and efficacy which constitute the world of magic and myth, it embodies a new step toward the truth' (PSF, II, 26). Earlier, in *Kants Leben und Lehre* (1918), Cassirer had written:

> The work of art is a unique and detached thing, independent and possessing it own end within itself — and yet there is portrayed therein a new 'whole', a new total image of reality and the spiritual cosmos itself. The individual does not refer in this instance to some abstract universal beyond itself but is this very universal itself because it grasps the sum and substance of it symbolically.[35]

And later, in *An Essay on Man*, Cassirer explained that 'the same classical formula', a 'unity in a manifold', could be applied to beauty as well as truth (*Essay*, p. 143), and defended beauty against Hume's claim that 'beauty is no quality in things themselves', 'it exists merely in the mind which contemplates them':[36]

> Beauty cannot be defined by its mere *percipi*, as 'being perceived'; it must be defined in terms of an activity of the mind, of the function of perceiving and by a characteristic direction of this function. It does not consist of passive precepts; it is a mode, a process of perceptualization. But this process is not merely subjective in character; on the contrary, it is one of the conditions of our intuition of an objective world. (*Essay*, p. 151)

According to Cassirer, in Romantic thought imagination is 'no longer that special human activity which builds up the human world of art', but acquires 'universal poetic value' (*Essay*, p. 155). No Romantic himself, the emphasis in Cassirer's philosophy is not imagination as having universal, but rather specifically *human* value. For Cassirer, 'art' is 'a symbolic language' (*Essay*, p. 168), which shapes our cultural environment — in other words, the way we see the world. According to Jung, 'psychology is concerned with the act of seeing' — *Die Psychologie befaßt sich mit dem Akt des Sehens* (CW, 12, §15) — and both Cassirer and Jung are concerned with how individual consciousness extends itself into 'collective', cultural forms. In the conclusion to 'On the Metaphysics of Symbolic Forms' (1928), part of the material for the fourth, uncompleted volume of *The Philosophy of Symbolic Forms*, Cassirer summed up the significance of the symbol as follows:

> Throughout the course of our investigation [. . .] we have sought to show how the course of human knowledge leads from 'representation' to 'signification', from the schematism of perception to the symbolic grasp of pure relationships and orders of meaning. All these orders, no matter how absolute we may take them to be, existing in and of themselves, are there 'for' man only to the extent that he participates in their development. Man's life in them cannot consist of passive awareness; his life is bound up with their production so that he raises these orders up into his consciousness by means of this course of knowledge. In this act of becoming conscious and of making himself conscious we do not find the power of fate which governs individual processes. Here we attain the

realm of freedom. The true and highest achievement of every 'symbolic form' consists in its contribution toward this goal; by means of its resources and its own unique way, every symbolic form works toward the transition from the realm of 'nature' to that of 'freedom'. (PSF, IV, 111)

In a Hegelian manner, Cassirer claimed in *The Problem of Knowledge in Philosophy and Science* [*Das Erkenntnisproblem in der Philosophie und Wissenschaft*] that '[i]f philosophy is to be the authentic and complete consciousness which Spirit has of itself [. . .] it must truly grasp everything within itself, all creative spiritual achievement in the whole of "objective spirit" as it presents itself in religion and in art, morality, law, in science and in the state';[37] in *The Philosophy of Symbolic Forms* that 'the pure *function* of the spirit itself must seek concrete fulfillment in the sensory world' (PSF, I, 87); and in an essay of 1945 that we should use the term *Geist* 'in a functional sense as a comprehensive name for all those functions which constitute and build up the world of human culture'.[38] In very much the same spirit, Jung wrote in his autobiographical work *Memories, Dreams, Reflections* (1961):

> Unconscious wholeness therefore seems to me the true *spiritus rector* of all bio-logical and psychic events. Here is a principle which strives for total realisation — which in man's case signifies the attainment of total consciousness. Attain-ment of consciousness is culture in the broadest sense, and self-knowledge is therefore the heart and essence of this process.

> [*Die unbewußte Ganzheit erscheint mir daher als der eigentliche spiritus rector alles biologischen und psychischen Geschehens. Sie strebt nach totaler Verwirklichung, also totaler Bewußtwerdung im Fall des Menschen. Bewußtwerdung ist Kultur im weitesten Sinne und Selbsterkenntnis daher Essenz und Herz dieses Vorgangs.*][39]

Notes

[1] See Paul Bishop, 'Speaking of Symbols: Affinities Between Cassirer's and Jung's Theories of Language', in Cyrus Hamlin and John Michael Krois (eds), *Symbolic Forms and Cultural Studies: Ernst Cassirer's Theory of Culture* (New Haven and London: Yale University Press, 2004), pp. 127–56.

[2] In this essay, the following abbreviations are used to refer to works by Cassirer and by Jung: PSF = Cassirer, *The Philosophy of Symbolic Forms*, trans. by Ralph Manheim, 3 vols (New Haven and London: Yale University Press, 1955–1957), and vol. 4, *The Metaphysics of Symbolic Forms*, ed. by John Michael Krois and Donald P. Verene, trans. by John Michael Krois (New Haven: Yale University Press, 1996) [cited with references to volume and page number]; CW = Jung, *Collected Works*, ed. by Sir Herbert Read, Michael Fordham, Gerhard Adler and William McGuire, 20 vols (London: Routledge and Kegan Paul, 1953–1983) [cited with references to volume and paragraph number]; PU = Jung, *Psychology of the Unconscious: A Study of the Transformations and Symbolisms of the Libido: A Contribution to the History of the Evolution of Thought* [translation of *Wandlungen und Symbole der Libido*], trans. by Beatrice M. Hinkle (London: Routledge, 1991).

[3] See Lucien Lévy-Bruhl, *Les Fonctions mentales dans les sociétés inférieures* (1912), a copy of which was owned by Jung.

[4] See Claude Lévi-Strauss, *La Pensée sauvage* (1962).

[5] This term, now firmly associated with Jacques Derrida, was earlier used by C. G. Carus in *Über Lebensmagnetismus* (1857), where he differentiated between a superficial, 'logozentrisch' way and a richer, 'biozentrisch' way of looking at the world (Raymond Furness, *Zarathustra's Children: A Study of a Lost Generation of German Writers* (Rochester, NY, and Woodbridge: Camden House, 2000), p. 121); and by Ludwig Klages (1872–1956), who uses the term extensively in *Der Geist als Widersacher der Seele* (1929–1932).

[6] See Immanuel Kant, *Kritik der Urteilskraft* [*Kritik of Judgement*], §9 (cf. §26) and §10.

[7] Cassirer and Klages. See PSF, IV, 23–27. On expression, see PSF, III, 67; and Krois, *Cassirer: Symbolic Forms and History* (New Haven and London: Yale University Press, 1987), pp. 57–62. For Klages, the expressive experience represents 'a kind of Archimedean point, from which he seeks to lift the world of ontology off its hinges' (PSF, III, 100), of the kind that neither Cassirer, nor Jung (see CW, 8, §421 and §437), believed their respective disciplines of philosophy and psychology enjoyed.

[8] Karl Phillip Moritz, *Götterlehre der Griechen und Römer*, ed. by Max Oberbreyer (Leipzig: Reclam, 1878), p. 11 (quoted in David Wellbery, *The Specular Moment: Goethe's Early Lyric and the Beginnings of Romanticism* (Stanford, CA: Stanford University Press, 1996), pp. 180 and 309).

[9] F. W. J. Schelling, *Ausgewählte Schriften*, 6 vols (Frankfurt am Main: Suhrkamp, 1985), vol. 5, p. 226.

[10] As paraphrased by Karl Kerényi in his 'Prolegomena' to C. G. Jung and Karl Kerényi, *Essays on a Science of Mythology* (Princeton, NY: Princeton University Press, 1963), p. 6.

[11] See *Kritik der reinen Vernunft*, A 118–A 126 (Immanuel Kant, *Kritik der reinen Vernunft*, ed. by Raymund Schmidt [Hamburg: Meiner, 1990], pp. 173a–184a; *Critique of Pure Reason*, trans. and ed. by Paul Guyer and Allen W. Wood [Cambridge: Cambridge University Press, 1997], pp. 238–41). In a footnote Kant observes that 'no psychologist has yet thought that the imagination is a necessary ingredient of perception itself' (*daß die Einbildungskraft ein notwendiges Ingredienz der Wahrnehmung selbst sei, daran hat wohl noch kein Psychologe gedacht*) (A 121, note). Whilst this might be true of eighteenth-century psychology, it is a deficit which Jung tries to make good.

[12] Martin Heidegger, *Kant and the Problem of Metaphysics*, trans. by James S. Churchill (Bloomington: Indiana University Press, 1962), p. 170.

[13] Eight years later, Jung would insist on the importance of *Phantasie* in similar terms in 'The Aims of Psychotherapy ['Ziele der Psychotherapie'] (1929), apparently equating *Phantasie* and *Einbildungskraft*: 'To me, phantasy is the maternally creative side of the masculine mind. When all is said and done, we can never rise above phantasy. It is true that there are unprofitable, futile, morbid, and unsatisfying fantasies whose sterile nature is immediately recognized by every person endowed with common sense; but the faulty performance proves nothing against the normal performance. All the works of Man have their origin in creative imagination. What right, then, have we to disparage phantasy? In the normal course of things, phantasy does not easily go astray; it is too deep for that, and too closely bound up with the tap-root of human and animal instinct. It has a surprising way of always coming out right in the end. The creative activity of imagination frees Man from his bondage to the "nothing but" and raises him to the status of one who plays. As Schiller says, Man is completely human only when he is at play' (*Phantasie ist mir in letzter Linie die mütterliche Schöpferkraft des männlichen Geistes. Im letzten Grunde sind wir nie erhaben über Phantasie. Gewiß gibt es wertlose, unzulängliche, krankhafte und unbefriedigende Phantasien, deren sterile Natur jeder mit gesundem Menschenverstand Begabte baldigst erkennen wird, aber Fehlleistungen beweisen bekanntlich nichts gegen Normalisierung. Alles Menschenwerk entstammt der schöpferischen Phantasie. Wie sollten wir da von der Einbildungskraft gering denken dürfen? Auch geht Phantasie normalerweise nicht in die Irre, dazu ist sie zu tief und zu innig verbunden mit dem Grundstock menschlicher und tierischer Instinkte. Sie kommt in überraschender Weise immer wieder zurecht. Die schöpferische Betätigung der Einbildungskraft entreißt den Menschen seiner Gebundenheit im "Nichts-als" und erhebt ihn in den Zustand des Spielenden. Und*

der Mensch ist, wie Schiller sagt, "nur da ganz Mensch, wo er spielt") (CW, 16, §98) (cf. Friedrich
Schiller, *On the Aesthetic Education of Mankind*, ed. and trans. by Elizabeth M. Wilkinson and
L. A. Willoughby, 2nd edn [Oxford: Clarendon Press, 1982], Letter 15, §9, pp. 106–07).

[14] Kant, *Kritik der Urteilskraft*, 'Einleitung', II (*Werke*, ed. by Wilhelm Weischedel, 10 vols
[Darmstadt: Wissenschaftliche Buchgesellschaft, 1975], vol. 8, pp. 247–48; *The Critique of
Judgement*, trans. by James Creed Meredith [Oxford: Clarendon Press, 1952], p. 14).

[15] Book I, §9; cf. §26.

[16] In other words, Schiller's aesthetic theory represents a reaction and a response to Kant. For
example, in §22 Kant claims that it is contradictory to assert that the imagination is both free
and conformable to a law, whereas Schiller, in On the Necessary Limitations of the Use of
Beautiful Forms' ['Über die notwendigen Grenzen beim Gebrauch schöner Formen'] and the
so-called 'Kallias-Briefe' (both referred to by Jung in *Psychological Types*) argues that this is
not so. For further discussion, see Jeffrey A. Gauthier, 'Schiller's Critique of Kant's Moral
Psychology: Reconciling Practical Reason and an Ethics of Virtue', *Canadian Journal of
Philosophy*, 27 (1997), 513–44.

[17] Kant, *Critique of Judgement*, §77, p. 526; trans. Creed, p. 65.

[18] Ernst Cassirer, *An Essay on Man: An Introduction to a Philosophy of Culture* (New Haven and
London: Yale University Press, 1972), p. 57. Henceforth cited as *Essay*.

[19] 'A thing [. . .] can relate to the totality of our various functions without being a definite
object for any single one of them: that is its *aesthetic* character' (*Eine Sache kann sich auf das
Ganze unsrer verschiedenen Kräfte beziehen, ohne für eine einzelne derselben ein bestimmtes Objekt zu
sein: das ist ihre* ästhetische *Beschaffenheit*) (Letter 20, §4, footnote; pp. 142–43).

[20] For further discussion, see Paul Bishop, *Analytical Psychology and German Classical Aesthetics*,
vol. 1, *The Development of the Personality* (London and New York: Routledge, 2008), chap. 4,
'Schiller and the problem of typology', pp. 126–56.

[21] See also PSF, III, 235: 'We have designated as symbolic pregnance the relation in consequence of which a sensuous thing embraces a meaning and represents it for consciousness:
this pregnance can be reduced neither to merely reproductive processes nor to mediated
intellectual processes — it must ultimately be recognized as an independent and autonomous
determination, without which neither an object nor a subject, neither a unity of the thing nor
a unity of the self would be given to us'. For further discussion, see Krois, *Cassirer: Symbolic
Forms and History*, pp. 50–57.

[22] *Die Traumdeutung*, in Sigmund Freud, *The Standard Edition of the Complete Psychological
Works*, ed. by James Strachey and Anna Freud, 24 vols (London: Hogarth Press, 1953–1974),
vol. 2/3, p. 283; *Gesammelte Werke: chronologisch geordnet*, 19 vols (Frankfurt am Main: S.
Fischer, 1952–1987), vol. 4, p. 277.

[23] 'Consider for a moment how depth psychology approaches a dream. To understand its
significance, we interpret the dream according to a posited *a priori* or *a posteriori* absolute. If
the therapist is committed to *a priori* ultimates, the significance of the case material comes
about through a reduction to such absolutes as drives, the Oedipus complex, archetypes,
biochemistry, the environment, family systems, childhood traumas, the analytic frame, and
so on. Notice how all these absolutes are temporally located in the past' (Paul Kugler, 'The
Unconscious in a Postmodern Depth Psychology', in: *C. G. Jung and the Humanities: Towards
a Hermeneutics of Culture*, ed. by Karin Barnaby and Pellegrino d'Acierno [London: Routledge,
1990], pp. 307–18 [p. 313]).

[24] 'The authority for the clinical interpretation might also be grounded in a posited absolute
located in the future. For example, the clinical material might be interpreted as moving
toward and referring to *a posteriori* ultimates such as the self, archetypes, wholeness, unity,
spirit, soul, death, and so forth. For these first principles to perform their function, they cannot
be implicated in the very system of thought and language they are being used to explain; nor
can their meaning have the same semantic status as the other meanings within the system.
Their semantic status must be something like the "meaning of meaning" or the "metaphor of

metaphors". These *a priori* and *a posteriori* "god" terms function as the linchpins for our Western theories of clinical interpretation' (Kugler, 'The Unconscious in a Postmodern Depth Psychology', p. 314).

[25] See 'Cryptomnesia' ('Kryptomnesie') (CW, 1, §184).

[26] In *Mythical Thought*, Cassirer writes: 'Folk beliefs show that this primordial force of the mythical imagination is still alive and active. In it is rooted the belief in the vast throng of nature demons who dwell in field and meadow, thicket and wood. In the rustling of the leaves, the murmuring and roaring of the wind, and the play and sparkle of the sunlight, in a thousand indefinable voices and tones the life of the forest first becomes perceptible to the mythical consciousness as the immediate manifestation of the innumerable elemental spirits who inhabit the woods: the woodsprites and elves, the spirits of tree and wind' (PSF, II, 201). According to Jung, the world of the early Renaissance thinker Paracelsus was one in which 'nature swarmed with witches, incubi, succubi, devils, sylphs, undines, etc.' (CW, 15 §12); and, echoing Weber's thesis of the 'disenchantment of the world' (*Entzauberung der Welt*), Jung writes in 'After the Catastrophe' (1945): 'For the first time since the dawn of history we have succeeded in swallowing the whole of primitive animism into ourselves, and with it the spirit that animated nature. Not only were the gods dragged down from their planetary spheres and transformed into chthonic demons, but, under the influence of scientific enlightenment, even this band of demons, which at the time of Paracelsus still frolicked happily in mountains and woods, in rivers and human dewlling-places, was reduced to a miserable remnant and finally vanished altogether. From time immemorial, nature was always filled with spirit. Now, for the first time, we are living in a lifeless nature bereft of gods [*Jetzt leben wir zum erstenmal in einer entseelten und entgötterten Natur*]' (CW, 10, §431).

[27] First described by Jung in *Wandlungen und Symbole der Libido* (see PU, §§245–47). Jung's source for this information is Konrad Theodor Preuss's 'Der Ursprung der Religion und Kunst', *Globus: Illustrierte Zeitschrift für Länder- und Völkerkunde*, 86 (1904), 355–63 and 87 (1905), 333–419, an article also referred to by Cassirer.

[28] For Cassirer, the logic of the sacrifice can also be understood within the framework of an energic metaphor as a method of canalization: 'Fundamentally, every sacrifice implies a negative factor: a limitation of sensory desire [*sinnlichen Begehrens*], a renunciation [*Verzicht*] which the I imposes on itself. [. . .] Yet all these forms of renunciation [*Entsagung*] and sacrifice have at first a purely egocentric purpose: by submitting to certain physical privations a man aims merely to strengthen his mana, his physical-magical power and efficacy. [. . .] A man's sensory wishes and desires [*die sinnlichen Wünsche und Begierden*] do not flow equally in all directions; he no longer seeks to transpose them immediately and unrestrictedly into reality; rather he limits them at certain points in order to make the withheld and, one might say, stored-up power free for other purposes [*damit die hier zurückgehaltene und gewissermaßen aufgespeicherte Kraft für andere Zwecke frei wird*]' (PSF, II, 221–22).

[29] By seeing alchemy and astrology as precursors of modern science (PSF, II, 66–67; CW, 8, §§88–91 and CW, 5, §213 and §226), Cassirer and Jung develop a position speculatively, even polemically, articulated by Nietzsche in *The Gay Science*, §300, in the form of a rhetorical question: 'Do you really believe that the sciences would ever have originated and grown if the way had not been prepared by magicians, alchemists, astrologers, and witches whose promises and pretensions first had to create a thirst, a hunger, a taste for hidden and forbidden powers?' ('Preludes of Science', in Friedrich Nietzsche, *The Gay Science* [1882], trans. by Walter Kaufmann [New York: Vintage Books, 1974], p. 240).

[30] In his emphasis in *Mysterium coniunctionis* (1955–1956) on 'the step beyond a merely aesthetic attitude' (*den Schritt über die bloß ästhetische Einstellung*) (CW, 14, §755), Jung follows Schiller and Wilhelm von Humboldt in distinguishing between Art and the merely Aesthetic (*bloß Ästhetische*) (see Humboldt's letters to Schiller of 13 February 1796 and 16 July 1797).

[31] 'I know of no creative person who was more hamstrung by his inability to write' (Anthony Storr, *Jung* [London: Fontana, 1973], pp. 37–38).

[32] For a counter-position that argues for Jung's stylistic mastery, see Susan Rowland, *Jung as a Writer* (London: Routledge, 2005).

[33] Letter 15, §2 (Schiller, *On the Aesthetic Education of Man*, pp. 100–01); cf. CW, 6, §§170–71; *Essay on Man*, pp. 151 and 166.

[34] See Letter 15, §2 (Schiller, *On the Aesthetic Education of Man*, pp. 100–01).

[35] PSF, I, 48; citing Cassirer, *Kants Leben und Lehre* (Berlin: B. Cassirer, 1928), p. 328.

[36] See Hume, 'Of the Standard of Taste', in *Essays: Moral, Political, and Literary*, ed. by T. H. Green and T. H. Grose, 2 vols (London: Longmans, Green, 1889), vol. 1, pp. 266–84 (p. 269).

[37] *Das Erkenntnisproblem in der Philosophie und Wissenschaft der neueren Zeit*, 3 vols (Berlin: B. Cassirer, 1906–1910), III, p. 365.

[38] Ernst Cassirer, 'Structuralism in Modern Linguistics', *Word: Journal of the Linguistic Circle of New York*, 1 (1945), 99–120 (p. 114).

[39] Jung, *Memories, Dreams, Reflections: Recorded and edited by Aniela Jaffé*, trans. by Richard and Clara Winston (London: Collins/Routledge and Kegan Paul, 1983), p. 356.

SYMBOLISM AND *BASISPHÄNOMENE*

By JOHN MICHAEL KROIS

Ernst Cassirer's magnum opus, the *Philosophie der symbolischen Formen*, has usually been taken to be a continuation of Kantian philosophy with new means. The theory of symbolism took the place of a transcendental investigation of forms of aesthetic and conceptual experience. In Cassirer's philosophy, symbolism refers to pre-cultural meaning as well as to conventional sign systems. To refer to this generalized conception of symbolism Cassirer coined the term 'symbolic pregnancy' or *symbolische Prägnanz*, which he described as 'the way in which a perception as a "sensory" experience contains at the same time a certain nonintuitive "meaning" which it immediately and concretely represents' (*die Art* [. . .], *in der ein Wahrnehmungserlebnis, als 'sinnliches' Erlebnis, zugleich einen bestimmten nicht-anschaulichen 'Sinn' in sich faßt und ihn zur unmittelbaren konkreten Darstellung bringt*).[1] According to this doctrine, there is no such thing as elementary phenomena, neither the sort that Carnap called 'Elementarerlebnisse' — momentary cross sections of a holistic empirical experience — nor in the sense of Husserl's phenomenological conception of hyle, the 'matter' of phenomenological reality. Instead, every sensory experience always already embodies particular symbolic values, so that *symbolische Prägnanz* is a ubiquitous phenomenon, which occurs in different ways — as expressive, representative, or pure significative symbolic values. The explication of *symbolische Prägnanz* in Cassirer's *Phänomenologie der Erkenntnis* deals with the pre-cultural organization of cognition, as did Kant's analyses of the *reine Anschauungsformen* and *reine Verstandesbegriffe*, but Cassirer took a different starting point than Kant did.

Instead of beginning with the fact of consciousness or apperception, Cassirer's investigations investigated the experience of the body. As he put it: 'The relation of body and soul represents the prototype and model for a purely symbolic relation' (*Das Verhältnis von Leib und Seele stellt das erste Vorbild und Musterbild für eine rein symbolische Relation dar*).[2] Even concrete bodily feelings express meanings that go beyond the momentary sensation: 'The basic qualities of the tactile sense — qualities such as "hard" and "soft", "rough" and "smooth" — arise only through motion, so that if we limit tactile sensations to a single moment, they can no longer be discerned as data' (*die grundlegenden Qualitäten des Tastsinns — Qualitäten wie 'hart' und 'weich', 'rauh' und 'glatt' [entstehen] erst kraft der Bewegung [. . .], so daß sie, wenn wir die Tastempfindung auf einen einzelnen Augenblick beschränkt sein lassen, innerhalb*

dieses Augenblickes als Data gar nicht aufgefunden werden können).[3] This emphasis
upon dynamic movement played a central role in Cassirer's philosophy of
symbolism, and in his theory of mythic thought he emphasized that cultural
sign systems emerge from actions, particularly through gestures and rituals.
He summarized this view in 1925: 'Not mere observation, but rather actions
provide the middle point from which, for human beings, the intellectual
organization of reality takes its beginnings' (*Nicht das bloße Betrachten, sondern
das Tun bildet vielmehr den Mittelpunkt, von dem für die Menschen die geistige
Organisation der Wirklichkeit ihren Ausgang nimmt*).[4] This emphasis upon the
primacy of movement, rather than upon static transcendental preconditions
was what so impressed Maurice Merleau-Ponty about Cassirer's *Phänomenologie der Erkenntnis*, and indeed Cassirer's philosophy of symbolism is in many
ways more akin to Merleau-Ponty's phenomenology of the body-subject
than to Kantianism.

In 1941 Cassirer wrote from America to his friend and former student,
Malte Jacobsohn, then governor (Landshövding) in Gothenburg, that he was
looking forward to returning to live there again.[5] Upon his return he
intended to see the unpublished texts he had left behind in Sweden through
to publication, but Cassirer's death on 13 April 1945 in New York City
resulted in his manuscripts remaining unknown for decades. Cassirer
had lived in Sweden from 1935 to 1941, during which time he published a
number of important works, such as *Determinismus und Indeterminismus in der
modernen Physik* or *Zur Logik der Kulturwissenschaften*, but he wrote much more
that never was published. Cassirer's publications after he left Germany in 1933
appeared to supplement his *Philosophie der symbolischen Formen* in particular
fields of investigation, but not to depart from its general framework.[6] This
was even true of his last works written in America after 1941. In his unpublished manuscripts, however, a new turn in his thought went far beyond an
application of his philosophy of symbolism.

The doctrine of *Basisphänomene*, which was the focus of his thinking during
his years in Sweden, is documented in the first five volumes of his *Nachgelassene Manuskripte und Schriften*. According to this doctrine, three irreducibly
different phenomena define the nature of reality or *Wirklichkeit* — prior to its
symbolic interpretation. Cassirer referred to these Basic phenomena by means
of the personal pronouns of *Ich, Du, Es* (I, Thou, It). These stand for three
dynamic processes, which he sometimes called life, action, and works. He
described them as (1) 'a "Being" that is not to be understood as at rest in itself,
but as a process, as movement' (*ein 'Sein', das aber nicht ruhend, sondern als
Prozess, als Bewegung zu verstehen ist*); (2) as 'action and reaction' (*Wirkung und
Gegenwirkung*); and (3) as 'works' (*Werke*), resulting from 'actions and deeds'
(*Handlungen und Taten*) rather than blind causal efficacy.[7]

The *Basisphänomene* doctrine was a 'realism', for it was concerned with real processes, not our words or thoughts about them. *Ich*, *Du*, and *Es* were not taken simply as pronouns, but as real phenomena independent of language. Cassirer is explicit about the reality of the *Basisphänomene*, for he stated explicitly that 'they are "prior" to all thought and inference and are the basis of both' (*sie sind 'vor' allem Denken und Schließen, liegen diesem selbst zu Grunde*).[8] To understand the force of this statement, taken from the text 'Über Basisphänomene' from the late 1930s, it is necessary to recall the basic position of the Marburg school of Neo-Kantianism, which historians of philosophy have always associated Cassirer with. For the Marburg school, philosophy begins with the view that 'Nothing is given to thought except thought itself' (*Nichts ist dem Denken gegeben außer dem Denken selbst*).[9] In Cohen's words, 'for thought nothing may be considered as given' (*dem Denken darf nichts als gegeben gelten*).[10] But Cassirer's doctrine of *Basisphänomene* denies this. The *Basisphänomene* are '[. . .] "vor" allem Denken und Schließen, liegen diesem selbst zu Grunde'. Here, Cassirer turned away from Marburg Kantianism to phenomenology. Whereas the philosophy of symbolic forms transformed Kantianism into a philosophy of inter-subjective meaning, the doctrine of *Basisphänomene* was not Kantian at all. It was not concerned with Kant's 'transcendental question' of the conditions of the possibility of the phenomena at hand, for basis phenomena are existential facts, and if a question could be raised about the conditions of their possibility, then we would, by definition, not be talking about *basic* phenomena anymore.

The thinking and sensing subject was not the focal point of the *Basisphänomene* doctrine, but the dynamic processes of organisms in interaction with each other and the world. This conception was already found in his treatment of symbolism in his writings of myth, but in the late 1930s Cassirer made this point even more generally. He compared the three basic phenomena to the first, second, and third person perspectives, and their irreducibility. He rejected the primacy of the first person perspective: 'Without the second and third person we do not have the first / and "in our thoughts" we cannot isolate the first person / for thoughts always have to be thoughts about something' (*Ohne die zweite und dritte Person haben wir auch die erste nicht - / und selbst 'in Gedanken' können wir die erste Person nicht isolieren / denn Gedanken müssen eben immer schon Gedanken von Etwas sein*).[11] To this he added: 'Knowledge about "me" is not prior to and independent of knowledge of the "thou" and the "it", but they all constitute one another' (*Das Wissen von 'mir' ist nicht vor und unabhängig vom Wissen des 'Du' und 'Es', sondern dies alles konstituiert sich nur miteinander*).[12]

Whereas Kantianism favorued the first-person perspective, Cassirer's doctrine of *Basisphänomene* is a kind of pluralistic realism. The *Basisphänomene* doctrine formulates what everybody is familiar with but which is incapable of explanation, because explanations always presuppose these basic phenomena.[13] Cassirer did not return to traditional realism (going back to Aristotle), for the basic phenomena were not things or *substances*. As he once put it: 'Life, reality, being, existence are nothing but different terms referring to one and the same fundamental fact. These terms do not describe a fixed, rigid, substantial thing. They are to be understood as names of a process'.[14] *Basisphänomene* were taken to be aspects of a dynamic process, while the function of symbolism consisted in giving this process an understandable form.

In 1928, Cassier called symbolism 'the fundamental problem in philosophical anthropology' (*das Grundproblem der philosophischen Anthropologie*).[15] The theoretical basis of Cassirer's thought appeared then to reside in his concept of *symbolische Prägnanz*, and the different symbolic values of *Ausdruck*, *Darstellung* and *reine Bedeutung*. Even in his philosophy of symbolism Cassirer did not begin with language or the thinking subject. Language was not merely co-emergent with gesture — a notion now widespread in cognitive linguistics — it presupposed a foundation in actions and expressive, emotional meaning. 'The narrative', Cassirer said, 'offers no key to an understanding of the cult; it is rather the cult which forms the preliminary stage and objective foundation of myth' (*So bietet nicht dieser Bericht den Schlüssel zum Verständnis des Kultus dar, sondern es ist vielmehr der Kult, der die Vorstufe des Mythos und seine 'objektive' Grundlage bildet*).[16] The so-called 'linguistic turn' in philosophy was predicated on the belief that language is prior to any thought that we articulate. By contrast, Cassirer's philosophical anthropology led him to emphasize that language presupposes *speakers*, and before they learn a language they are able to understand and to communicate with one another and interact with the world — by means of facial expressions, gestures, and by mimetic forms of behaviour, particularly with ritual. This approach seemed also to limit philosophy to philosopical anthropology — a theory of reality per se seemed missing from Cassirer's philosophy — until he developed the doctrine of *Basisphänomene*.

But the doctrine of *Basisphänomene* does not break with or contradict Cassirer's philosophy of symbolism — it explicates its presuppositions. Cassirer always avoided the term ontology, for although the presuppositions that Cassirer analyses (*Ich – Du – Es*) could be conceived of as ontological givens, he rejected substance ontology in the most radical way. In his early philosophy of symbolic forms, he reinterpreted the metaphyical basis of logic — rejecting the concept of substance in favour of the concept of function — and regarding the logic of relation as the basis of logic rather than the logic of classes.

Unlike linguistically inspired, structuralist conceptions of symbolism, Cassirer's theory of symbolic forms was based upon a triadic notion of symbolic processes rather than on the static, dual relation of signifier and signified. Language and other cultural sign systems depend upon activities, which he termed 'Energien des Geistes' that differently link sensory signs and meanings.[17]

The doctrine of the three basic phenomena describes the background for the emergence of such cultural symbolic forms, with gesture and the understanding of expressivity on the border between natural phenomena and cultural activities. In his writings on philosophical anthropology, Cassirer delineated the break between the human ability to create and understand symbols and the understanding of signals in animals, about which his colleague in Hamburg, Jakob von Uexküll, conducted pioneering research. But the doctrine of *Basisphänomene* did not deal with meaning, they were more fundamental than any symbolic interpretation, for they formulate the phenomena which, as Cassirer put it, 'we have to assume, in order to gain access to "reality"' (*von denen wir ausgehen müssen, um irgend einen Zugang zur 'Wirklichkeit' zu gewinnen*).[18] The dynamic action metaphors of 'ausgehen von' and 'Zugang gewinnen' indicate how Cassirer understood these Basic phenomena to reside in dynamic processes of action and bodily accessibility.

Cassirer's willingness to adopt such a doctrine was not as abrupt as it seems. When Cassirer's interpretation of quantum theory appeared in 1936, reviewers were taken aback by what they considered to be its inexplicable break with his supposed philosophical orientation. In a review in the *Physikalische Zeitschrift*, Carl Friedrich von Weizäcker criticized Cassirer for upholding conceptions that could not be reconciled with Neo-Kantianism because he abandoned the causal principle that was appropriate for classical mechanics in which Kant believed.[19] Weizäcker was not alone with this reaction. Max von Laue wrote to Cassirer on 26 March 1937 in reaction to his book:

> As far as I remember the *Critique of Pure Reason*, causality is supposed to make possible the organization of objective events in time and space, in fact, it ensures these placement and organization by itself alone. If we retain this idea of complementarity as Bohr characterized it, *as Cassirer does*, you will abandon, it seems to me, the foundations of Kant's epistemology forever. And really the fundamentals, not any kind of secondary, historically-conditioned aspects of Kant's writings.

> [*Soweit ich mich an die Kritik der reinen Vernunft erinnere, soll doch die Kausalität gerade die Einordnung der objektiven Geschehnisse in Raum und Zeit ermöglichen, ja sogar allein diese Einordenbarkeit gewährleisten. Wenn man diesen von Bohr geprägten Gedanken der Komplementarität beibehält* wie Cassirer es tut, *verläßt man m. E. die Grundlagen der Kantischen Erkenntnislehre auf Nimmerwiedersehen. Und zwar wirklich die Grundlagen, nicht irgend welche sekundären, zeitbedingten Züge der Kantischen Schriften*].[20]

This is why Weizäcker wrote in his review that Cassirer was 'not allowed as a Neo-Kantian' to think the way he did. The book on indeterminism offered hints at what was going on in Cassirer's philosophizing since he had moved to Sweden.

Upon his arrival in Gothenburg in 1935 Cassirer was confronted with the 'Uppsala school' of philosophy, headed by Axel Hägerström. The Uppsala school sought to establish a logical and realistic philosophy in strict opposition to any kind of subjective orientation or Idealism. In 1939 Cassirer addressed this topic in a lecture entitled 'Was ist Subjectivismus?', in which he sought to avoid asserting either a subjectivistic position or siding with the radical anti-subjective position of the Uppsala school. His approach so enraged the Uppsala philosophers that the discussion afterwards lasted needed to be continued the next day and went on for a total of four hours. Cassirer commented in a letter (to Åke Petzäll) afterwards that a mutual understanding about Realism appeared finally to have been reached, when he stated that 'Realität' needed to be taken as given — yet should not simply be asserted in a naive and dogmatic way.[21] However, the philosopher Ingemar Hedenius reacted by objecting that the Uppsala school was 'consciously-dogmatic' (*bewusst dogmatisch*) and Konrad Marc-Wogau even added that it was 'consciously naïve' (*bewusst naiv*).[22] The Uppsala philosophers took Cassirer to be speaking in a contradictory way, in their terms: neither declaring himself to be a naive realist nor admitting that he was a subjectivist in line with German idealism. Cassirer's theory of *Basisphänomene*, was his answer to the Uppsala philosophers; for it could not be subsumed under either of their alternatives.

In the late 1930s Cassirer wrote a critical study of the Vienna Circle of Logical Positivism.[23] Cassirer disagreed with the Vienna Circle philosophers on specific issues (such as their physicalism), but he praised their critical attitude towards dogmatic thinking,[24] which they were able to put into praxis — for, in the German-speaking academic world, the Vienna Circle school of philosophy stood out in its immunity to enthusiasm for the Nazi world view.[25] Cassirer's doctrine of the *Basisphänomene* was developed at least in part in reaction to the political situation. In Cassirer's inaugural lecture at Gothenburg on 19 October 1935[26] about 'The Concept of Philosophy as a Philosophical Problem',[27] he announced that he was going to embark on a new programme of research. He stated that he now regarded philosophy differently than he did before, asserting that philosophy had a duty to examine social and political reality, to which he had himself given too little attention, and that among other things he would examine the question whether there are trans-cultural ethical claims.

Two things caused Cassirer to rethink his philosophy during his years in Sweden. One was the state of European politics, and the other was his exposure to contemporary Swedish philosophy. The Uppsala school, like the Vienna Circle of Logical Positivism, radically opposed traditional metaphysical philosophy and drew far-ranging consequences from this, especially in regard to practical philosophy. Both adopted emotivist conceptions of ethics. That is, ethical statements for them were mere verbal emotional outbursts without any claim to a basis in reality. They were neither true nor false, and therefore meaningless.

Unlike the Vienna Circle, which gave pride of place to the philosophy of science, the Uppsala school, and Hägerström in particular, focused upon ethics and legal philosophy. Hägerström and the Vienna Circle both held that 'objectivity' was limited to the sphere of spatially extended physical objects. This meant that the observable phenomenological difference between things and persons fell by the wayside, even though the perception of expression (such as seeing a smile or a frown) is an undeniable fact. This strictly physicalistic conception of objectivity led Hägerström to conceive of ethics and normative claims as matters of momentary feeling: immediate like and dislike. Hägerström's position became known as *value nihilism*, yet it did not deny the social importance of values, only it claimed that the metaphysical underpinnings that philosophers offered for them, such as a 'general will', were mere fabrications.[28]

Cassirer disagreed, emphasizing that just as a written law prejudices the future, so too individual value judgements are not momentary events, but relational in nature.[29] Value judgements involve temporality: an overview of the past, present, and future.[30] By contrast, feelings are simply momentary events.[31] Cassirer's insistence on the irreducibility of value judgements to momentary feelings depended upon his claim that the perception of persons was different from but just as objective as the perception of things.[32] For Cassirer, perceiving was never mere sensation, but always exemplifies some type of symbolism, either expressive or representational. Now he wanted to base ethical claims upon this difference. This required him to talk about the 'objectivity' of the perception of expression as our insurance of the 'reality' of persons as distinguished from things. The ability to recognize emotion and the reality of 'the Other' was a presupposition of ethics, but instead of claiming that this is a matter of immediate intuition, Cassirer argued that it was a symbolic process that took place without conscious interpretative activity. The ability to distinguish between things and persons depended upon the objectivity of the expressive function of symbolism, but it was also an aspect of reality — the Basic phenomenon of the Other — *das Du*.

In Cassirer's book about Hägerström he countered the reduction of ethics to momentary feelings by offering an alternative analysis of evaluation and developing a conception based upon commitments expressed by the oral and written use of language. But in Cassirer's unpublished texts on the objectivity of expression,[33] he offered an even more fundamental dimension for his conception of the objectivity of ethics. Against physicalism, Cassirer claimed

that both our perception of 'the Other' and of physical objects are equally
real, *basic* phenomena. Cassirer no longer depended like Kant upon a rational
subject as the source of moral law. The perception of the Other as a living
person was the basis for ethics and this perception was in turn due to the fact
that the 'Thou' was a basic phenomenon like that of the 'I' or the world or
'It'. Life processes are visibly different from merely physical ones. Expressions
of anticipation (fear or joy) are temporal in a way that natural processes are
not, and these phenomena require us to distinguish between persons and
things and so to recognize the dignity of the Other.

The doctrine of *Basisphänomene* outlines Cassirer's conception of reality, or
'Wirklichkeit'. One of the unpublished manuscripts he completed in Sweden
was entitled *Ziele und Wege der Wirklichkeitserkenntnis*.[34] The first sentence of
the book set the tone for his approach: 'Thomas Hobbes hat einmal gesagt,
daß von allen Erscheinungen, die uns umgeben, das "Erscheinen selbst" die
merkwürdigste und wunderbarste Tatsache sei'.[35] This claim, Cassirer adds,
was remarkable coming from Hobbes, who was perhaps the most consistent
materialist and mechanistic thinker in the history of philosophy. Cassirer's
point was that a phenomenological approach was compatible with even the
most radical empiricism. But Cassirer also regarded human existence as subject to different conflicting symbolic interpretations. This made it imperative
to investigate whether there could be an ethics that could claim applicability
in different, conflicting cultures. Here the doctrine of the *Basisphänomene*
was to come to his aid, for the reality of the Thou and the objectivity of the
perception of expression were taken to be invariant in the flux of cultural
differences. Hägerström and the positivists regarded linguistic statements
as meaningless insofar as they were not true or false,[36] but for Cassirer
philosophical or metaphysical statements about reality are problematic for a
different reason: they were reductionistic in that they took some particular
perspective to offer a characterization of reality in general.[37] In this way, even
Hägerström and the Vienna Circle philosophers themselves fell into metaphysics by taking the basis phenomenon of the *Es* or 'It' to be the *only* truly
real phenomenon — at the expense of the other basis phenomena, especially
that of *das Du*, or *the Other*. Without such an objective basis for ethics, it
would be impossible to assert the validity of any universal ethical claims.

The doctrine of basis phenomena presents problems for the interpretation
of Cassirer's philosophy. It does not appear to follow from — or even to fit
—his earlier thought, at least not under the long-prevailing assumption that
Cassirer's philosophy represented Marburg Neo-Kantianism. The doctrine of
the *Basisphänomene* was not only not a subjectivism; it was directed against
monistic theoretical philosophy. It showed why a pluralistic philosophy
of different 'symbolic forms' was needed to explicate 'reality' (*Wirklichkeit*):
the three irreducible symbolic functions of expressive, representative,

significative meaning were not simply matters of interpretation, but related to dimensions of reality: life, natural things, and cultural 'works'. These were co-relative and irreducible to one another. This meant that Cassirer's philosophy ultimately was not a type of Kantianism. Rather, it derived from Cassirer's reception of Goethe, especially from Goethe's morphological conception of form.[38]

Instead of beginning with fixed a priori principles, categories, or even mathematical certainties, an approach which Cassirer called the 'mathematical spirit', and which construed the role of reason to consist in *unification*,[39] he began with what he termed the order of the concrete. In the order of the concrete there was unity without uniformity. In *Die Philosophie der Aufklärung* he spoke of reality as 'a "pluralistic universe"',[40] in which even elementary unitary realities are 'dynamic'. Cassirer asserted that this dynamism meant that the fundamental motive dominating philosophy is 'only apparently that of identity', whereas it is actually the principle of 'continuity'. 'Continuity', Cassirer stressed, 'means unity in multiplicity, being in becoming, constancy in change'.[41] This repeats a claim that he had made thirty years earlier in his book *Leibniz' System*, that Leibniz's philosophy offered a vindication of qualitative individuality. With Leibniz, the idea of rigid, fixed form was broken down, and supplanted by the idea of 'development' or 'Entwicklung'.[42] 'Form' means 'continuity in development', so that individuality and generality are no longer opposites. The motivating impetus stemmed for Cassirer's thinking and his doctrine of *Basisphänome* stemmed from Leibniz and Goethe's notion of morphology.

The *Basisphänomene* doctrine does not constitute a radical break in Cassirer's philosophical development, but its completion. The doctrine of *Basisphänomene* should not be regarded in isolation, as something special, divorced from his earlier thought or from his other concerns in the late 1930s. Indeed, the doctrine was crucial for Cassirer's late investigations of ethics, and it entered into his philosophical anthropology as well.

Cassirer began work on his philosophical anthropology while he was still in Hamburg, where he came under the influence of Jakob von Uexküll's theoretical biology, who was his colleague there after 1926. Cassirer's philosophical anthropology was based upon a conception of the organism as acting in its 'world' (*Umwelt*).[43] Cassirer wrote an extensive explication of theoretical biology while he was in Sweden — the chapter on 'biology' in *The Problem of Knowledge*, volume four.[44] This chapter showed that biology was an integral part of his philosophy, combining his interests in Uexküll's and Goethe's conceptions of life, especially the emergence of species. Cassirer generalizes his conception of biological emergence in the fourth study in *Zur Logik der Kulturwissenschaften*, on 'The Problem of Form and the Problem of Cause'. There Cassirer extrapolates from the emergence of species in biology in order to claim that both in nature and in culture, processes of development cannot be explained causally.[45]

Cassirer was deeply interested in history, so much so that he has sometimes been regarded exclusively as a historian. But his writings on history and on historiography from his years in Sweden show that he also regarded history in terms of his doctrine of *Basisphänomene*. His text 'Geschichte'[46] begins with the assertion that '*historical* knowledge also must be considered in regard to the three Ground phenomena (Basic phenomena) and it will only be seen in its full content when it is regarded equally in the light of all these different *dimensions*' (*auch* historische *Erkenntnis muss in Rücksicht auf die drei Grundphaenomene (Basisphaenomene) betrachtet werden und erhält erst ihren vollen Gehalt durch die gleichmässige Berücksichtigung aller dieser verschiedenen* Dimensionen).[47] He calls these three dimensions historical *Gedächtnis*, *Wirkung* and *Entwicklung* — i.e., memory, influence, and development.

Cassirer's various interests during his years in Sweden — theoretical biology and philosophical anthropology and his seemingly new conception of *Basisphänomene* derived from his earliest intellectual interests: Goethe's morphological conception of form and theory of symbolism. One cannot read Cassirer's Gothenburg Goethe-*Vorlesungen* without sensing the impact which Goethe's work had on Cassirer as a young man. He did not agree with Goethe's rejection of mathematics nor his denigration of interventional experiments, or his reliance upon imaginative vision over historical study, but Goethe's morphological conception of form and the idea of *Urphänomene* — not to mention the symbol — left an indelible mark on his philosophy. The *Basisphänomen* doctrine was not a kind of sudden mutation in Cassirer's thought.[48]

With the doctrine of 'Basis phenomena', Cassirer was trying to develop what Kant called the 'world conception' of philosophy — philosophy as it matters to everyone, rather than its 'school conception', as it concerns academic standpoints.[49] In the doctrine of *Basisphänomene*, Cassirer sought to exhibit the basis of the different dimensions of civilization — art, science, morality and politics, history, and philosophy — at a time when they appeared to be disintegrating as never before. This doctrine avoids the pathos of philosophical Romanticism (Heidegger) and the intellectual confinements of Positivism (Carnap).[50] Its emphasis on action and development can perhaps be best understood in comparison with Merleau-Ponty's later phenomenology of the body-subject or Charles Peirce's earlier formulations of his doctrine of the categories, which he first discussed under the headings of the personal pronouns I —You — It. These two renegades from Kantianism agreed upon the dynamic nature of form, continuity, and even the reality of emergent novelty, although neither took cognizance of the other. Merleau-Ponty, we know, was directly influenced by his reading of Cassirer.

On 29 July 1934 Cassirer wrote to his former doctoral students including — to name only a few: Erich Weill, Paul Oskar Kristeller, and Leo Strauss — that he had never acted as a philosophy teacher in the traditional sense because, as he put it: 'I lacked a belief in the possibility and necessity of school ties in the field of philosophy' (*Mir fehlte der Glaube an die Möglichkeit und Notwendigkeit schulmässiger Bindungen im Gebiet der Philosophie*).[51] In his later years Cassirer wrote with a new definiteness, so that what was often only vaguely recognizable now became evident: that the philosophy of symbolic forms ignored the boundaries separating different philosophical schools of thought. The *Philosophie der symbolischen Formen* is able to combine the linguistic turn in philosophy with a phenomenological theory of reality that explicates what it is that is given ymbolic form.

Notes

[1] Ernst Cassirer, *Philosophy of Symbolic Forms*, vol. 3, *The Phenomenology of Knowledge*, trans. by R. F. C. Hull (New Haven and London: Yale University Press, 1957), p. 202; *Philosophie der symbolischen Formen*, vol. 3, *Phänomenologie der Erkenntnis* [*Gesammelte Werke: Hamburger Ausgabe*, vol. 13], ed. by Julia Clemens (Hamburg: Meiner, 2002), p. 231.

[2] Cassirer, *Philosophy of Symbolic Forms*, vol. 3, *The Phenomenology of Knowledge*, p. 100; *Philosophie der symbolischen Formen*, vol. 3, *Phänomenologie der Erkenntnis*, p. 113.

[3] Cassirer, *The Phenomenology of Knowledge*, p. 178; *Phänomenologie der Erkenntnis*, p. 202.

[4] Ernst Cassirer, *The Philosophy of Symbolic Forms*, vol. 2, *Mythical Thought*, trans. by Ralph Manheim (New Haven and London: Yale University Press, 1955), p. 157 [translation corrected]; Cassirer, *Philosophie der symbolischen Formen*, vol. 2, *Das mythische Denken* [*Gesammelte Werke: Hamburger Ausgabe*, vol. 12], ed. by Claus Rosenkranz (Hamburg: Meiner, 2002), p. 183.

[5] Ernst Cassirer, *Ausgewählter wissenschaftlicher Briefwechsel*, ed. by John Michael Krois (Hamburg: Meiner, 2009), p. 222.

[6] Cassirer, 'Naturalistische und humanistische Begründung der Kulturphilosophie', *Göteborgs Kungl. Vetenskaps- och Vitterhets-Samhälles Handlingar*, Issue 5, Series A, vol. 7, no. 3 (1939), 1–28; see *Aufsätze und kleine Schriften (1936–1940)* [*Gesammelte Werke: Hamburger Ausgabe*, vol. 22], ed. by Claus Rosenkranz (Hamburg: Meiner, 2006), pp. 140–65.

[7] See Ernst Cassirer, 'On Basis Phenomena', in *The Philosophy of Symbolic Forms*, vol. 4, *The Metaphysics of Symbolic Forms*, ed. by John Michael Krois and Donald P. Verene, trans. by John Michael Krois (New Haven: Yale University Press, 1996), pp. 128–30; 'Über Basisphänomene', in *Zur Metaphysik der symbolischen Formen* [*Nachgelassene Manuskripte und Texte*, vol. 1], ed. by John Michael Krois *et al.* (Hamburg: Meiner, 1999), pp. 123–25.

[8] See Cassirer, 'On Basis Phenomena', in *The Philosophy of Symbolic Forms*, vol. 4, *The Metaphysics of Symbolic Forms*, p. 137; 'Über Basisphänomene', in *Zur Metaphysik der symbolischen Formen*, p. 132.

[9] This was the credo of the Marburg School. See Cassirer on Cohen in *Aufsätze und kleine Schriften 1941–1946* [*Gesammelte Werke: Hamburger Ausgabe*, vol. 24], ed. by Claus Rosenkranz (Hamburg: Meiner, 2007), p. 168.

[10] Hermann Cohen, *Logik der reinen Erkenntnis* [*System der Philosophie*, vol. 2], 2nd edn (Berlin: Bruno Cassirer, 1914), p. 26; cf. Cassirer, *Aufsätze und kleine Schriften 1902–1921* [*Gesammelte Werke: Hamburger Ausgabe*, vol. 9], ed. by Marcel Simon (Hamburg: Meiner, 2001), p. 504.

[11] This text will appear in Ernst Cassirer, *Über symbolische Prägnanz, Ausdrucksphänomen und 'Wiener Kreis'* [*Nachglessene Manuskripte und Texte*, vol. 4], ed. by Christian Möckel (Hamburg: Meiner, forthcoming [2010]).

[12] Cassirer, *Über symbolische Prägnanz, Ausdrucksphänomen und 'Wiener Kreis'* [*Nachglessene Manuskripte und Texte*, vol. 4], forthcoming.

[13] Cassirer distanced himself from Husserl, who as a follower of Descartes granted subjectivity the main role in philosophy. Cassirer wanted with his phenomenology neither to create a new kind of philosophical science or first philosophy outfitted with special methods as Husserl did nor did he conceive phenomenology as Heidegger did, with the aim of establishing a philosophy of existence in opposition to empirical natural or cultural sciences. See 'On Basis Phenomena', in *The Philosophy of Symbolic Forms*, vol. 4, *The Metaphysics of Symbolic Forms*, pp. 171–72; 'Über Basisphänomene', in *Zur Metaphysik der symbolischen Formen*, pp. 171–72.

[14] Ernst Cassirer, 'Language and Art II', in Ernst Cassirer, *Symbol, Myth, and Culture: Essays and Lectures of Ernst Cassirer 1935–1945*, ed. by Donald Philip Verene (New Haven: Yale University Press, 1979), pp. 166–95 (pp. 193–94).

[15] See 'The Problem of the Symbol as the Fundamental Problem of Philosophical Anthropology', in *The Philosophy of Symbolic Forms*, vol. 4, *The Metaphysics of Symbolic Forms*, pp. 34–111; 'Das Symbolproblem als Grundproblem der philosophischen Anthropologie', in *Zur Metaphysik der symbolischen Formen*, pp. 32–109.

[16] Cassirer, *The Philosophy of Symbolic Forms*, vol. 2, *Mythical Thought*, pp. 219–20; *Philosophie der symbolischen Formen*, vol. 2, *Das mythische Denken*, pp. 258–59.

[17] On Cassirer's notion of the *Energien des Geistes*, see Ernst Cassirer, 'Der Begriff der symbolischen Form im Aufbau der Geisteswissenschaften' [1923], in *Aufsätze und kleine Schriften (1922–1926)* [*Gesammelte Werke: Hamburger Ausgabe*, vol. 16], ed. by Julia Clemens (Hamburg: Meiner, 2003), pp. 75–104 (p. 79).

[18] See Cassirer, 'On Basis Phenomena', in *The Philosophy of Symbolic Forms*, vol. 4, *The Metaphysics of Symbolic Forms*, pp. 136–37; 'Über Basisphänomene', in *Zur Metaphysik der symbolischen Formen*, p. 131.

[19] C. F. von Weizäcker, '[Review of] Determinismus und Indeterminismus in der modernen Physik by Ernst Cassirer', *Physikalische Zeitschrift*, 38 (1937), 860–61.

[20] Letter of Max von Laue to Ernst Cassirer of 26 March 1937; *Ausgewählter wissenschaftlicher Briefwechsel*, p. 167.

[21] Letter of Ernst Cassirer to Åke Petzäll of 28 February 1939; *Ausgewählter wissenschaftlicher Briefwechsel*, p. 197.

[22] Cassirer to Petzäll, 28 February 1939; *Ausgewählter wissenschaftlicher Briefwechsel*, p. 197.

[23] This text will appear in *Über symbolische Prägnanz, Ausdrucksphänomen und 'Wiener Kreis'* [*Nachglessene Manuskripte und Texte*, vol. 4].

[24] See John Michael Krois, 'Ernst Cassirer und der Wiener Kreis', in Friedrich Stadler (ed.), *Elemente moderner Wissenschaftstheorie: Zur Interaktion von Philosophie, Geschichte und Theorie der Wissenschaften* (Vienna and New York: Springer, 2000), pp. 105–21.

[25] To quote one of the Vienna School's chief proponents, Otto Neurath: 'Nobody can use logical Empiricism to establish an argument for totalitarianism. It does not offer a single hiding place for dogmatism. Pluralism is the backbone of my thinking. Metaphysical attitudes often lead to totalitarianism, but I do not know a single logical Empiricist, who as such has arrived at a totalitarian outlook' (*Niemand kann den logischen Empirismus zur Begründung eines totalitären Arguments benutzen. Er bietet nicht ein einziges Schlupfloch für Dogmatismus. Pluralismus ist das Rückgrat meines Denkens. Metaphysische Haltungen führen oft zum Totalitarismus, aber ich kenne keinen einzigen logischen Empiristen, der als solcher zu einer totalitären Auffassung gelangt ist.*); cited from Horace M. Kallen, 'Postscript – Otto Neurath 1882–1945', *Philosophy and Phenomenological Research*, 6.4 (June 1946), 529–33 (p. 533).

[26] See 'Göteborgs Högskolas Matrikel, 1916–1941', in *Göteborgs Högskolas Årsskrift*, 6 (1942), 16.

[27] See the English translation of the lecture under this title in Cassirer, *Symbol, Myth, and Culture*, ed. by Verene, pp. 49–63.

[28] See Axel Hägerström, 'Is Positive Law an Expression of Will?', in Axel Hägerström, *Inquiries into the Nature of Law and Morals*, ed. by Karl Olivecrona (Stockholm: Almqvist & Wiksell, 1953), pp. 17–55. Compare with Cassirer's assessment in *Axel Hägerström: Eine Studie zur schwedischen Philosophie der Gegenwart* (Göteborg: Elander, 1939), pp. 106–08.

[29] See Cassirer, *Axel Hägerström*, pp. 53–65. Cassirer began his work in philosophy with a criticism of tradtional logic, which was based upon the principle of subsumption and the concept of classes, arguing that relations and the concept of function are the true basis of logic. See *Substance and Function*, in *Substance and Function and Einstein's Theory of Relativity*, trans. by William Curtis Swabey and Marie Collins Swabey (New York: Dover, 1953), pp. 1–346.

[30] Cassirer, *Axel Hägerström*, p. 65.

[31] Cassirer's book on Hägerström is sympathetic but critical, and his arguments there, as he wrote in the preface, deal with matters he had neglected before (Cassirer, *Axel Hägerström*, pp. 6–7).

[32] The distinction between the perception of expression and the perception of things is the topic of the first study in his book on *The Logic of the Cultural Sciences*. See 'The Object of the Science of Culture', in *The Logic of the Cultural Sciences*, trans. by S. G. Lofts (New Haven, NJ, and London: Yale University Press, 2000), pp. 1–33.

[33] See Cassirer, 'Zur Objektivität der Ausdrucksfunktion', in *Kulturphilosophie: Vorlesungen und Vorträge 1929–1941* [*Nachgelassene Manuskripte und Texte*, vol. 5], ed. by Rüdiger Kramme and Jörg Fingerhut (Hamburg: Meiner, 2004), pp. 105–99.

[34] See Ernst Cassirer, *Ziele und Wege der Wirklichkeitserkenntnis* [*Nachgelassene Manuskripte und Texte*, vol. 2], ed. by Klaus Christian Köhnke and John Michael Krois (Hamburg: Meiner, 1999).

[35] Cassirer, *Ziele und Wege der Wirklichkeitserkenntnis* [*Nachgelassene Manuskripte und Texte*, vol. 2], p. 3.

[36] Cassirer, *Axel Hägerström*, pp. 16–17. For a survey of the Uppsala school and philosophy in Sweden generally, see Svante Nordin, *Från Hägerström till Hedenius: Den Moderna Svenska Filosofin* (Lund: Doxa, 1983). A general survey of Cassirer's encounter with the Uppsala School can be found in Jonas Hansson and Svante Nordin, *Ernst Cassirer: The Swedish Years* (Berne: Lang, 2006).

[37] Cassirer, *Axel Hägerström*; and *The Philossophy of Symbolic Forms*, vol. 4, *The Metaphysics of Symbolic Forms*, pp. 153–66; *Zur Metaphysik der symbolischen Formen*, pp. 150–65.

[38] Supporters of this reading, to which I also subscribe, include Cyrus Hamlin, 'Goethe as Model for Cultural Values: Ernst Cassirer's Essay on Thomas Mann's Lotte in Weimar', in Cyrus Hamlin and John Michael Krois (eds), *Symbolic Forms and Cultural Studies* (New Haven: Yale University Press, 2004), pp. 185–99; Barbara Naumann, *Philosophie und Poetik des Symbols: Cassirer und Goethe* (Munich: Fink, 1998); Oswald Schwemmer, 'The Variety of Symbolic Worlds and the Unity of Mind', in *Symbolic Forms and Cultural Studies*, pp. 3–18; and R. H. Stephenson, '"Eine zarte Differenz": Cassirer on Goethe on the Symbol', in *Symbolic Forms and Cultural Studies*, pp. 157–84. Cf. John Michael Krois, 'Urworte — Cassirer als Goethe-Interpret', in *Kulturkritik nach Ernst Cassirer* [Cassirer-Forschungen, vol. 1] (Hamburg: Meiner, 1995), pp. 297–324; and 'Die Goetheschen Elemente in Cassirers Philosophie', in Barbara Naumann and Birgit Recki (eds), *Cassirer und Goethe: Neue Aspekte einer philosophisch-literarischen Wahlverwandtschaft* (Berlin: Akademie-Verlag, 2003), pp. 159–72, as well as the other contributions to this volume.

[39] Ernst Cassirer, *The Philosophy of the Enlightenment*, trans. by Fritz C. A. Koelln and James P. Pettegrove (Princeton, NJ: Princeton University Press, 1951), p. 23; *Die Philosophie der Aufklärung* [*Gesammelte Werke: Hamburger Ausgabe*, vol. 15] (Hamburg: Meiner, 2009), p. 23.

[40] Cassirer, *The Philosophy of the Enlightenment*, p. 29; *Die Philosophie der Aufklärung* [*Gesammelte Werke: Hamburger Ausgabe*, vol. 15], p. 30.

[41] Cassirer, *The Philosophy of the Enlightenment*, p. 29; *Die Philosophie der Aufklärung* [*Gesammelte Werke: Hamburger Ausgabe*, vol. 15], p. 30.

[42] Cassirer, *Die Philosophie der Aufklärung* [*Gesammelte Werke: Hamburger Ausgabe*, vol. 15], p. 45; translated as 'evolution' in Cassirer, *The Philosophy of the Enlightenment*, p. 34.

[43] This text was found together with his text 'Über Basisphänomene' in envelope 184 of his papers, and were published together in *Nachgelassene Manuskripte und Texte*, vol. 1, *Zur Metaphysik der symbolischen Formen*, and translated in *The Philosophy of Symbolic Forms*, vol. 4, *The Metaphysics of Symbolic Forms*.

[44] Cassirer wrote the manuscript of this book between 9 July and 26 November 1940; see Charles W. Hendel's preface to Cassirer's *The Problem of Knowledge*, trans. by William H. Woglom (New Haven: Yale University Press, 1950,) p. ix. The original German text was not published until 1957. The new edition of this volume in the ECW, *Das Erkenntnisproblem in der Philosophie und Wissenschaft der neueren Zeit IV* [*Gesammelte Werke: Hamburger Ausgabe*, vol. 5], ed. by Tobias Berben and Dagmar Vogel (Hamburg: Meiner, 2000), includes a complete bibliography of the large literature on biology cited in the book.

[45] See 'The Problem of Form and the Problem of Cause', in *The Logic of the Cultural Sciences*, p. 102.

[46] See Ernst Cassirer, *Geschichte. Mythos* [*Nachgelassene Manuskripte und Texte*, vol. 3], ed. by Klaus Christian Köhnke, Herbert Koop-Oberstebrink and Rüdiger Kramme (Hamburg: Meiner, 2002), pp. 4–174.

[47] Cassirer, *Geschichte. Mythos* [*Nachgelassene Manuskripte und Texte*, vol. 3], p. 3.

[48] In his earlier works Cassirer appealed to Goethe's notion of the *Urphänomen* again and again without ever explicating its place in his own thought. The expressive function of meaning is an *Urphänomen* (*Philosophy of Symbolic Forms*, vol. 3, *Phenomenology of Knowledge*, p. 87; *Philosophie der symbolischen Formen*, vol. 3, *Phänomenologie der Erkenntnis*, p. 102), the experience of the living human body is an *Urphänomen* (*Philosophy of Symbolic Forms*, vol. 3, *Phenomenology of Knowledge*, pp. 99–103; *Philosophie der symbolischen Formen*, vol. 3, *Phänomenologie der Erkenntnis*, pp. 116–21), so too is the 'person' (Cassirer, 'William Stern: Zur Wiederkehr seines Todestages', *Acta Psychologia*, 5 (1940), 1–15 (p. 9); reprinted in Ernst Cassirer, *Aufsätze und kleine Schriften (1941–1946)* [*Gesammelte Werke: Hamburger Ausgabe*, vol. 24], ed. by Claus Rosenkranz (Hamburg: Meiner, 2007), pp. 585–96 [p. 591]). And time is an *Urphänomen* (*Phenomenology of Knowledge*, p. 205; *Phänomenologie der Erkenntnis*, p. 176).

[49] See Immanuel Kant, *Critique of Pure Reason*, A 838–39/B 866–67.

[50] For a discussion of this direction in Cassirer's philosophy, see Michael Friedman, *A Parting of the Ways: Carnap, Cassirer, Heidegger* (Chicago and La Salle, IL: Open Court, 2000).

[51] Ernst Cassirer to Paul Oskar Kristeller, Leo Strauss, and others, in *Ausgewählter wissenschaftlicher Briefwechsel*, p. 139.

WORK AND TECHNOLOGY IN ERNST CASSIRER: OR, THE REHABILITATION OF INSTRUMENTAL REASON

By BIRGIT RECKI

'We are born for action', said Michel de Montaigne in around 1580, citing Ovid, '*Cum moriar, medium solvare inter opus*' (When I die, may I be in the midst of work).[1] In so doing, he expresses a judgement that he is by no means alone in our culture in holding. Luther, the founder of the Protestant Church might not agree with Montaigne, the Catholic humanist, as far as his respect for work is concerned, but he would wholeheartedly agree with his esteem for the activity associated with it. A good half century earlier, in his translation of Psalm 90, *Und wenn's köstlich gewesen ist, so ist's Mühe und Arbeit gewesen* (rendered in the Authorized Version, 'And yet is their strength labour and sorrow'), Luther had made this emphatically clear — even though, in his doctrine of the justification of the Christian *sola fide* (through faith alone), he spoke out decisively against justification through works.

We live in a cultural world that is founded on science and its technology — and it is by no means uncommon for us to find that our contemporaries, who have, following Luther, wanted to take his valuation of work into the canon of human rights or who, like Montaigne, extol the pleasure of work as the highest of feelings, nevertheless at the same time despise technology or at least are afraid of it. One encounters a kind of double schizophrenia: telephone answering-machines are said to be soulless machines, to whose communicative level one is not prepared to sink; in contrast to the ubiquitousness of communication via e-mail, a veritable nostalgia for paper and ink comes to the fore; computer games appear to be a sign of nothing less than the decline of Western civilization. These reservations about technology are not so strongly held, when one's husband or one's wife suffers a heart attack and is rushed by ambulance to casualty and given an electrocardiogram, or when a child born prematurely is placed in an incubator.

At the beginning of the twenty-first century, we are not the first ones who have to come to terms with this syndrome; in fact, we stand in a tradition of scepticism, even enmity, towards technology. For example:

> One would like to ask: is there, then, no positive gain in pleasure, no unequivocal increase in my feeling of happiness, if I can, as often as I please, hear the voice of a child of mine who is living hundreds of miles away or if

I can learn in the shortest possible time after a friend has reached his destination
that he has come through the long and difficult voyage unharmed? Does it
mean nothing that medicine has succeeded in enormously reducing infant
mortality and the danger of infection for women in childbirth, and, indeed,
in considerably lengthening the average life of a civilized man? And there is a
long list that might be added to benefits of this kind which we owe to the
much-despised era of scientific and technical advances.

*Man möchte einwenden, ist es denn nicht ein positiver Lustgewinn, ein unzweideutiger
Zuwachs an Glücksgefühl, wenn ich beliebig oft die Stimme des Kindes hören kann, das
Hunderte von Kilometern entfernt von mir lebt, wenn ich die kürzeste Zeit nach
der Landung des Freundes erfahren kann, daß er die lange, beschwerliche Reise gut
bestanden hat? Bedeutet es nichts, daß es der Medizin gelungen ist, die Sterblichkeit
der kleinen Kinder, die Infektionsgefahr der gebärenden Frauen so außerordentlich
herabzusetzen, ja die mittlere Lebensdauer des Kulturmenschen um eine beträchtliche
Anzahl von Jahren zu verlängern? Und solcher Wohltaten, die wir dem vielgeschmähten
Zeitalter der wissenschaftlichen und technischen Fortschritte verdanken, können wir noch
eine große Reihe anführen.*[2]

'But' — and thus our contemporary, conscious of the problem, continues:

But here the voice of pessimistic criticism makes itself heard and warns us that
most of these satisfactions follow the model of the 'cheap enjoyment' extolled
in the anecdote — the enjoyment obtained by putting a bare leg from under
the bedclothes on a cold winter night and drawing it in again. If there had been
no railway to conquer distances, my child would never have left his native
town and I should need no telephone to hear his voice; if travelling across the
ocean by ship had not been introduced, my friend would not have embarked
on his sea-voyage and I should not need a cable to relieve my anxiety about
him. What is the use of reducing infantile mortality when it is precisely that
reduction which imposes the greatest restraint on us in the begetting of children, so that, taken all round, we nevertheless rear no more children than in
the days before the reign of hygiene, while at the same time we have created
difficult conditions for our sexual life in marriage, and have probably worked
against the beneficial effects of natural selection? And, finally, what good to us
is a long life if it is difficult and barren of joys, and if it is so full of misery that
we can only welcome death as a deliverer?

*Aber da läßt sich die Stimme der pessimistischen Kritik vernehmen und mahnt, die
meisten dieser Befriedigungen folgten dem Muster jenes „billigen Vergnügens", das in
einer gewissen Anekdote angepriesen wird. Man verschafft sich diesen Genuß, indem
man in kalter Winternacht ein Bein nackt aus der Decke herausstreckt und es dann
wieder einzieht. Gäbe es keine Eisenbahn, die die Entfernungen überwindet, so hätte
das Kind die Vaterstadt nie verlassen, man brauchte kein Telephon, um seine Stimme
zu hören. Wäre nicht die Schiffahrt über den Ozean eingerichtet, so hätte der Freund
nicht die Seereise unternommen, ich brauchte den Telegraphen nicht, um meine Sorge
um ihn zu beschwichtigen. Was nützt uns die Einschränkung der Kindersterblichkeit,
wenn gerade sie uns die äußerste Zurückhaltung in der Kinderzeugung aufnötigt, so daß
wir im ganzen doch nicht mehr Kinder aufziehen, als in den Zeiten vor der Herrschaft*

der Hygiene, dabei aber unser Sexualleben in der Ehe unter schwierige Bedingungen gebracht und wahrscheinlich der wohltätigen, natürlichen Auslese entgegengearbeitet haben? Und was soll uns endlich ein langes Leben, wenn es beschwerlich, arm an Freuden und so leidvoll ist, daß wir den Tod nur als Erlöser bewillkommnen können?[3]

At this point it becomes clear: the fictional debate being carried on here dates from some time ago, since the critic of scientific-technical progress is not yet able to add to the developmental spiral the achievements of modern contraception and — at the risk of appearing sarcastic — the modern entertainment industry. Aside from this limitation to its spectrum of experience, what Sigmund Freud in 1929 in this passage from *Civilization and its Discontents* (*Das Unbehagen in der Kultur*) argues, might still be said to be relevant to our current situation. Now, as then, we experience — in defiance of all kinds of broader cultural impact and sub-cultural sophistication in how we accommodate ourselves to technology — the debate between Rousseauistic critics who regard culture with contempt and those who have come to appreciate a more profound perspective: that, without culture, the *human* being would not be even be what he is — a *humane* being.

For Freud, culture is 'the whole sum of the achievements and the regulations which distinguish our lives from those of our animal ancestors and which serve two purposes — namely to protect men against nature and to adjust their mutual relations' (*die ganze Summe der Leistungen und Einrichtungen* [. . .], *in denen sich unser Leben von dem unserer tierischen Ahnen entfernt und die zwei Zwecken dienen: dem Schutz des Menschen gegen die Natur und der Regelung der Beziehungen der Menschen untereinander*).[4] And he goes on: 'We recognize as cultural all activities and resources which are useful to men for making the earth serviceable to them, for protecting them against the violence of the forces of nature, and so on' (*Als kulturell anerkennen wir alle Tätigkeiten, die dem Menschen nützen, indem sie ihm die Erde dienstbar machen, ihn gegen die Gewalt der Naturkräfte schützen u. dgl.*), and so 'the first acts of civilization were the use of tools, the gaining of control over fire and the construction of dwellings' (*die ersten kulturellen Taten waren der Gebrauch von Werkzeugen, die Zähmung des Feuers, der Bau von Wohnstätten*).[5]

In Freud's concept of culture, as his choice of examples shows, technology has its place right from the beginning. Nevertheless our own discourses about civilization and its discontents proceed along lines more or less similar to Freud's in his exposition of a hostility towards culture. *Technology* is, in the eyes of many contemporaries of the scientific-technical age, something that makes them feel uneasy. For our discussion we can take up Freud's concerns with no discernable break, albeit with attention to a complicating factor that testifies to the ambiguity, indeed, the fracture in the contemporary relation to culture: not a few of those who, with good reason, take a stand against any fundamentalist critique of culture and against all Rousseauistic tendencies, and who bring forward arguments in the defence of culture, nevertheless make a notable distinction within culture between the value they attach to its different spheres. They know all too well how to place a high value on all kinds of *works* — but as far as *technology* itself is concerned, without which there would be no works at all, they would prefer it if, in line with Karl Marx's analysis of its relation to the production of goods, labour were to disappear into its product without a trace.

Now, this sceptical, frequently schizophrenic and escapist attitude to technology is not entirely unfounded — after all, participation in the steps of its progress has its price. It demands intelligence, presence of mind, patience, and effort to keep up with its level of development, in order to benefit from its achievements. Even when the longed-for kitchen appliance has at last been introduced, one has to read the instructions first; if one wants to understand the functions of a mobile phone, reading about it can acquire something of the form of study; and who can describe the human dramas that sometimes take place, when someone of an advanced age — possibly under the pressure of time to catch a particular train — is confronted at the station with the latest model of electronic ticket machine and has to articulate his wishes on a touch screen? Just how much redundant effort really is spared when we write a text on a personal computer can be gauged by those who have written their theses or dissertations on electronic typewriters; yet so often it seems that they simply do not want to — the effort required to get used to a new word-processing programme is more recent and seems so much greater. We all have this kind of experience, and we know the difficulties it can cause.

In short, *technology, which is supposed to make life easier, is — paradoxically enough — also a burden for the user.* We have an ability to forget that, after a phase of acclimatization, we owe to such efforts something that lightens our load, and we bemoan the source of such efforts as if we were still living in the age of mythical consciousness. Our relationship to technology is a fetishistic one, which seems to be caused by frustrating experiences in our encounters when dealing with technology. The characteristics of cost, effort, investment are also things that technology has in common with culture. But in great works the expectation that has just been described appears largely to have disappeared, so that the effort — not only the effort required by their production, but also the effort demanded by its reception — in the end vanishes without a trace in the result of their greatness. This is a process to whose successful conclusion the high intellectual prestige of such works has much to contribute.

Why, in the eyes of so many, does technology not enjoy the prestige of the great intellectual achievement or intellectual greatness? One reason is that technology's achievements have the tendency to become a *second nature*, and thus the loss of character deprives them of the positive judgement that they really deserve. And if technology does not — in a fatal catch-22 situation — succeed in making itself transparent, this is precisely when we are reminded all too directly of the effort of mastering it. Is the way the modern individual is prepared to feel alienated greater when the gratification of trouble and effort consists only in having made an effort to solve a problem? Is there in the rejection of technology a manifestation of an otherwise well-hidden truth about our relation to work? Whatever the case may be, philosophical enlightenment on this matter consists of replacing prejudices with well-founded judgements arrived at by methodical reflection. Thus the concept of technology requires a fundamental reconsideration.

The Kantian Foundations of Technology

In his third critique, the *Critique of Judgement* (*Kritik der Urteilskraft*), Immanuel Kant draws attention to a implication of his practical philosophy that has been rarely remarked upon when he defines 'culture' (*die Cultur*) as 'the production in a rational being of an aptitude for any ends whatever of his own choosing, consequently of the aptitude of a being in his freedom' (*die Hervorbringung der Tauglichkeit eines vernünftigen Wesens zu beliebigen Zwecken überhaupt (folglich in seiner Freiheit)*).[6] At this point the cultural implication becomes clear of the pre-moral and subsequent understanding of freedom that Kant developed after the *Critique of Pure Reason* (*Kritik der reinen Vernunft*) in the concepts of negative freedom and freedom of the will alike: that is to say, the self-evident link between *the determination of goals through reason, freedom, and culture* results in a concept of culture, which is ultimately concerned with everything that the human being makes of himself through the best use of his powers in the circumstances in which he finds himself. To his critique of reason, whose methodical exposition of the foundations of certain knowledge, moral behaviour, and sensory impressions has led, in the history of its reception, to a concentration on the higher, the 'pure' achievements of reason, Kant thus adds the dimension of the pragmatic as a realm of the cultural formation of life. In other words, we are talking here about the *cultural dimension of reason*, and this refers not simply to the freedom of determination of the self in one's actions, but also to the freedom to determine one's own relations in what one does and what one makes. In the foundation of morality, alongside the claim to normative validity of the categorical imperative, there corresponds to the insight associated with this dimension the recognition of *advice as to how to lead one's life* and *rules of skilful behaviour* — in other words, of hypothetical imperatives — as elements of ethics. If one considers this strand of the Kantian critique of reason which has, up until now, largely been ignored, one will no longer find it surprising that Kant ascribes to the reason of the human being as a sensory being with needs 'an office which it cannot refuse, namely, to attend to the interest of his sensible nature' (*allerdings einen nicht abzulehnenden Auftrag von Seiten der Sinnlichkeit, sich um das Interesse derselben zu bekümmern*).[7]

Indeed, these reflections are to be reconstructed, in the first place, as a rehabilitation of instrumental reason from the self-understanding of freedom, and, in the second, as one of the systematic origins of a modern philosophy of culture. Using a Kantian foundation of culture, such as becomes available in harmony with the development of a teleological concept of nature, an objective and methodical alternative to a Rousseauistic critique of culture can be sketched. This also means that in the foundational acts of cultural philosophical modernity there is a serious alternative to the inevitable consequence of Rousseauism as a result of which culture, through its opposition to nature, is pushed onto the metaphysical defensive. In culture, the sensory needs of the human being assert themselves through being transformed into strategies of freely chosen goals. Thus Kant's concept of reason also includes pragmatic — indeed, instrumental — reason. In his early text criticizing the fantasies of the purely intellectual or spiritual, this step is already anticipated when, in his summary of his discussion of the pretensions of spirituality, Kant writes:

> Before we were wandering like Democritus in empty space, where the butterfly-wings of metaphysics had lifted us, and conversing with spirit forms. Now that the styptic power of self-knowledge has folded these silken wings, we see ourselves back on the low ground of experience and common sense, happy if we regard it as our assigned place from which we may never depart with impunity and which contains everything that can satisfy us, so long as we stay with what is useful.

> *Vorher wandelten wir wie Demokrit im leeren Raume, wohin uns die Schmetterlingsflügel der Metaphysik gehoben hatten, und unterhielten uns daselbst mit geistigen Gestalten. Jetzt, da die stiptische Kraft der Selbsterkenntniß die seidene Schwingen zusammengezogen hat, sehen wir uns wieder auf dem Boden der Erfahrung und des gemeinen Verstandes; glücklich! wenn wir denselben als unseren angewiesenen Platz betrachten, aus welchem wir niemals ungestraft hinausgehen, und der auch alles enthält, was uns befriedigen kann, so lange wir uns am Nützlichen halten.*[8]

So long as we stay with what is useful! However important, from the perspective of a realistic relation to things in the world, utility is, for the foundation of morality, which increasingly comes to dominate his interest, it could not remain the last word — unless, in questions of morality, Kant were to have adopted a utilitarianism of the kind that he knew from several varieties of sensualist as well as rationalist forms of Enlightenment philosophy. We know that Kant, in the following decades until 1785, the year of the publication of his *Foundation of the Metaphysics of Morals (Grundlegung zur Metaphysik der Sitten)*, will distinguish the moral from the paradigm of what is useful as well as from mere knowledge, and that finally in 1788, in his *Critique of Practical Reason* (*Kritik der praktischen Vernunft*), he will, in the context of his doctrine of the highest good, argue for a concept of happiness that postulates more than simply 'staying with what is useful'. But this does not mean that the recognition of the pragmatic has to be abandoned in its entirety — nor is it entirely abandoned by Kant. For he still considers it to be good, insofar as it is possible for us, to stay with what is useful, as long as we do not confuse this with being moral.

A direct path runs from Kant and the cultural — indeed, the pragmatic — dimension of his concept of reason and freedom to the cultural philosophy of the twentieth century,[9] and to Ernst Cassirer's *The Philosophy of Symbolic Forms* (*Philosophie der symbolischen Formen*), written in the 1920s and the 1930s. Cassirer's philosophy of culture, founded on the theory of the symbol, is a fundamental contribution to *anthropology as cultural philosophy*. At the same time it enables the Kantian legacy of a theory of rationality and freedom to become fruitful for the programme of rehabilitating instrumental reason. In a key passage in the introduction to the first volume of *The Philosophy of Symbolic Forms*, Cassirer characterizes his own systematic outline as a transformation of the critique of reason into a critique of culture.[10] This does not mean abandoning any claim to reason, but rather the contextualization of reason by means of an internal extension of the concept of reason by including the perception of the multiplicity of rational functions. His systematic outline also contains a constructive contribution to an understanding of technology as something essential to culture, and in this theory of technology the inclusion of the instrumental dimension in the concept of reason exemplifies this very contextualization and extension of the concept of reason. In what follows, the contribution made by Cassirer will be presented in accordance with the following fundamental outline: (1) What is culture? The approach of a philosophy of symbolic forms; (2) The work as an element of culture; and (3) Technology as a form of freedom.

WHAT IS CULTURE? THE APPROACH OF A PHILOSOPHY OF SYMBOLIC FORMS

Cassirer's philosophy of culture is a doctrine of a theory of meaning that explains the formation of reality through human beings: for man is the *animal symbolicum*, a being that creates symbols,[11] and 'culture' here means nothing other than the system of all possible ways of producing meaning through symbolization. This broad concept, as broad in its fundamental conception as it is in the scope of its application, which stands in opposition to a concentration of the understanding of culture to the greatest products of high culture, has its methodological roots in the breadth of the concept of the symbol. In contrast to the more specific concept of the symbolic encountered in, for

instance, art history or in literary studies, a more general understanding lies at
the basis of Cassirer's concept of the symbol as 'the expression of something
mental through sensuous "signs" and "images", in the broadest sense'
(*Ausdruck eines Geistigen durch sinnliche 'Zeichen' und 'Bilder', in seiner weitesten
Bedeutung*).[12] Cassirer understands symbolization in general as the mediation
of the sensuous and the intellectual, a mediation that takes place in all
kinds of different materials and media — in the articulated cry, in pictures, in
material objects, in rituals, ceremonies, and practices, in all different kinds of
actions, in institutions, in formulas. The symbol thus resides in all the different
ways of *making meaning sensuous*. As his principal witnesses for this concept
of the symbol, Cassirer presents various predecessors, from Nicolas of Cusa,
via Leibniz, Kant, and Goethe, to Heinrich Hertz;[13] it is evident that Hegel
belongs to this tradition, for in his *Lectures on Aesthetics* (*Vorlesungen über die
Ästhetik*) he defines the symbol in general as the formed *expression* (*Ausdruck*)
of a *meaning* (*Bedeutung*).[14] In the context of his characterization of artistic
beauty we find in Hegel in the following famous formulation:

> 'Sense' is this wonderful word that can be used in two opposing meanings. On
> one hand, it signifies the organs of immediate apprehension, on the other we
> also describe as meaning the significance, the thought, the general aspect of a
> thing. And so meaning relates on one hand to the immediate exteriority of
> existence, on the other hand to its inner essence. *A sensible consideration does not
> separate these two aspects, but by concentrating on one it also captures the other, and
> apprehends in immediate sensory perception both the essence and the concept at the same
> time.*

> *'Sinn' nämlich ist dies wunderbare Wort, welches selber in zwei entgegengesetzten
> Bedeutungen gebraucht wird. Einmal bezeichnet es die Organe der unmittelbaren
> Auffassung, das andere Mal aber heißen wir Sinn: die Bedeutung, den Gedanken, das
> Allgemeine der Sache. Und so bezieht sich der Sinn einerseits auf das unmittelbar
> Äußerliche der Existenz, andererseits auf das innere Wesen derselben.* [Eine sinnvolle
> Betrachtung nun scheidet die beiden Seiten nicht etwa, sondern in der
> einen Richtung enthält sie auch die entgegengesetzte und faßt im sinnlichen
> unmittelbaren Anschauen zugleich das Wesen und den Begriff auf.][15]

This injunction, not to separate the two aspects of something externally
sensuous and something intellectually meaningful, but to establish them as an
unavoidable *concretion* for a being capable of meaning, as *the growing-together
of sensuousness and meaning*, is followed by Cassirer in his theory of cultural
symbolisms, which he always understands as the unity of an 'intellectual
meaning' (*geistiger Bedeutungsgehalt*) and a 'sensory sign' (*sinnliches Zeichen*).

The main point of this theory lies in its view of symbolization as nothing
rare or special, something that occurs here and there in elevated spheres. The
autonomous symbolic activity of the human being takes place from the
process of elementary perception right up to the most highly developed

works. Wherever we do something that involves our senses and our under-standing, we are doing something that is symbolic. Even everything that is sensuously perceived is, according to this view, 'as a sensory experience [. . .] always the vehicle of a meaning' (*als sinnliches Erlebnis immer schon Träger eines Sinnes*),[16] what is perceived is immediately perceived *as* meaningful. Cassirer's concept of the symbol and hence his whole approach thus claims to explain how for us, as beings that shape and give form to our reality, in principle anything can become a vehicle of meaning — indeed, it *must* become a vehicle of meaning.

From its very inception this fundamental and quite general programme opens up a systematic opportunity to grasp the entire complexity and diffe-rentiation in which culture is available to us: right from the beginning we are dealing with a conception of the historical and contemporary *multiplicity* of cultural forms. Accordingly, culture is not conceivable as a monoculture, but it is rather always characterized by an internal plurality, it reveals itself as (1) a multiplicity of ways of giving form — in this respect it is not a random cluster or aggregate, but (2) a *system* of ways of giving form.

It is the regularly observable or typical forms of symbolization, which become as it were institutionalized into an area of their own, that Cassirer calls 'symbolic forms' and defines as follows:

> By a 'symbolic form' should be understood every energy of the mind through which a content of intellectual meaning is connected to a concrete, sensory sign and made to adhere internally to it.

> *Unter einer 'symbolischen Form' soll jede Energie des Geistes verstanden werden, durch welche ein geistiger Bedeutungsgehalt an ein konkretes sinnliches Zeichen geknüpft und diesem Zeichen innerlich zugeeignet wird.*[17]

This brings us to the central concept of Cassirer's entire philosophy of culture. It is not, as we can immediately see, the single formed vehicle of meaning that is described as *symbolic form*. Rather, symbolic forms are the mental or intel-lectual 'energies of formation' (*Energien des Bildens*),[18] by means of which symbolization takes place. So we could also call them the mental or intellec-tual energies that give form (i.e., *die formgebenden geistigen Energien*), which manifest themselves in cultural achievements, as regular, typical means of understanding and of producing meaning. The insight that comes into its own in this conception is that it is mental or intellectual energy (*geistige Energie*) that is articulated in all kinds of formation.

Cassirer usually mentions as symbolic forms myth and religion, language, art, and science, but he also understands law and morality, the economy and history as symbolic forms — and, as I shall demonstrate, technology. These 'energies of formation' (*Energien des Bildens*)[19] are also called by Cassirer 'mental or intellectual forms' (*geistige Formen*),[20] or 'mental/intellectual basic functions' (*geistige Grundfunktionen*),[21] and in view of the richness of his historical and systematic account of the development of culture, it is not surprising that his aim is to provide 'a philosophical system of the spirit' (*eine philosophische Systematik des Geistes*).[22] These remarks and others, as well as the architecture in the multiplicity of symbolic forms — myth, religion, language, art, and science — not only remind one of Kant's theoretical programme, but also display striking methodological similarities to Hegel. Indeed, Cassirer refers explicitly to Hegel's phenomenology of mind, when he sketches the general area of culture: 'Language, myth, and theoretical knowledge are all taken as fundamental forms of the objective spirit' (*Die Sprache, der Mythos, die theoretische Erkenntnis: sie alle werden hier als Grundgestalten des 'objektiven Geistes' genommen*).[23] In view of the suspicion that frequently greets the concept of the spirit, it is surely worth mentioning that Cassirer in his theory of culture, just like Hegel, self-evidently does not imagine spirit (*Geist*) as something ethereal, as something hovering over the waters. According to his theory, spirit (*Geist*) only ever consists in a materialized form, only ever in concrete, sensuous forms, woven into the products arising from our formative activities. Spirit, or *Geist*, is material as it takes shape in us, the formative energy realized in a medium, and it is never to be found elsewhere than in shaped or formed material. For we can only recognize spirit (*Geist*) inasmuch as it gives expression to itself, and it has to express itself in a medium:

> The concept of *Geist* is correct; but we should not use it as a name for a substance — for a thing, *quod in se est et in se concipitur.*[[24]] We should use it in a functional sense as an all-embracing name for all those functions which constitute and construct the world of human culture.

> *Der Begriff 'Geist' ist korrekt; aber wir dürfen ihn nicht als Namen einer Substanz gebrauchen − für ein Ding 'quod in se est et in se concipitur.' Wir sollten ihn in einem funktionellen Sinne gebrauchen als einen umfassenden Namen für alle jene Funktionen, die die Welt der menschlichen Kultur konstituieren und aufbauen.*[25]

THE WORK AS AN ELEMENT OF CULTURE

Metaphysical insight into the 'functional meaning' (*funktionellen Sinn*) of the concept of spirit (*Geist*) is traditionally represented by the expression 'work' (*Werk*). The work, which Cassirer understands to be synonymous with the concept of the symbol,[26] stands, as the achievement of the *animal symbolicum*,[27] at the centre of his philosophical concerns:[28] as the vehicle of meaning, it is the chief element of the world that humans make. Thus, according to Cassirer, a philosophy informed by the science of culture (*Kulturwissenschaft*) will find in its analysis of the work its 'true, fundamental level' (*eigentliche tragende Grundschicht*).[29] In the work we find the fusion of material substance and spiritual form, but in the work we also find an exemplary case of what Hegel sees as the concretion of sensuousness and meaning. Thus the human work is always a medium of communication. Cassirer highlights this aspect in his discussion of Simmel's thesis of the tragedy of culture (*Tragödie der Kultur*) — in a nutshell, the thesis that, in the autonomous dynamic of a culture based on the division of labour, the works created by human beings escape the control of those who have created them. By means of an analysis of the tripartite relation realized in the work between ego (*Ich*), other (*Du*), and object (*Objekt*), he can not only understand the processual nature of permanent production to be constitutive: he can also emphasize the social element of mediated communication, by means of which in the production of a work its actual result is always transcended. The work is, according to Cassirer, a 'human deed, which has become condensed into being' (*menschliche Tat, die sich zum Sein verdichtet hat*),[30] and as such it is 'not an "absolute"' (*kein 'Absolutes'*), but 'a point of transition' (*ein Durchgangspunkt*): and thus it is 'the bridge that leads from the ego–point over to the other' (*die Brücke, die von einem Ichpol zum andern hinüberführt*).[31]

As a result, he emphasizes the provisional nature of all productive engagement with works, which turn out to be, in the culturally constitutive necessity of permanent recreation though their appropriation, 'mediators between the ego and the other' (*Vermittler zwischen Ich und Du*).[32] In terms of his discussion of Simmel's influential thesis, this means that one cannot speak of a 'tragedy of culture', in the sense that human productions become independent of those who produce them, because such independence is only ever provisional, only ever a transitional phase in the continual process of communicative appropriation and production. The permanently communicative production of works that takes place in social integration can only be understood by Cassirer as an action or deed (*Tat*), and hence also as an effect of freedom (*Freiheit*). With reference to the productive formation in processes of symbolization Cassirer always emphasizes a decisive moment: in the objectivization that is part of the production and the reception alike of symbols, the human being puts distance between himself and his impressions, as well as their relation to each other; and gaining this distance in the production of the work, he achieves a moment of freedom. For by distancing himself from the object, at the same time he distances himself from himself, and both open up scope for action. By means of every act of symbolization we gain, in the distancing objectivization, scope for fresh possibilities, which enable us to set out and to undertake new deeds. In the realization of meaning that finds expression in every human articulation, we find a reciprocal interaction of *poiesis* and *praxis* in a state of constant transitional flux: by means of them we make our world, as we make something of ourselves, and we do this together with each other.

TECHNOLOGY AS A FORM OF FREEDOM

There is nothing particularly original about Cassirer's admiration for work as an element of culture. The 'ergological' criterion of culture, that goes back to Aristotle's concept of *poiesis*, namely the insight that culture is the permanent world of things that constitutes itself in and through human works, was already being vigorously discussed in the 1920s and 1930s, after having become a common topos of cultural philosophy in the nineteenth century; it had already formed the basis of the philosophy of history developed by Giambattista Vico; indeed, ever since Plato's mythical story of Prometheus and Epimetheus in the *Protagoras* it has been part of every discussion of the splendour and misery of the human situation. But Cassirer has given this insight a particular twist. The novelty and the orginality of his philosophy of culture lies not in its emphasis on the concept of the work, but, *firstly*, in the theoretical status of meaning that he consistently attributes to the character of work in human production by means of its theoretically symbolic status; and, *secondly*, in his high evaluation of the human creation of works as the origin of human freedom.[33] Of chief significance on this basis for the question posed here about technology is how Cassirer does not concentrate in his characterization of works in terms of the theory of meaning, of the symbol, and of freedom, on the outstanding intellectual achievements of an aestheticist high culture. Language, myth, religion, art, science — all these areas of productive designated by Cassirer as symbolic forms are just as much areas of work-production. Nor are these the only ones. Law and morality, too, as well as history, the economy, and — technology — are understood by Cassirer as symbolic forms.

Cassirer's point of access to technology is one of such a fundamental nature and such profundity that it is, at first glance, entirely independent of the positive or negative assessment of its achievements. Technology is — in accordance with the concept of the symbolic form — understood instead as one of the 'basic powers of the spirit' (*Grundmächte des Geistes*). It is not a direct question of the wholly positive conclusion, as Freud is so swift in the passage, cited above, to set against the Rousseauistic criticism of scientific and cultural progress. Rather, Cassirer is concerned 'to enquire into the conditions of possibility of technological activity and technological formation' (*nach den Bedingungen der Möglichkeit des technischen Wirkens und der technischen Gestaltung zu fragen*),[34] or in other words to understand the *principle of technology* and its fundamental function of meaning in the entirety of culture. Of course, it is inevitable that participation in technology becomes conscious in the spirit of culture. For Cassirer says:

> The question of the merits and demerits of technology cannot be decided by reckoning the 'usefulness' and 'disadvantage' of technology and balancing each against the other — by contrasting the benefits it brings mankind with the idyll

of a pre-technological 'state of nature' and regarding them, thus held in balance, as too insufficient. This is not a question of pleasure or pain, of happiness or sorrow, but a question of freedom or the lack of freedom.

> *Die Frage über Wert und Unwert der Technik kann nicht dadurch entschieden werden, daß man 'Nutzen' und 'Nachteil' der Technik erwägt und gegeneinander aufrechnet — daß man die Glücksgüter, mit denen sie die Menschheit beschenkt, dem Idyll eines vortechnischen 'Naturzustandes' entgegenhält und sie, in dieser Abwägung, zu leicht befindet. Hier geht es nicht um Lust oder Unlust, um Glück oder Leid, sondern um Freiheit oder Unfreiheit.*[35]

According to the general conditions of establishing scope for development through an objectivization that is productive and generative of meaning, this option requires only a brief explanation. This basic thought can be considered just as fundamental in the case of language as it is in the case of technology, which is what Cassirer does in his great essay of 1930 about *Form and Technology* (*Form und Technik*), in which he rigorously pursues an analogy between the achievements of technology and those of language. After he has repeatedly used language as an example of the function of a symbolic form, not just in the first part of *The Philosophy of Symbolic Forms*, but also in numerous treatises, such as in 'Die Sprache und der Aufbau der Gegenstandswelt' (1931), he now attends to the use of words and the use of tools as equivalent means of creating meaning and thus giving form to reality. In his fundamental approach to the formation of meaning as the elementary function of giving form to reality through intellectual or mental activity, Cassirer places technology and language on the same level, declaring that 'the human spirit has created for itself in language and in the tool the most important means of its liberation' (*der menschliche Geist in der Sprache und im Werkzeug die wichtigsten Mittel der Befreiung sich geschaffen hat*).[36] Just as the word created a fundamental effect of distancing from the sense impressions that threaten to overwhelm the individual and prevent their articulation, so does the tool; just as the word can only do this through the creation of meaning, so, too, does the tool.

Cassirer explains in detail how technology, through its own form of giving shape, makes a contribution to the objectivizing tendency of thought:

> It is no exaggeration to say that in the transition to the first tool there lies not only the first step to a new *domination* of the world, but there is also a global change in our knowledge. In the means of indirect action that has now been gained, that form of mediatedness that belongs to the essence of thought is founded and consolidated for the first time. All thought is, according to its purely logical form, mediated — it is reliant on the discovery and gaining of means of mediation that link together the beginning and the end, the initial principle and the conclusion of a logical chain. The tool fulfils the same function, found here in the sphere of logic, in the *objective* sphere: it is, so to speak, the middle term apprehended in objective intuition, not mere thought. It stands *between* the first initiative of the will and the goal.

Es ist nicht zuviel gesagt, wenn man behauptet, daß in dem Übergang zum ersten Werkzeug nicht nur der Keim zu einer neuen Weltbeherrschung liegt, sondern daß hier auch eine Weltwende der Erkenntnis einsetzt. In der Weise der mittelbaren Handelns, die jetzt gewonnen ist, gründet und festigt sich erst jene Art von Mittelbarkeit, die zum Wesen des Denkens gehört. Alles Denken ist seiner rein logischen Form nach mittelbar — ist auf die Entdeckung und Gewinnung von Mittelgliedern angewiesen, die den Anfang und das Ende, den Obersatz und den Schlußsatz einer Schlußkette miteinander verknüpfen. Das Werkzeug erfüllt die gleiche Funktion, die sich hier in der Sphäre des Logischen darstellt, in der gegenständlichen *Sphäre: Es ist gleichsam der in gegenständlicher Anschauung, nicht im bloßen Denken erfaßte 'terminus medius'. Es stellt sich zwischen* den ersten Ansatz des Willens und das Ziel.[37]

On the basis of his own theory of the indispensability of rendering sensuous — which means, embodying — meaning, and more precisely on the basis of such considerations as those cited above, Cassirer has not the slightest reason to dissociate himself from the definition of technology that he cites from Max Eyth, so that we can accept it without further ado as Cassirer's own definition of technology: 'Technology is everything that gives a bodily form to the human will' (*Technik ist alles, was dem menschlichen Wollen eine körperliche Form gibt*).[38]

Thus Cassirer can also understand technology as an essentially liberating force. And this liberation is realized, in a very specific way that is connected with the relation of the human individual to his body, in exactly the reciprocal sense that Cassirer always explicitly emphasizes, namely the simultaneous change of one's consciousness of the object and of one's self.[39] For this reason Cassirer thinks it important 'that technological activity, when directed externally, always represents at the same time a declaration of confidence on the part of mankind and thereby a medium of his self-knowledge':[40]

In the tool and its use [...] the longed-for goal is moved to a certain extent for the first time into the distance. Instead of looking, as if spellbound, at this goal, man learns to 'look away' from it — and precisely this looking-away becomes the means and the condition of its attainment.

Im Werkzeug und seinem Gebrauch [...] wird gewissermaßen zum ersten Male das erstrebte Ziel in die Ferne gerückt. Statt wie gebannt auf dieses Ziel hinzusehen, lernt der Mensch von ihm 'abzusehen' — und ebendieses Absehen wird zum Mittel und zur Bedingung seiner Erreichung.[41]

Following on from such reflections as these it becomes clear what Cassirer means when he describes the implicit meaning of all technology as 'freedom through servitude' (*Freiheit durch Dienstbarkeit*). And with this characteristic it does not stand alone, but rather technology is, as we have seen, the extension of thought into the realm of the practical; in relation to our knowledge of nature it is also *the praxis of theory*. One specific dimension of how technology becomes practical reveals itself in its relation to art. Hence the reference in

Cassirer's essay to Leonardo da Vinci, the exemplary figure of the union of scientific research, artistic design, and technological invention that characterizes the spirit of the modern age. But this reference also captures the insight, illustrated with particular clarity in the form of Leonardo, that our culture has developed itself, from the elementary achievements of coping with the demands of life to the highest and most sophisticated works of art, as a rationally formed world. In this world, the three authoritative forms of structuring activity that lead to discoveries and provide meaning — science, technology, art — form a unity.[42]

One is reminded of Robert Musil's characterization of art by means of an innovative *meaning of possibility* (*Möglichkeitssinn*), when in this context Cassirer defines technology as follows:

> Technology does not enquire in the first instance into what it is, but rather into what could be. [It teaches us] time and again that the circle of the 'objective', of what is determined by firm and general laws, by no means coincides with the circle of what is present, of what has been sensuously realized.

> *Die Technik fragt nicht in erster Linie nach dem, was ist, sondern nach dem, was sein kann. [Sie belehrt uns] fort und fort darüber, daß der Umkreis des 'Objektiven', des durch feste und allgemeine Gesetze Bestimmten, keineswegs mit dem Umkreis des Vorhandenen, des sinnlich Verwirklichten zusammenfällt.*[43]

In technology possibilities are tried out, possibilities are made real, and something new is created: 'The technician is in this respect the very image of that activity which Leibniz, in his metaphysics, attributes to the divine "demiurge"' (*Der Techniker ist hierin ein Ebenbild jenes Wirkens, das Leibniz in seiner Metaphysik dem göttlichen 'Demiurgen' zuspricht*).[44] Let us remind ourselves: what does the demiurge do? Out of the material available it forms — a world. What is being offered in this passage is more than a sober explication of the concept of technology. Through his echo of the myth of the demiurge, we have the apotheosis of Cassirer's own philosophical approach to the creation of works, and it is worth noticing that this explanatory hyperbole occurs to him in the context of a theoretical tribute to technology.

The recognition of technology as an elementary, culture-creating power, which arises from this discussion of its meaning-function within the context of the philosophy of symbolic forms, should now be beyond question, and the associated esteem in which it is held should be hard to surpass. Moreover, surely Cassirer's reflections offer a way to a possible solution of the problem presented at the beginning of this essay, and a suggestion as to how to increase the prestige and thus the acceptance of technology? The question as to whether technological works can be beautiful is answered by Cassirer with a highly suggestive reference to the difference between 'work-beauty' (*Werk-Schönheit*) and 'expressive beauty' (*Ausdrucks-Schönheit*). The latter is reserved

for art, in which, in the midst of coming to terms with an objective problem
of giving shape, one is also trying to illustrate the conditions of the human
inner life. But:

> if one takes the norm of what is beautiful in a sense so wide that one can
> speak of beauty wherever there is a victory of 'form' over 'matter', of the 'idea'
> over the 'material', *then there can be no doubt* about the large extent to which
> precisely technology participates in this.

> [f]aßt man die Norm des Schönen so weit, daß man überall dort von ihr spricht, wo ein
> Sieg der „Form" über den „Stoff", der „Idee" über die „Materie" hervortritt, so kann
> kein Zweifel *daran sein, in welch hohem Maße gerade die Technik an ihr Anteil
> hat.*[45]

This is how, at the beginning of the 1930s, Cassirer voices a conviction that
the contemporary reader of today, in the twenty-first century, may well
share with him. To offer a solution to the problem of prestige mentioned at
the beginning of this essay, it is necessary, as well as having an appropriate
philosophical theory of technology, to ensure that the resources of design are
used to help technology cope with its problems in a form that is not only
appropriate, but also attractive — and thus to make us aware in a sensuous
form of precisely the freedom it helps to realize.

Translated by Paul Bishop

Notes

[1] Michel de Montaigne, 'To philosophize is to learn how to die' (*Essays*, Book 1, chapter
20, in *The Complete Essays*, ed. and trans. by M. A. Screech (Harmondsworth: Penguin, 2003),
p. 99.

[2] Sigmund Freud, *Civilization and its Discontents*, in Freud, *Civilization, Society and Religion*
[*Penguin Freud Library*, vol. 12], ed. by Albert Dickson (Harmondsworth: Penguin, 1991),
pp. 243–340 (p. 276); Sigmund Freud, *Das Unbehagen in der Kultur* [1929], in *Gesammelte
Werke: chronologisch geordnet*, 19 vols (Frankfurt am Main: Fischer, 1952–1987), vol. 14,
pp. 419–506 (p. 447).

[3] Freud, *Civilization and its Discontents*, pp. 276–77; *Das Unbehagen in der Kultur*, p. 447.

[4] Freud, *Civilization and its Discontents*, p. 278; *Das Unbehagen in der Kultur*, p. 448.

[5] Freud, *Civilization and its Discontents*, p. 278; *Das Unbehagen in der Kultur*, p. 449.

[6] Immanuel Kant, *Critique of Judgement* [1790], §83, in *The Critique of Judgement*, trans.
by James Creed Meredith (Oxford: Clarendon Press, 1986), p. 94; *Kritik der Urtheilskraft*, in
Gesammelte Schriften, ed. by Königliche Preußische Akademie der Wissenschaften, 29 vols
(Berlin: Reimer; de Gruyter, 1902–1980) [known as the Akademie-Ausgabe], vol. 5, p. 431.

[7] Immanuel Kant, *Kritik der praktischen Vernunft* (1788), Akademie-Ausgabe, vol. 5, p. 61.

[8] Immanuel Kant, *Dreams of a Spirit-Seer, Elucidated through Dreams of Metaphysics*, in *Dreams
of a Spirit-Seer and Other Writings*, ed. by Gregory R. Johnson, trans. by Gregory R. Johnson
and Glenn Alexander Magee (West Chester, Pennsylvania: Swedenborg Foundation
Publishers, 2002), p. 57; *Träume eines Geistersehers, erläutert durch Träume der Metaphysik* (1766),
Akademie-Ausgabe, vol. 2, p. 368.

[9] Siehe Ernst Cassirer, *Kants Leben und Lehre* [1918], in *Gesammelte Werke* [Hamburger
Ausgabe, vol. 8] (Hamburg: Meiner, 2001).

[10] 'Thus the critique of reason becomes the critique of culture. It seeks to understand and to show how every content of culture, in so far as it is more than a mere isolated content, in so far as it is grounded in a universal principle of form, presupposes an original act of the human spirit' (*Die Kritik der Vernunft wird damit zur Kritik der Kultur. Sie sucht zu verstehen und zu erweisen, wie aller Inhalt der Kultur, sofern er mehr als bloßer Einzelinhalt ist, sofern er in einem allgemeinen Formprinzip gegründet ist, eine ursprüngliche Tat des Geistes zur Voraussetzung hat*) (Ernst Cassirer, *The Philosophy of Symbolic Forms*, vol. 1, *Language*, trans. by Ralph Manheim (New Haven and London: Yale University Press, 1975), p. 80; *Philosophie der symbolischen Formen*, vol. 1, *Die Sprache* [*Gesammelte Werke: Hamburger Ausgabe*, vol. 11] (Hamburg: Meiner, 2001), p. 9.

[11] Ernst Cassirer, *An Essay on Man: An Introduction to a Philosophy of Human Culture* [1944] (New Haven and London: Yale University Press, 1972), p. 26.

[12] Ernst Cassirer, 'Der Begriff der symbolischen Form im Aufbau der Geisteswissenschaften' [1923], in *Aufsätze und kleine Schriften (1922–1926)* [*Gesammelte Werke: Hamburger Ausgabe*, vol. 16] (Hamburg: Meiner, 2003), pp. 75–104 (p. 78).

[13] Cassirer makes repeated reference to Heinrich Hertz; see *The Philosophy of Symbolic Forms*, vol. 1, *Language*, pp. 75–76 and 85; *Philosophie der symbolischen Formen*, vol. 1, *Die Sprache*, pp. 3–4 and 15.

[14] Georg Wilhelm Friedrich Hegel, *Vorlesungen über die Ästhetik I*, in: *Werke in zwanzig Bänden*, ed. by Eva Moldenhauer and Karl Markus Michel (Frankfurt am Main: Suhrkamp, 1970), vol. 13, p. 394.

[15] Hegel, *Vorlesungen über die Ästhetik I*, p. 173.

[16] Ernst Cassirer, *The Philosophy of Symbolic Forms*, vol. 3, *The Phenomenology of Knowledge*, trans. by Ralph Manheim (New Haven and London: Yale University Press, 1957), p. 200; *Philosophie der symbolischen Formen*, vol. 3, *Phänomenologie der Erkenntnis* [*Gesammelte Werke: Hamburger Ausgabe*, vol. 13] (Hamburg: Meiner, 2002), p. 228.

[17] Cassirer, 'Der Begriff der symbolischen Form im Aufbau der Geisteswissenschaften', p. 79.

[18] Cassirer, 'Der Begriff der symbolischen Form im Aufbau der Geisteswissenschaften', p. 104.

[19] Cassirer, 'Der Begriff der symbolischen Form im Aufbau der Geisteswissenschaften', p. 79.

[20] See 'Foreword' to *The Philosophy of Symbolic Forms*, vol. 1, *Language*, p. 71; *Philosophie der symbolischen Formen*, vol. 1, *Die Sprache*, p. ix.

[21] See 'Foreword' to *The Philosophy of Symbolic Forms*, vol. 1, *Language*, p. 72; *Philosophie der symbolischen Formen*, vol. 1, *Die Sprache*, p. xi.

[22] *The Philosophy of Symbolic Forms*, vol. 1, *Language*, p. 12; *Philosophie der symbolischen Formen*, vol. 1, *Die Sprache*, p. 12.

[23] Ernst Cassirer, *The Philosophy of Symbolic Forms*, vol. 3, *The Phenomenology of Knowledge*, p. 49; *Philosophie der symbolischen Formen*, vol. 3, *Phänomenologie der Erkenntnis*, p. 54.

[24] I.e., 'that which is in itself and is conceived by itself', a reference to Spinoza's definition of substance in his *Ethics*, Part 1, definition 3 (see Benedict de Spinoza, *On the Improvement of the Understanding; The Ethics; Correspondence*, trans. by R. H. M. Elwes (New York: Dover, 1955), p. 45) [Editorial note].

[25] Ernst Cassirer, 'Strukturalismus in der modernen Linguistik' [1945], in *Geist und Leben: Schriften zu den Lebensordnungen von Natur und Kunst, Geschichte und Sprache*, ed. by Ernst Wolfgang Orth (Leipzig: Reclam, 1993), pp. 317–48 (p. 337). See also Ernst Cassirer, '"Geist" und "Leben" in der Philosophie der Gegenwart' (1930), in *Aufsätze und kleinere Schriften (1927–1931)* [*Gesammelte Werke: Hamburger Ausgabe*, vol. 17] (Hamburg: Meiner, 2004), pp. 185–205.

[26] See Ernst Cassirer, 'Naturbegriffe und Kulturbegriffe', in *Zur Logik der Kulturwissenschaften: Fünf Studien* [1942], in *Aufsätze und kleinere Schriften (1941–1946)* [*Gesammelte Werke: Hamburger Ausgabe*, vol. 24] (Hamburg: Meiner, 2007), pp. 414–45 (p. 444).

[27] Cassirer, 'Naturbegriffe und Kulturbegriffe', pp. 444–45.

[28] Cassirer, *The Philosophy of Symbolic Forms*, vol. 1, *Language*, pp. 93–94 and 218; *Philosophie der symbolischen Formen*, vol. 1, *Die Sprache*, pp. 25 and 172.

[29] Ernst Cassirer, 'Formproblem und Kausalproblem', in *Zur Logik der Kulturwissenschaften*, pp. 446–61.

[30] Ernst Cassirer, 'Die "Tragödie der Kultur"', in *Zur Logik der Kulturwissenschaften*, pp. 462–86 (p. 486).

[31] Cassirer, 'Die "Tragödie der Kultur"', in *Zur Logik der Kulturwissenschaften*, p. 469; see Birgit Recki, *Kultur als Praxis: Eine Einführung in Ernst Cassirers Philosophie der symbolischen Formen* (Berlin: Akademie-Verlag, 2004), chap. C.III, 'Das Ethos der Freiheit: Ernst Cassirers ungeschriebene Ethik und ihre Postulatenlehre', pp. 172–88.

[32] Cassirer, 'Die "Tragödie der Kultur"', in *Zur Logik der Kulturwissenschaften*, p. 469; see Oswald Schwemmer, *Ernst Cassirer: Ein Philosoph der europäischen Moderne* (Berlin: Akademie-Verlag, 1997), pp. 197–219.

[33] How little self-evident this metaphysical nomenclature is, can be seen from a glance at Hannah Arendt's view of human activity. In *The Human Condition* (1958), she distinguishes between the *vita activa* as working, as creating, and as acting. Working is the cyclical return of the ever-same activities to satisfy needs that maintain the status quo of life: the metabolic process with nature, that does not lead to any permanent product. Purposive goal-oriented production is the productive creation of a permanent human world: in other words, culture. But only (in Arendt's view) with action taken with no specific purpose in mind, or in other words genuine political interaction between human beings to arrive at a common understanding of the meaning of their shared world, does freedom arise. Now, here we find a noticeably different conception of the human world from the one proposed by Cassirer: not least in the way the hierarchical division of achievements, based on the unusual reservation of the concept of purpose for product-oriented creation, disappears, where in the context of a theoretical foundation of action the insight into the *symbolic productivity of all human activities*, right from the act of consciousness to far more elaborate productions, becomes decisive.

[34] Ernst Cassirer, *Form und Technik* [1930], in *Aufsätze und kleinere Schriften (1927–1931)* [*Gesammelte Werke: Hamburger Ausgabe*, vol. 17], pp. 139–83 (p. 142).

[35] Ernst Cassirer, *Form und Technik*, pp. 172–73.

[36] Cassirer, *Form und Technik*, p. 161.

[37] Cassirer, *Form und Technik*, p. 158.

[38] Cassirer, *Form und Technik*, p. 144.

[39] Cassirer, *Form und Technik*, p. 167.

[40] Cassirer, *Form und Technik*, p. 168.

[41] Cassirer, *Form und Technik*, p. 159.

[42] In an essay of 1951, Hans Blumenberg referred to Leonardo in a similar way, but supplemented, in order to develop his theory of rationality, the triad of science, technology, and art, with the concept of power. See also Jürgen Mittelstraß, *Leonardo-Welt: Über Wissenschaft, Forschung und Verantwortung* (Frankfurt am Main: Suhrkamp, 1992).

[43] Cassirer, *Form und Technik*, p. 176.

[44] Cassirer, *Form und Technik*, p. 176.

[45] Cassirer, *Form und Technik*, p. 178. Emphasis by the author, Birgit Recki.

CONSTRUCTING THE WORLD IN SYMBOLS: ABY M. WARBURG AND ERNST CASSIRER ON IMAGERY

By ISABELLA WOLDT

Even as a young man, Aby M. Warburg was regarded as being an emotionally sensitive individual. He had decided early on against a career in the family business. The oldest son of Moritz and Charlotte Warburg, Aby was to have assumed the chairmanship of M. M. Warburg & Co., the family's commercial banking enterprise. Instead, he chose to study art history and archaeology in Bonn and Strasbourg.[1] His primary interests were in Renaissance art and the reception of antiquity. Under the influence of his teacher Hermann Usener, Warburg turned to researching the psychological background of the origins of art.[2] Henceforth he regarded art as a symbolic occurrence of humanity's passionate struggle to reconcile irrational, emotive influences with the rational. The pictorial realization of these struggles served humanity (and Warburg personally) by providing orientation in the world, indeed, the cosmos. Warburg recognized that the Pictorial (Imagery) is articulated not only as an iconic form, but also finds its formal expression in other kinds of media such as writing, music, and language. He initially demonstrated how these various media interact in his dissertation on Sandro Botticelli's *Primavera* and *The Birth of Venus* which he had presented to Hubert Janitschek in Strasbourg in 1893.[3] Warburg describes there how Botticelli had been inspired by the painterly compositions in poems by the poet Angelo Poliziano, which in turn had been influenced by Ovid's *Metamorphoses*.

Scholars have already investigated the significance of pictographic elements and imagery in Warburg's research.[4] But a conclusive answer to this question cannot be given because Warburg's masterwork – his *Mnemosyne Atlas*, the collection of panels seen as the culmination of his research — remains unfinished.[5] In this *Mnemosyne Atlas*, Warburg attempted to visualize the pictorial character of human knowledge. On over sixty vertically formatted panels one can see numerous reproductions of different graphic media such as paintings, textiles, illustrations, newspaper clippings, etc. These images from Warburg's research range from astrology to war propaganda. Grouped thematically, they are meant to illustrate the core of Warburg's cultural research. A volume with comments had been planned but was never realized.[6] Indeed, insufficient insight into the world of images is offered by the Introduction provided.

Warburg characterizes artistic figuration here as 'distance consciously achieved between itself and the outside world' [*bewußtes Distanzschaffen zwischen sich und der Außenwelt*] and that this 'likely denotes one of the basic acts of human civilization' [*darf man wohl als Grundakt menschlicher Zivilisation bezeichnen*].[7] Warburg sees humankind as fluctuating back and forth between emotional and mathematical ideologies. The resulting tension creates forms of expression, which like a stamping press — 'engrams of passionate experience' [*Engramme leidenschaftlicher Erfahrung*], become 'imprinted' [*eingeprägt*] into memory and emerge in the process of creation again and again. Warburg compares this process to the supplementation of Indo-Germanic languages. He refers here to Hermann Osthoff, whose work demonstrated that adjectives and verbs in either their comparative or conjugational forms lead to the omission of original basic expression, but that the entry of foreign expressions nevertheless causes an intensification of the original meaning.[8] A similar procedure can also be seen in the process of artistic figuration. Imprinted forms of expression are taken up for the purpose of elevating meaning. Warburg delineated these forms of expression as so-called pathos-formulae [*Pathosformel*]. The highest valued of these — 'gesture language' [*Gebärdensprache*], the origin of which is found in the gestures of classical art —is used reiteratively as a genotype and survives over time in the memory. These *pathos-formulae* should not be characterized as merely utterances of motivation, devoid of meaning and sense, but rather as the bearers of human passions.[9]

For Warburg, Ovid — the classical poet — represented one of the most substantial cultural-historical sources of the graphic translation of the aforementioned human passions. Warburg wrote on 4 February 1927, while preparing a lecture on *Sources of Passionate Gesture-Language* [*Urworte leidenschaftlicher Gebärdensprache*] that he gave on 6 February at his Library of Cultural Sciences in Hamburg [Kulturwissenschaftliche Bibliothek Warburg = KBW]:

> Ovid is the treasure chest, the safety deposit box whose active or passive fervor for cultural memory continually mints value in the imitation of the past.

> [*Ovid ist der Schatzbehälter, der Tresor, der durch die Goldwährung seiner aktiven oder passiven Leidenschaftlichkeit die Erinnerungsbilder, Nachahmung der Vergangenheit wertbeständig machen kann*].[10]

While the *Mnemosyne Atlas* was supposed to be an inventory of classical aesthetic types representing moving life within the arts, the aforementioned lecture should be seen as part of its genesis. By the end of the century Warburg had already investigated the survival of ancient symbolic language — specifically in his thesis on Botticelli, for example. In the art of early modern times, Warburg concluded, that motion was being pictorially displayed to new, livelier effect, which finds its roots in the art of Antiquity. The chief aim of the Botticelli paper was to describe the artists of the *Quattrocentro* and their interest in such archaic elements of motion in classical art, and how those elements survived in the literature and pictorial art of the early Renaissance:

> It can be traced here step by step how the artists and their advisors saw an increasing, external movement in the models of Antiquity and how they borrowed from those works when their representations dealt with external accessories such as clothing and hair.
>
> [*Es lässt sich nämlich hierbei Schritt für Schritr verfolgen, wie die Künstler und deren Berater, in 'der Antike' ein gesteigerte äußere Bewegung verlangendes Vorbild sahen und sich an antike Vorbilder anlehnten, wenn es sich um Darstellung äußerlich bewegten Beiwerks — der Gewandung und der Haare — handelte*].[11]

In this process of adopting specific pictorial forms and motifs Warburg recognizes an 'aesthetic act of empathy in becoming formative stylistic power' [*den ästhetischen Akt der 'Einfühlung' in seinem Werden als stilbildende Macht*].[12]

Warburg's research into *Nachleben* — the survival and inheritance of classical symbolic language — was formally conceived in his aforementioned lecture on *Sources of Passionate Gesture-Language*, the 1927 exhibition on Ovid's *Metamorphoses* imparting a particularly concise expression of that idea. The passions evoked in Ovid's narrative are described on the basis of different image-archetypes from the early Renaissance to the Baroque period. In his lecture and introduction to the exhibition, Warburg denoted Ovid's *Metamorphoses* as a source of both the pathos-formulae and as the source of his research into the concept of *Nachleben* (the survival of classical motifs), albeit oftentimes in the fragmentary manner of written notes jotted in hermetic compression, as, for example, in the following:

> This issue of Antiquity's influence leads to the examination of how the vehicles of classical religious systems introduced and carried this influence into European modes. For centuries the chief travel agency for travelling gods obviously lay in the hands of the esteemed firm of Ovid & Co.
>
> [*Das Problem nach dem Einfluss der Antike hat im Lauf der Jahre natürlicherweise dazu geführt, die Hauptvehikel, auf denen die antike Götterwelt in die europäische einfährt zu untersuchen. Das Hauptverkehrsbüro für reisende Götter lag Jahrhunderte lang offenbar in den Händen der bewährten Firma: Publius Ovidius Naso u(nd) Epigonen*].[13]

For Warburg, Ovid's archetypes fulfilled the visualization of spiritual dynamics that contributed to the development of seminal forms of stylistic expression. Warburg accompanied his remarks with an exhibition of panels, on which he mounted illustrations of different pictorial media, and sometimes also books. It is especially this form of presentation I wish to denote as Warburg's mode of 'constructing the world in symbols'. Warburg's *Mnemosyne Atlas*, realized after Kreuzlingen, encompassing his methodology of presentation and remaining his greatest contribution to posterity, was conceived of earlier. While preparing a lecture to be delivered at the 1912 Conference of Art Historians on the astrological frescoes found at the Palazzo Schofanoja in Ferrara, Italy,[14] Warburg intimated to his friend and intellectual compatriot, the classical scholar Franz Boll, that he had been surrounded with an exhibition of images for his lecture.[15] The method of presentation that Warburg developed — the comparative preparation of attaching selected reproductions of works to panels — made visible the diverse transformations and dialectic processes of cultural movements that are passed down in pictorial representation. Warburg's continuous work on the panels corresponds to the transformations within the images. (As his still-unfinished *Mnemosyne Atlas* was delivered in various manifestations, several variations of the Ovid exhibition exist.)

The entire image collection (six panels) for the Ovid *Metamorphoses* show, dated 6 February 1927, were erected to the left and right of the entry-way into the reading room of Warburg's Library of Cultural Sciences (or the KBW) in Hamburg. A large and varied amount of illustrations was arranged on panels, and books were also laid open on display. The panels were provided with captions. From left to right we can read the following: *The Chase* (Daphne) [*Verfolgung*] and *The Metamorphosis* (Actaeon) [*Verwandlung*], *The Rape* (Proserpina) [*Raub* ...], *The Sacrifice* (Orpheus) [*Opfertod* ...], *Human Sacrifice* (Medea) [*Menschenopfer* ...]. The sixth panel is captioned *The Sacrificial Dance* and *The Lament* [*Opfertanz Klage*]. Even though the photographic record does not present the whole sixth panel, it is known beyond doubt through documentation that this panel was partitioned in two.[16] The captions for the works refer to the Ovidian stories: the kidnapping of Daphne, Actaeon and his transformation, the death of Orpheus and the death of Jason's sons, as well as Medea's filicide. For Warburg these works represent a typology — transformative examples of the very language of expression — and are instances of classical motifs influencing European cultural history, particularly since the Renaissance.

Individual photographs of each of the panels, much like Warburg's notes, indicate that the disposition of the images was changed many times. For the second presentation of the exhibition on 12 February, Warburg combined *The Chase* with *The Metamorphosis* into one panel (see Fig. 1). Concentrating on the story of Daphne and Apollo, the combined images create what is considered to be the prototypical chase scene while also illustrating the ultimate symbol of disassociated love. Several contain various Renaissance

FIGURE 1. Aby M. Warburg, Ovid-Exhibition, Plate 1, KBW, 1927 (© The Warburg Institute Archive, London)

representations of Daphne's escape from Apollo. These illustrations mostly show the instant the nymph turns into a laurel tree while trying to flee the Olympian god whose love she could not reciprocate. Yet Warburg continues to think beyond the merely historical by viewing the image of Apollo and the dragon as typifying the cause of the pursuit. The gesture of archery seen in Bernardo Buontalenti's drawings, as already noted, can be assessed as having future impact: Warburg originally dedicated a singular panel to the metamorphosis with the caption *Actaeo*. As an art historian, he was referring to the transformation-story where the ancient hunter is turned into a deer for having seen the goddess Diana bathing. It clearly did not disturb Warburg to remove this panel in order to unite the narrative of Apollo and Daphne with the metamorphosis-motif. The iconographic contents of these reproductions exhibit transformative dynamics that become visible in the incessant rearranging of the images. Warburg deals with his illustrations as if they constituted an ever-changing image-laboratory that continually leads in its outcome to new variations in content and constructs, in turn, again and again constructing new, contextualizing worlds.

With this dynamic understanding of the works and their function as a kind of process of constructing the world by orienting imagery, Warburg is possibly alluding to (the concept of) the symbol and to how Ernst Cassirer understood it. Cassirer was one of the most influential personalities in Warburg's circle in Hamburg, and his close friend.[17] Already central to the *Philosophy of Symbolic Forms* — which, in its three parts, articulates human understanding as a path from mythical to scientific understanding — the very notion of symbolism had also been formulated by Warburg circa 1927 in the Introduction to the *Mnemosyne Atlas* — in relation to the idea, already discussed, that mankind fluctuates between religious and mathematical worldviews. Thus Warburg's ideas on this matter can be seen as having occurred around approximately the same time as Cassirer's.

My aim is not to undertake anew a comparison of the two thinkers. On the contrary I would much rather deal with Cassirer's understanding of symbolism and, in that context, try to comprehend Warburg's handling of the artworks in his exhibitions. The symbol and its expression are of fundamental importance to Cassirer, which he designates as *mutable*: 'a symbol is not only universal but extremely variable', he wrote, reflecting on the study of symbols in his *Essay On Man*.[18] Furthermore, he stated, 'I can express the same meaning in various languages; and even within the limits of a single language a certain thought or idea may be expressed in quite different terms'.[19]

As we have seen, Warburg conceived his pathos-formulae as based on transformation and the functional possibilities of language, but not really as discursive and progressive. Both Warburg's and Cassirer's thoughts converge here. Warburg realized the transformation of pictorial elements, understood as symbols, on his panels in long graphical rows without start or end. His rearranging of the images is a method Warburg borrowed from the works themselves, since they were already functioning variably as symbols. Through alternating arrangements, changing the disposition, the inter-relationships of the images, their contents are in that way constantly redefined with regard to each other, and enhanced — thus producing a world of relationships, that helps us to understand the world by means of imagery. When it comes to the symbol, meaning and form are found in this shuffling. It becomes a matter not of the identity between the sign and the signified, but rather the mediation between, on the one hand, the infinite and absolute reason and, on the other, the detail and the limitation of concrete form. In contrast to the mere sign where the link between content and form is arbitrary, the exterior contents of the symbol are comprehended simultaneously. Cassirer differentiated between the 'functional' conception of the symbol and 'substantial' conception of signs. In theoretical cognition substance-conceptualizations are replaced by functional conceptions in a series. These modifications in fact lead to an open-ended experience of scientific knowledge arranged by one another in a series and thus converted into coherent theories that always seek to be improved and modified. The individual experience always already represents the general idea of experience. This relationship has never before been given this articulation, but has rather emerged in the very structure of a series. This also represents an ordering schema that Cassirer uses in his *Philosophy of Symbolic Forms* [*Philosophie der symbolischen Formen*] as the foundation for logical reasoning in the humanities, in order to construct a general system for understanding mankind's reality. The symbolic, revealed by Cassirer in the function of mental faculties, is from here on referred to as 'symbolic form'. These so-called 'systems of order' or 'relational structures' that Cassirer posits for the natural sciences and the humanities can also be transferred to Warburg's methodology because the arrangement of the pictures consists essentially of ordered series of images, open to reiterative modifications. By thus defining symbols, Cassirer does not deal with the interpretations of single items, but rather with their arrangement within the context of a structuring principle. It is also revealing that Cassirer deduces his conception of relational symbolism from the work of Friedrich Theodor Vischer, who designated the symbol as a 'shape-shifting Proteus' [*gestaltwechselndes Proteus*], as well as from the scientific view of physical mathematics developed, for example, by Heinrich Hertz.[20] Heinrich Hertz understood mathematical symbols as signs that necessarily link reality with the presentation of appearances. The physical mathematical signs of space, time and mass are 'illusory images' [*Scheinbilder*] of sensory phenomena that do not correspond to the shape and form of these phenomena.[21] Cassirer can also obtain the meaning of this symbolic system from Galileo in the natural sciences and from Leibniz in philosophy. There the symbol serves the anchoring of content and definition. In his own account Cassirer states that each natural law does not take on the shape of a general formula for our thinking, but rather each can be represented differently by the linkage of general and specific conditions.[22] The founding principle of knowledge therein takes specific, contextual shape and always evokes the general in the particular, the particular in the general. The semiotic principle, found within the symbol or sign, that is required to link the general with the particular, lies for Cassirer not solely in the sciences, but works equally in the philosophy of symbolic forms in respect of fundamental cognition, languages, the arts, religion and myth.[23] This is the case because these forms would only be brought to bear in accordance with particular modes and conceptions, creating a sensory substrate as is, for example, determined by phonograms in language and by comprehensible and palpable figures in the arts and mythology. Thus, the content of the spiritual can only be made accessible via its particular expression. 'The ideal form will only be recognized in and for itself in the epitome of sensory signs which it avails itself of in expression' [*Die ideelle Form wird erkannt nur an und in dem Inbegriff der sinnlichen Zeichen, deren sie sich zu ihrem Ausdruck bedient*].[24]

Cassirer does not define the sensory in accordance with the dogma of sensationalism, which states that all modes of cognition originate from sensuous experience and thereby neglects the formal, but instead in terms of Goethe's 'precise sensory imagination' [*exakte sinnliche Phantasie*]. Sensory factors are not simple, sensuous things but 'a system of manifold sensations that are created by any free process of formation' [*ein System sinnlicher Mannigfaltigkeiten, die in irgendeiner Form freien Bildens erschaffen wurden*].[25] This principle of symbol-formation is valid for all the humanities but particularly so for the arts. The re-producer of reality does not place this principle alongside the aforementioned epistemological overcoming of the dualism of the 'world' and the 'image of reality'. But as Cassirer said, 'all conceptions of the aesthetically formed sensory world' [*alle Auffassung einer ästhetischen Form am Sinnlichen*] are 'only possible [. . .] if we ourselves constitute the foundational elements of the form' [*nur dadurch möglich {. . .}, daß wir selbst die Grundelemente der Form bildend erzeugen*].[26] In this view the world is the result of the 'archetype of reality' [*Vorbilden von Wirklichkeit*] in the mind, thereby exemplifying the basic artistic principle, i.e., the figuration or forming of symbols is the fundamental principle of cognition.

From the perspective of the background of Warburg's collection of images, his form of presentation was developed as a scientific methodology that presupposed an inherent transformation-mechanism that originated in the arrangement of the images, a method that, in turn, continually transformed meaning and content. Not only were the individual panels subject to modification, but the stocks or the arrangement of the selected reproductions were also altered, from works that were passed down to the entire collection. On the 'Human Sacrifice' panel in the Ovid exhibition, one of the books bearing Medea illustrations, originally displayed in the lower region as eight books instead of nine, was evidently taken to the centre, possibly so that the entire stock could remain identical as the arrangement was changed. The arrangement of the works on the panels is not accidental. Again, in respect of the panel for 'The Chase' and 'The Metamorphosis', Warburg arranged various graphic representations of Daphne and Apollo in the upper area while having a separate series of printed editions of Ovid's *Metamorphoses* down below. The central perspective point thereby remains Botticelli's *Primavera*. This image and its unique evolutionary history became for the art historian the epitome of Antiquity's heritage as well as the assimilation of passionate forms of movement in Renaissance painting. Warburg assumed that the right, outer group — the one depicting the erotic pursuit — resulted from Ovid's description of Daphne's escape before being pursued by Apollo. And he understands the dynamic representation of the painters as 'capturing the images of moving life' [*Festhalten der Bilder des bewegten Lebens*].[27] The books displayed in the lower area of the panels are arranged chronologically from the oldest to the most recent (dating from the late seventeenth century) and show illustrations of Daphne's escape and/or transformation. Warburg concludes this series of images with an edition from the Baroque period, because for him this clearly provides the stylistic highpoint of motion within the symbolism in this context. As for the conclusion of the lower row, Warburg inserted an illustration of Gianlorenzo Bernini's sculpture *Apollo and Daphne* dating from 1622–1625, whose *Figura serpentinata*, with its dramatic upward turn, unites internal and outward movement. As Warburg noted in his explanation of the Ovid exhibition, the classical imprinting in the Baroque sculpture conveys 'heightened cognitive dynamics' [*gesteigerte seelische Dynamik*] leading to a 'Baroque style of communicative and heighetened pathos-formulae' [*zu einem Barockstil mitteilsamer und erregter Pathosformeln*].[28] On the other hand, the need to express graphically the internal turmoil within the spectacle and its actual production of movement 'discharges the epic-poetic lyrical dynamic within into the drama of the modern age' [*Einmünden der dichterisch-epischen lyrischen Dynamik in das reale Drama der Neuzeit*].[29] The panel containing *The Sacrifice* describes this transposition of the death of Orpheus graphically represented on an Attic vase to the title page of Ottavio Rinuccini's *Euridice* as well as to the staging of the myth in Monteverdi's early opera.

In his notes from 4 February 1927, Warburg records a further and, for him, crucial stylistic intersection:

> The entrance of a highly idealized movement-motif takes place during the attempt to liberate the ancient world of art from oriental-astrological Hellenistic and courtly Burgundian masking.

[Eintritt des idealistischen hohen Bewegungsstils findet statt beim Befreiungsversuch der Antike aus orientalisch-astrologisch hellenistischer burgundisch-höfischer Maskierung].[30]

Warburg saw this form of language metamorphosis in the planet representations that Baccio Baldini had developed *c.* 1465, Warburg noting the 'Entrance of the stylization of classical phenomenon circa 1465, Baldini's *Planet Calendar*' [*Eintritt der Umstillisierung der antikischen Erscheinung c. 1465 Baldini Planetenkalender*].[31] Even if these thoughts had been noted before his first show on 6 February 1927, they received no response in the lecture fragments from that day but rather first, as the entries from 12 February 1927 suggest, in Warburg's second presentation, when the exhibition stocks had been supplemented with a panel containing images of Botticelli's *Birth of Venus* and Baldini's Calendar. The Venus from the Baldini Calendar, robed in contemporary Burgundian garb rising to the idealized ancient nakedness of Botticelli's *The Birth of Venus*, is to be taken quite literally on the basis of the compositional arrangement of the reproductions. At the end of the lecture Warburg had composed an image dialogue, one that quite seriously placed cultural historical perspectives before the observers' very eyes, i.e., the idea of transitioning to 'Antiquity's idealized style' [*antikisierender Idealstil*] as liberation of the Renaissance.[32]

Thanks to Warburg's intensive transformational achievement an exhibition was created, one that stressed at its core the methodological possibilities of figurative argumentation. Between 1924 and 1929 Warburg prepared more than ten such presentations, the culmination of which is the *Mnemosyne Atlas*. The mobility in the metamorphosis of the pictures exhibited, through Warburg's methods of visualization, creates a rich symbolic character, and represents therefore an echoing of Cassirer's philosophy of symbolic forms. Due to the rearranging of the ordering of the presentations, the images become augmented through the handling method. Warburg thus attempted, by means of a scientific logic, to contain the mutability of images, which are naturally resistant to linear human rationality, by utilizing interactive ordering structures.

The gaps in knowledge that are revealed in this presentation technique, as opposed to the apparent totality of, say, an artistic manifesto, show simultaneously that the art-works function as symbols, reflecting their metamorphosis of generally validated cultural values and creating a world as space for orientation.

Notes
[1] Ernst Gombrich, *Aby Warburg: Eine intellektuelle Biographie* (Frankfurt am Main: Europäische Verlagsgesellschaft, 1981 [English, [1]1970]), pp. 35–36.
[2] Gombrich, *Aby Warburg*, pp. 35–36.

[3] Aby M. Warburg, *Sandro Botticellis 'Geburt der Venus' und 'Frühling': Eine Untersuchung über die Vorstellungen von der Antike in der italienischen Renaissance* [1893], in *Gesammelte Schriften: Studienausgabe*, ed. by Horst Bredekamp and Michael Diers, I.1, *Aby Warburg: Die Erneuerung der heidnischen Antike: Kulturwissenschaftliche Beiträge zur Geschichte der europäischen Renaissance* [1932] (Berlin: Akademie Verlag, 1998), pp. 1–58.

[4] See Georges Didi-Huberman, *L'image survivante: Histoire de l'art et temps des fantômes selon Aby Warburg* (Paris: Minuit, 2002); Philippe-Alain Michaud, *Aby Warburg and the Image in Motion* (New York: Zoone Books, 2004 [French, 1998]).

[5] Edited posthumously by Martin Warnke in *Gesammelte Schriften: Studienausgabe*, ed. by Horst Bredekamp and Michael Diers, II.1 (Berlin: Akademie Verlag, 2000). This publication illustrates the last authorized version of the *Mnemosyne Atlas* by Warburg.

[6] Letter from Fritz Saxt to the publisher B. G. Teubner (Leipzig), 1930, in *Gesammelte Schriften: Studienausgabe*, ed. by Horst Bredekamp and Michael Diers, II.1 (Berlin: Akademie Verlag, 2000), p. xix.

[7] Aby M. Warburg, *Mnemosyne: Einleitung*, in *Gesammelte Schriften: Studienausgabe*, ed. by Horst Bredekamp and Michael Diers, II.1 (Berlin: Akademie Verlag, 2000), p. 3.

[8] Warburg, *Mnemosyne*, p. 3.

[9] For further discussion of the concept of the *Pathosformel*, see Fritz Saxl, *Die Ausdruckgebärden der bildenden Kunst* [1932], in *Aby M. Warburg: Ausgewählte Schriften und Würdigungen*, ed. by Dieter Wuttke (Baden-Baden: Verlag Valentin Koerner, 1979), pp. 13–25; Götz Pochat, 'Zum Problem der Pathosformeln: Imitation and Assimilation', in Götz Pochat and Lars Olof Larsson (eds), *Kunstgeschichtliche Studien zur Florentiner Renaissance: Kunsthistorische Beiträge anläßlich einer Dreiländerexkursion unter der Schirmherrschaft der European Cultural Foundation der kunsthistorischen Institute in Stockholm* (Vienna, Würzburg, Stockholm: European Cultural Foundation, 1980), pp. 258–63; Ulrich Port, '*Katharsis des Leidens*: Aby Warburgs *Pathosformeln* und ihre konzeptionellen Hintergründe in Rhetorik, Poetik und Tragödientheorie', *Deutsche Vierteljahresschrift für Literaturwissenschaft und Geistesgeschichte*, 73 (1999), 1–42; Joachim Knape, 'Gibt es Pathosformeln? Überlegungen zu einem Konzept von Aby M. Warburg', in Wolfgang Dickhut (ed.), *Muster im Wandel: Zur Dynamik topischer Wissensordnungen im Spätmittelalter* [Berliner Mittelalter und Frühneuzeitforschung, vol. 5] (Göttingen: V. & R. Unipress, 2008), pp. 115–37.

[10] WIA [Warburg Institute Archive, London] III, 97.1.1, fol. 18 (Notation on 4 February 1927).

[11] Warburg, *Sandro Botticellis 'Geburt der Venus' und 'Frühling'*, in *Gesammelte Schriften*, I.1, p. 5.

[12] Warburg, *Sandro Botticellis 'Geburt der Venus' und 'Frühling'*, in *Gesammelte Schriften*, I.1, p. 5.

[13] WIA III, 97.3, fol. 1.

[14] Aby M. Warburg, *Italienische Kunst und internationale Astrologie im Palazzo Schifanoja zu Ferrara* [1912], in *Gesammelte Schriften: Studienausgabe*, ed. by Horst Bredekamp and Michael Diers, I.2, *Aby Warburg: Die Erneuerung der heidnischen Antike: Kulturwissenschaftliche Beiträge zur Geschichte der europäischen Renaissance* [1932] (Berlin: Akademie Verlag, 1998), pp. 459–81.

[15] Letter by Aby Warburg to Franz Boll, 14 August 1912, WIA, GC [= General Correspondence].

[16] WIA III, 97.2 [small size], WIA III, 108.7.2 [bigger size].

[17] Warburg corresponded with Cassirer during his stay in Kreuzlingen from 1921, but they met each other for the first time in spring 1924, also in Kreuzlingen; see Ernst Cassirer, *Ausgewählter wissenschaftlicher Briefwechsel*, ed. by John Michael Krois [Ernst Cassirer, *Nachgelassene Manuskripe und Texte*, vol. 18] (Hamburg: Meiner, 2009), pp. 53, 57, 59, 61, 64, 65 and 67.

[18] Ernst Cassirer, *An Essay on Man: An Introduction to a Philosophy of Human Culture* [*Gesammelte Werke: Hamburger Ausgabe*, vol. 23] (Hamburg: Meiner, 2006), p. 58.

[19] Cassirer, *An Essay on Man*, p. 58.

[20] See Ernst Cassirer, *Das Symbol und seine Stellung im System der Philosophie* [1927], in *Aufsätze und kleine Schriften 1927–1931*, ed. by Birgit Recki [*Gesammelte Werke: Hamburger Ausgabe*, vol. 17] (Hamburg: Meiner, 2004), pp. 253–82 (pp. 253–56); and Ernst Cassirer, *Philosophie der symbolischen Formen*, vol. 1, *Die Sprache* [1923] (Darmstadt: Wissenschaftliche Buchgesellschaft, 1994), 'Introduction and Presentation of the Problem', pp. 1–51 (pp. 5 and 16–18).

[21] Cassirer, *Philosophie der symbolischen Formen*, vol. 1, *Die Sprache*, p. 17.

[22] Cassirer, *Philosophie der symbolischen Formen*, vol. 1, *Die Sprache*, p. 18.

[23] Cassirer, *Philosophie der symbolischen Formen*, vol. 1, *Die Sprache*, p. 18.

[24] Cassirer, *Philosophie der symbolischen Formen*, vol. 1, *Die Sprache*, pp. 18–19.

[25] Cassirer, *Philosophie der symbolischen Formen*, vol. 1, *Die Sprache*, p. 20.

[26] Cassirer, *Philosophie der symbolischen Formen*, vol. 1, *Die Sprache*, p. 21.

[27] Warburg, *Sandro Botticellis 'Geburt der Venus' und 'Frühling'*, in *Gesammelte Schriften*, I.1, pp. 45–46.

[28] WIA III, 97.3, fol. 3.

[29] WIA III, 97.1.1, fol. 40.

[30] WIA III, 97.1.1, fol. 19 (entry of 4 February 1927).

[31] WIA III, 97.1.1, fol. 20 (entry of 3 February 1927).

[32] See Ernst H. Gombrich, 'Aby Warburg 1866–1929', in *Aby Warburg: Von Michelangelo bis zu den Puebloindianem*, ed. by Kulturforum Warburg [Warburger Schriften, vol. 5] (Warburg: Hermes, 1991), pp. 9–21 (p. 18).

APPENDIX
A LIST OF THE PUBLICATIONS AND
PAPERS GIVEN BY R. H. STEPHENSON

PUBLICATIONS

2010

1. *Studies in Weimar Classicism: Writing as Symbolic Form* (Bern: Lang, 2010).

2009

2. 'Ernst Cassirers Stilbegriff zwischen Philosophie und Literatur', in Birgit Recki (ed.), *Philosophie der Kultur — Kultur der Philosophie: Ernst Cassirer im 20. und 21. Jahrhundert* (Berlin: Akademie-Verlag, 2009).

2008

3. *Cultural Studies and the Symbolic*, vol. 3, *The Persistence of Myth* (co-edited with Paul Bishop (Leeds: Maney, 2008).

4. 'The Levels and Modes of Symbolism: Myth, Art, and Language in Cassirer, with special reference to Goethe's *Urworte. Orphisch*', *Cultural Studies and the Symbolic*, vol. 3, *The Persistence of Myth*, pp. 243–62.

2007

5. 'Schiller the Philosopher' [review of Frederick Beiser, *Schiller as Philosopher: A Re-Examination,* by Frederick Beiser (Oxford: Oxford University Press, 2005); *Schiller's 'On Grace and Dignity in its Cultural Context: Essays and a New Translation*, ed. by Jane V. Curran and Christophe Fricker (Rochester, NY: Camden House. 2005); Paul Barone, *Schiller und die Tradition des Erhabenen* (Berlin: Erich Schmidt Verlag, 2004)], *Modern Language Review*, vol. 102, no. 3 (2007), 878–83.

6. [review of] Hans-Gerd von Seggern, *Nietzsche und die Weimarer Klassik* (Tübingen: Narr Francke Attempto Verlag, 2005), in *Modern Language Review*, vol. 102, no. 3 (2007), 893.

7. Final Report on the AHRC Large Research-Project, 'Conceptions of Cultural Studies in Cassirer's Theory of Symbolic Forms' (B/RG/AN 8191/ APN 14590): www.ahrc.ac.uk/ - 23k (with Graham Whitaker).

2006

8. *Cultural Studies and the Symbolic*, vol. 2, *The Paths of Symbolic Knowledge* (co-edited with Paul Bishop) (Leeds: Maney, 2006).

9. 'Schiller's "Concrete" Theory of Culture: Reflections on the 200th Anniversary of his Death', in *Cultural Studies and the Symbolic*, vol. 2, *The Paths of Symbolic Knowledge*, pp. 92–117.

10. 'Violence and Aesthetic Identity in Weimar Classicism', in Helen Chambers (ed.), *Violence, Culture and Identity: Essays on German and Austrian Literature, Politics and Society* (Bern: Lang, 2006), pp. 101–23.

11. 'The Diachronic Solidity of Goethe's *Faust*', in Paul Bishop (ed.), *A Companion to Goethe's 'Faust': Parts I and II* (Rochester, NY: Camden House, 2001), pp. 243–70 [paperback version].

2005

12. *Friedrich Nietzsche and Weimar Classicism* (Rochester, NY: Camden House, 2005) (with Paul Bishop).

13. '"Binary Synthesis": Goethe's Aesthetic Intuition in Literature and Science', *Science in Context*, 18 (2005), 553–81.

14. 'The Aesthetics of Weimar Classicism, Ernst Cassirer, and the German Tradition of Thought', *Publications of the English Goethe Society*, NS 74 (2005), 67–82.

15. 'Nietzsche ist mein Bruder, Goethe mein Vater', *denkbilder*, 19 (2005), 55–57.

16. [Review of] Franziska Schoessler, *Goethe's 'Lehr'- und 'Wanderjahre': Eine Kulturgeschichte der Moderne* (Tübingen: Francke, 2002), *Modern Language Review*, 100 (2005), 863–65.

17. 'The Novel in Weimar Classicism: Symbolic Form and Symbolic Pregnance', in Simon Richter (ed.), *The Literature of Weimar Classicism* (Rochester, NY: Camden House, 2005), pp. 211–35.

2004

18. '"Eine zarte Differenz": Cassirer on Goethe on the Symbol', in Cyrus Hamlin and John Michael Krois (eds), *Symbolic Forms and Cultural Studies* (New Haven: Yale University Press, 2004), pp. 157–84.

19. 'Goethe's Late Verse', in Dennis F. Mahoney (ed.), *The Literature of German Romanticism* (Rochester, NY: Camden House, 2004), pp. 307–26 (with Paul Bishop).

20. 'Cassirer, Ernst. (1874–1945)', in Robert Clarke *et al.* (eds), *The Literary Encyclopedia and Literary Dictionary*, available at http://www.Literary Encyclopedia.com [accessed 8 July 2004] (with Stefanie Hölscher and Paul Bishop).

21. Annual Progress Report (Year 2) on the AHRB Large Research-Project, 'Conceptions of Cultural Studies in Cassirer's Theory of Symbolic Forms' (B/RG/AN 8191/APN 14590): www.ahrc.ac.uk/ - 23k (with Graham Whitaker).

2003

22. *Cultural Studies and the Symbolic*, vol. 1 (co-edited with Paul Bishop) (Leeds: Northern Universities Press, 2003).

23. 'Elizabeth Mary Wilkinson, 1909–2001', *Proceedings of the British Academy*, 120 (2003), 471–89.

24. '"Geeinte Zwienatur": Il Rapporto Tra Poesia (Scientifica) E Prosa (Letteraria) in Goethe', in Alberto Destro (ed.), *Scienza E Poesia in Goethe* (Bologna: Il Capitello del Sole, 2003), pp. 21–42.

25. 'The Proper Object of Cultural Study: Ernst Cassirer and the Aesthetic Theory of Weimar Classicism', in *Cultural Studies and the Symbolic*, vol. 1, pp. 82–114.

26. 'The Political Import of Goethe's *Reineke Fuchs*', in Kenneth Varty (ed.), *Reynard the Fox: Cultural Metamorphoses and Social Engagement in the Beast Epic from the Middle Ages to the Present* (Oxford: Berghahn, 2003), pp. 191–207 [paperback version].

27. 'Goethe and the Divine Feminine in the Light of the Spanish Kabbalah', *Quaderni di Lingue e Letterature Straniere*, 12 (2003), 299–334 (with Patricia D. Zecevic).

28. 'Conceptions of Cultural Studies in Ernst Cassirer's Theory of Cultural Studies: An AHRB Large Research-Project in the University's Centre for Intercultural Studies', *Avenue Magazine* (University of Glasgow: Glasgow, December 2003), p. 5.

29. 'What's Wrong with Cultural Studies? A Modest Proposal', *minnesota review*, 58–60 (2003), 195–206.

30 Annual Progress Report (Year 1) on the AHRB Large Research-Project, 'Conceptions of Cultural Studies in Cassirer's Theory of Symbolic Forms' (B/RG/AN 8191/APN 14590): www.ahrc.ac.uk/ - 23k (with Graham Whitaker).

2002

31. '"Ein künstlicher Vortrag": Die symbolische Form von Goethes naturwis-senschaftlichen Schriften', in Barbara Naumann and Birgit Recki (eds), *Cassirer und Goethe* (Berlin: Akademie Verlag, 2002), pp. 27–42.

32. 'Goethe's Influence in America', *GSLG Newsletter*, 32 (2002), 6–12.

33. [Review of] Nicholas Boyle, *Goethe: The Poet and the Age, vol 2: Revolution and Renunciation (1790–1803)* (Oxford: Oxford University Press, 2000), *Modern Language Review*, 97 (2002), 484–87.

34. 'Weimar Classicism's Debt to the Scottish Enlightenment', in Nicholas Boyle and John Guthrie (eds), *Goethe and the English-Speaking World* (Rochester, NY: Camden House, 2002), pp. 61–70.

2001

35. 'Zarathustras Evangelium des Schönen', *Sprachkunst: Zeitschrift der österreichischen Akademie*, 27 (2001), 1–26 (with Paul Bishop).

36. 'School of Modern Languages and Cultures', *University of Glasgow Newsletter*, 28 September 2001, p. 4.

37. 'The Diachronic Solidity of Goethe's *Faust*', in Paul Bishop (ed.), *A Companion to Goethe's 'Faust': Parts I and II* (Rochester, NY: Camden House 2001), pp. 243–70.

38. 'What is Intercultural Study?', *University of Glasgow Philosophy Magazine*, 1 (2001), pp. 8–9.

39. [Review of] Robert E. Norton, *The Beautiful Soul: Aesthetic Morality in the Eighteenth Century* (Cornell University Press: Ithaca and London, 1995), *Modern Language Review*, 96 (2001), 806–9[1].

40. [Obituary:] 'Elizabeth Mary Wilkinson', *German Life and Letters*, 54 (2001), iii–iv.

41. Foreword to Patricia Zecevic, *The Speaking Divine Woman: Lopez de Ubeda's 'La Picara Justina' and Goethe's 'Wilhelm Meister'* (Peter Lang: Oxford, 2001), pp. 13–14.

2000

42. *Goethe 2000: Intercultural Readings of his Work* (co-edited with Paul Bishop) (Leeds: Northern Universities Press, 2000).

43. 'The Cultural Theory of Weimar Classicism in the Light of Coleridge's Doctrine of Aesthetic Knowledge', in *Goethe 2000: Intercultural Readings of His Work*, pp. 150–69.

44. 'Goethe's Achievement as Aphorist, illustrated by Comparison with La Rochefoucauld, Lichtenberg, Novalis and Friedrich Schlegel', in Giulia Cantarutti (ed.), *Configurazioni dell' Aforisma*, 3 vols (Clueb: Bologna, 2000), vol. 1, pp. 84–105.

45. 'Über naïve und sentimentalische Rezeption: Goethe und die Briten — Eine fruchtbare interkulturelle Beziehung?', in Thomas Jung and Birgit Mühlhaus (eds), *Osloer Beiträge zur Germanistik*, vol. 27 ((Peter Lang: Bonn, 2000), pp. 81–91.

46. 'The Ethical Basis of Goethe's *Reineke Fuchs*', in T. J. Reed, Martin Swales and Jeremy Adler (eds), *Goethe at 250: London Symposium* (Munich: iudicium, 2000), pp. 265–72.

1999

47. 'Ansätze interkultureller Germanistik in Schottland', *Jahrbuch Deutsch als Fremdsprache*, 25 (1999), 377–82 (with Paul Bishop).

48. 'Modern German Thought', *GSLG Newsletter*, 26 (1999), 21–26 (with Paul Bishop).

49. 'Nietzsche and Weimar Aesthetics', *German Life and Letters*, 52 (1999), 412–29 (with Paul Bishop).

50. 'Senate Hits its 90-Minute Target Undeterred by "Triumph and Disaster" or Even by GONGOs', *University of Glasgow Newsletter*, 3 March 1999, p. 8.

51. 'Senate's Time-Machine Hears of Students' Preference for "Real-Live" Lecturers and Day-Time Exams', *University of Glasgow Newsletter*, 1 April 1999, p. 6.

52. 'Senate Gathers in Force for Teaching-Strategy Debate', *University of Glasgow Newsletter*, 2 June 1999, p. 8.

53. 'Short and Sweet', *University of Glasgow Newsletter*, 14 July 1999, p. 9.

1998

54. 'Goethe on Memory as Aesthetic Experience of the Particular', in Frank Brinkhuis and Sascha Talmor (eds), *Memory, History and Critique: European Identity at the Millenium. Proceedings of the Fifth Conference of the International Society for the Study of European Ideas, at the University for Humanist Studies, Utrecht, The Netherlands, 19–24 August 1996* (ISSEI/University for Humanist Studies: Utrecht, 1998) [CD-ROM].

55. 'Articulating the Particular: J.W. Goethe', *La Questione Romantica*, 5 (1998), 183–93.

1997

56. 'Die ästhetische Gegenwärtigkeit des Vergangenen: Goethes "Maximen und Reflexionen" über Geschichte und Gesellschaft, Erkenntnis und Erziehung', *Goethe Jahrbuch*, 114 (1997), 101–12, 382–84.

57. 'Lobrede auf Hans Siegbert Reiss', *Goethe Jahrbuch*, 114 (1997), 371–72.

58. 'Goethe's Prose Style', *Publications of the English Goethe Society*, NS 66 (1997), 33–42.

1996

59. 'Goethe in English Translation', *Translation and Literature*, 5 (1996), 242–50.

60. 'Goethe's "Faust" as World Literature: An Intercultural Reading', *La Questione Romantica*, 2 (1996), 79–89.

1995

61. *Goethe's Conception of Knowledge and Science* (Edinburgh: Edinburgh University Press, 1995).

62. 'Schiller's "An die Freude"', in *The Reference Guide to World Literature* (London: St James Press), 1995.

63. 'Goethe's "Götz von Berlichingen"', in *The Reference Guide to World Literature* (London: St James Press, 1995).

64. 'Admissions, Volunteers, and Professorial Storms', *University of Glasgow Newsletter*, 18 January 1995, p. 12.

65. 'The Deputy, the Gordian Knot and No Ordinary Degree', *University of Glasgow Newsletter*, 8 March 1995, p. 9.

66. 'Money: Funding, Cuts, and Rewards', *University of Glasgow Newsletter*, 5 April 1995, p. 8.

67. 'Future Prospects, Holidays, and IT in the Dock', *University of Glasgow Newsletter*, 7 June 1995, p. 8.

68. 'Flat Projections, Model Senates, and Numerous Farewells', *University of Glasgow Newsletter*, 12 July 1995, p. 8.

69. 'New Voices in Modern Languages', *University of Glasgow Newsletter*, 13 December 1995, p. 2 (with Cathy Dowling).

1994

70. '"Man nimmt in der Welt jeden, wofür er sich gibt": The Presentation of Self in Goethe's *Wahlverwandtschaften*', *German Life and Letters*, 48 (1994), 400–07.

71. 'Rumours, Reports, and "Real" Professors', *University of Glasgow Newsletter*, 24 January 1994, p. 9.

72. 'Union, Unity, and Cosmic Levels', *University of Glasgow Newsletter*, 21 March 1994, p. 8.

73. 'Wheat, Chaff, and Semesterisation', *University of Glasgow Newsletter*, 18 April 1994, p. 8.

74. 'Tightened Belts and Pro-Active Steering', *University of Glasgow Newsletter*, 13 June 1994, p. 8.

75. 'New Blood, Possible Partings, and Student-Aid', *University of Glasgow Newsletter*, 9 November 1994, p. 9.

76. 'Brevity, New Blood, and Good Tidings', *University of Glasgow Newsletter*, 7 December 1994, p. 8.

77. 'Academic Arias and Dramatic Exits', *University of Glasgow Newsletter*, 13 July 1994, p. 8.

1993

78. '"Das Was Bedenke . . .": On the Content, Structure and Form of Goethe's *Wilhelm Meister*', in Martin Swales (ed.), *London German Studies*, vol. 5 (Institute of Germanic Studies: London), 1993, pp. 79–94 (with Patricia D. Zecevic).

79. 'Drop-Outs, Foreign Codes, and Lean Libraries', *University of Glasgow Newsletter*, 25 January 1993, p. 9.

80. 'Headroom, Poverty, and Completion-Rates', *University of Glasgow Newsletter*, 22 February 1993, p. 9.

81. 'Images, Headroom, and Next Year's Students', *University of Glasgow Newsletter*, 19 April 1993, p. 8.

82. 'Flowering Thistles and "Failing Better"', *University of Glasgow Newsletter*, 14 June 1993, p. 8.

83. 'Chairs, Calculators, and Student-Expectations', *University of Glasgow Newsletter*, 16 November 1993, p. 8.

84. 'Harmony and Coda in the Face of Adversity', *University of Glasgow Newsletter*, 13 December 1993, p. 8.

85. 'Die Aneignung des "Fremden" durch ästhetische Gestaltung — anhand von Goethes "Faust"', in Bernd Thum and Gonthier-Louis Frank, *Praxis interkultureller Germanistik* (iudicium: Munich, 1993), pp. 789–97.

1992

86. 'Pankraz der Schmoller mit britischen Augen gelesen', *Jahrbuch Deutsch als Fremdsprache*, 18 (1992), 1–9 (with Susan Sirc).

87. 'Plain English, IT, and Farewell SUCE', *University of Glasgow Newsletter*, 16 November 1992, pp. 9 and 12.

88. 'Pay, Pence, and Penury for the Enablers', *University of Glasgow Newsletter*, 14 December 1992, p. 9.

1991

89. 'The Idea of Revolution in Goethe's Thinking', *Strathclyde Modern Language Studies*, Special Issue (1991), 5–22.

90. 'Die Wiedervereingung aus britischer Sicht', *Jahrbuch Deutsch als Fremdsprache*, 17 (1991), 325–34.

1990

91. Various contributions, including those on 'lecture', 'seminar', and 'tutorial', to The Student-Guide to the Faculty of Arts (University of Glasgow: Glasgow, 1990).

1989

92. 'Theorizing to Some Purpose: "Deconstruction" in the Light of Goethe and Schiller's Aesthetics — the Case of *Die Wahlverwandtschaften*', *Modern Language Review*, 84 (1989), 381–92.

1987

93. 'On the Function of A Delphic Ambiguity in Goethe's *Urworte Orphisch* and Kafka's *Ein Hungerkünstler*', *Quinquereme*, 10 (1987), 165–79.

1986

94. *Goethe's 'Maximen und Reflexionen': Selected and Translated, with an Introduction and Notes* (Glasgow: Scottish Publications in German Studies, 1986).

1984

95. 'Goethe: Last Universal Man or Wilful Amateur? On Goethe's Natural Philosophy', in Elizabeth M. Wilkinson (ed.), *Goethe Revisited* (London: John Calder, 1984), pp. 53–71.

1983

96. *Goethe's Wisdom Literature. A Study in Aesthetic Transmutation* (Bern, Frankfurt am Main, New York: Lang, 1983).

1982

97. 'Goethe's Transmutation of Commonplaces', *Jahrbuch für Internationale Germanistik*, 7 (1982), 111–16.

1981

98. 'Goethe Scholarship 1945–77', *Germanic Notes*, 12 (1981), 2–7.

1980

99. 'The Poem as Presentational Symbol', in Roland Hagenbüchle and Joseph T. Swann (eds), *Poetic Knowledge: Circumference and Centre* (Bonn: Bouvier, 1980), pp. 114–21.

100. 'On the Widespread Use of an Inappropriate and Restrictive Model of the Literary Aphorism', *Modern Language Review*, 75 (1980), 1–17.

1979

101. 'Goethe's *Sprüche in Reimen*: A Reconsideration', *Publications of the English Goethe Society*, NS 49 (1979), 102–30.

102. 'The Coherence of Goethe's Political Outlook', in Charles Phillip Magill, Brian Alan Rowley and Christopher J. Smith (eds), *Tradition and Creation: Essays in Honour of Elizabeth M. Wilkinson)* (Leeds: Maney, 1978), pp. 77–88.

In preparation

Goethe and Schiller's Conception of Classicism.

PAPERS GIVEN

2007

1. 'The Jacks Chair and German at Glasgow', William Jacks, German, and Glasgow: A Centenary Celebration, University of Glasgow, 7 December 2007.

2. 'Nietzsches Schönheitsbegriff', University of Groningen, 7 November 2007.

3. 'Ernst Cassirers Stilbegriff zwischen Philosophie und Literatur', Philosophie der Kultur – Kultur des Philosophierens, international conference held in the University of Hamburg, 4–6 October 2007.

[Vorlesungen im Rahmen der Ernst-Cassirer-Gastprofessur 2007

Zum Thema: '"Cultural Studies" und das Symbolische: Der Fall Ernst Cassirer':]

4. (11.4.) Was ist eigentlich 'Cultural Studies'?

5. Das eigentliche Objekt der Kulturtheorie: Zeichen oder Symbol?

6. (25.4.) Cassirer über das Symbol bei Goethe.

7. Cassirers Schiller-Lektüre.

8. Ebenen und Modalitäten des Symbolischen bei Cassirer

9. (16.5.) Die 'symbolische Form' der Sprache.

10. Die 'symbolische Form' des Mythos.

11. (13.6.) Die 'symbolische Form' der Kunst.

12. (20.6.) Die 'symbolische Prägnanz', bzw. das Ästhetische.

13. (27.6.) Cassirers Begriff der (Kultur als) Komödie.

14. 'Cultural Studies' als (fröhliche) Kulturwissenschaft.

2006

15. 'Aesthetic Approximation in Nietzsche', Institute of Germanic and Romance Studies, University of London, 16 February 2006.

2005

16. 'Ernst Cassirer's Reading of Schiller', Aesthetic Theory and Dramatic Production, international colloquium held in the University of Yale, 4–6 November 2005.

17. 'The Levels and Modes of Symbolism: Myth, Art, and Language in Cassirer', The Persistence of Myth as Symbolic Form, international conference held in the University of Glasgow, 16–18 September 2005.

18. 'Nietzsches "ältester Adel der Welt"', University of Zurich, 18 May 2005.

19. 'Goethes epigrammatischer Stil', University of Fribourg, 20 June 2005.

2004

20. 'The Adventures of a Symbolic Form. Or What Happened to Weimar Classicism?' Woodward Lecture, Yale University, 2 March 2004.

21. 'Ernst Cassirer, Weimar Classicism, and Modern Philosophy', The Institute of Germanic Studies, University of London, 25 March 2004.

22. 'Ebenen und Modalitäten des Symbolischen bei Cassirer', University of Hamburg, 30 September– 4 October 2004.

2003

23. 'Biography in Review' (with Paul Bishop), French and German Seminar Series, University of Glasgow, 5 March 2003.

24. 'What Is Scholarship? A Biographical Approach', French and German Seminar Series, University of Glasgow, 22 October 2003.

25. 'Masterclass on Ernst Cassirer', conducted at the Department of Philosophy, University of Groningen, 18 November 2003.

26. 'What Is a Symbol? — Cassirer on Goethe on Symbolism', University of Groningen, 19 November 2003.

27. 'Ernst Cassirer and Modern German Thought: The Case of "True Illusion"', University of Sheffield, 3 December 2003.

2002

28. 'Goethe in the Pub', Glasgow University Philosophy Society, 16 January 2002.

29. '*Kulturwissenschaft* and "Cultural Studies": The renewed relevance of Cassirer's "symbolic pregnance"', University of Maynooth, 16 April 2002.

30. 'The Aphorism and Foucault's *Epistéme*', Inaugural Conference of the School of Modern Languages and Cultures, University of Glasgow, 23 May 2002.

31. 'Cassirer's Conceptions of Cultural Studies', French and German Seminar Series, University of Glasgow, 30 October 2002.

2001

32. 'Goethe and America', GSLG Conference held in the University of Glasgow, 30 August–1 September 2001.

33. 'The Diachronic Solidity of Goethe's *Faust*: A Footnote', English Goethe Society, University of London, 31 May 2001.

34. 'The Scottish Enlightenment and Weimar Classicism', The Scottish Enlightenment in its European Context, international conference held in the University of Glasgow, 3–6 April 2001.

35. 'In Praise of Elizabeth M. Wilkinson', University College London, 16 March 2001.

36. 'What is Weimar Classicism?', The Centre for Intercultural Studies, The University of Glasgow, 20 February 2001.

2000

37. 'The Diachronic Dimension of Goethe's *Faust*', University of Liverpool, 12 December 2000.

38. 'Goethe's Indebtedness to Scottish Philosophy', German Department Research Seminar, University of Glasgow, 7 December 2000.

39. 'What's Wrong with Cultural Studies? — The Resistance to Hierarchy', The Seeds of Liberation, international conference held at Stony Brook University, New York, 5–7 October 2000.

1999

40. 'Geeinte Zwienatur: scienza et poesia in Goethe', Scienza e Poesia in Goethe, international conference held at the University of Bologna, 1–2 December 1999.

41. 'Where would we be without Goethe?', University of Edinburgh, 16 November.

42. '"Ein künstlicher Vortrag": Die symbolische Form von Goethes naturwissenschaftlichen Schriften', Cassirer und Goethe, international colloquium held in the University of Hamburg, 12–13 November 1999.

43. 'Goethe on the "*Urphänomen*": Morphology as Self-Manifestation', Goethe and Modern Culture, international conference held at Yale University, 8–10 October 1999.

44. 'Weimar Classicism's Debt to the Scottish Enlightenment', Goethe and the English-Speaking World, international conference held at the University of Cambridge, 22–25 September 1999.

45. 'The Ethical Basis of Reineke's Rhetoric', Goethe at 250, international conference held in the University of London, 20–23 April 1999.

46. 'Weimar Classicism and Coleridge', Intercultural Readings of Goethe, international colloquium held in the University of Glasgow, 19–21 April 1999.

47. 'Goethe und die Briten', Über die Grenzen Weimars hinaus, international colloquium held in the University of Oslo, 8 March 1999.

1998

48. 'Goethe, Schiller, and Coleridge on Art', Harvard University, 13 October 1998.

49. 'What's Classical about "Weimar Classicism"?', Stony Brook University, New York, 8 October 1998.

1997

50. 'Goethe's *Maximen und Reflexionen*', University of Freiburg, 11 June 1997.

51. 'Die ästhetische Gegenwärtigkeit des Vergangenen', Goethe-Gesellschaft, Weimar, 22 May 1997.

52. 'Schiller's *Maria Stuart*: The Will-to-Beauty', Associazione Italo-Britannica, Bologna, 30 January 1997.

53. 'Goethe in America', University of Pescara, 29 January 1997.

54. 'Goethe and Science', University of Pescara, 29 January 1997.

55. 'Goethe the Aphorist: Making Sense of Sense', University of Genoa, 28 January 1997.

56. 'Goethe and (the) English', Centro Interdisciplinare di Studi Romantici, University of Bologna, 22 January 1997.

57. 'Goethes *Werther*: Zu seinem Brief vom 10. Mai', Department of German, University of Bologna, 21 January 1997.

58. 'Goethe and "the White Goddess": His erotico-aesthetic mysticism', The British council, Bologna, 20 January 1997.

59. 'Goethe's *Faust* as a "Diachronic" Work of Art', Department of English, University of Bologna, 20 January 1997.

1996

60. 'Goethe on Memory as Aesthetic Experience of the Particular', University of Utrecht, 20 August 1996.

61. 'Goethe's Style', English Goethe Society, University of London, 30 May 1996.

1995

62. 'The Intercultural Texture of Goethe's *Faust*', University of Naples, 31 March 1995.

1994

63. 'Towards Establishing the Significance of Goethe's Science', German Department Research Seminar, University of Glasgow, 9 March 1994.

64. 'Wie man Nietzsche missverstehen kann', University of Edinburgh, 24 November 1994.

1993

65. 'Was heißt interkulturelle Germanistik im britischen Kontext?', University of Bayreuth, 22 June 1993.

1992

66. 'Kleists *Erdbeben in Chili*: Structuralist Deconstruction?', CUTG, University of Bath, 14 April 1992.

67. 'The Presentation of Self in Goethe', University of Glasgow, One-Day Conference on *Die Wahlverwandtschaften*, 28 March 1992.

68. 'Nietzsche's Dionysian-Apollonian Distinction', The Alexandrian Society, University of Glasgow, 25 November 1992.

1991

69. 'Die ästhetische Gestaltung von Goethe's *Faust*', University of Strasbourg, 5 September 1991.

70. 'Keller's *Pankraz der Schmoller*: Eine Textanalyse', University of Bayreuth, 3 September 1991.

71. '"Assemblage" as the Organizing Principle of Goethe's *Wilhelm Meister*', The Institute of Germanic Studies, University of London, 21 February 1991.

1990

72. 'Hermeneutics and Scholarship', German Research Seminar, University of Glasgow, 26 October 1990.

1989

73. 'Goethe and the French Revolution', Germany and the French Revolution, international colloquium held in the Universities of Glasgow and Strathclyde, 14 October 1989.

1988

74. '*Die Wahlverwandtschaften* Deconstructed', CUTG, University of Sheffield, 29 March 1988.

1987

75. 'Theorizing, Deconstruction, and Aesthetics', University of Stony Brook, New York, 24 April 1987.

1986

76. '*Maria Stuart*, Freud, and Sublimation', Goethe Institute, Glasgow, 24 September 1986.

1985

77. 'Goethe's *Faust* as a Whole', Goethe Institute, Glasgow, 9 November 1985.

1984

78. 'Cutting *Faust* Down to Size', Goethe Institue, Glasgow, 24 March 1984.

79. 'The Berliner Ensemble's Production of Goethe's *Faust, Part One*', Edinburgh Festival Lecture, 30 August 1982.

1982

80. 'Goethe: Jack-of-all-trades, Master of None?', University of Glasgow (Lunchtime Lecture), 16 March 1982.

81. 'Text and Image: Goethe's *Faust, Part One*', Goethe Institute, Glasgow, 18 October 1982.

1980

82. 'History of Literature as "Context of Discovery" and as "Context of Justification"', Modern Languages Methodology Seminar, University of Glasgow, 5 November 1980.

1979

83. 'Goethe's *Spruchdichtung*', English Goethe Society, University of London, 7 June 1979.

84. 'Goethe's Philosophical Poetry', CUTG, University of Manchester, 4 April 1979.

1978

85. 'Aesthetics and Poetics: The Case of Goethe's *weltanschauliche Gedichte*', University of Wuppertal, 11 November 1978.

1976

86. 'Goethe's Politics', University of Stirling, 31 January 1976.

1974

87. 'Foucault's *epistéme* and Literary History', Modern Languages Methodology Seminar, University of Glasgow, 16 October 1974.

1971

88. 'Goethe the Sage?', University College London, 6 December 1971.

Note

[1] For earlier reviews, see: *Journal of Eighteenth Century Studies*, 1996, 101–02 : *Modern Language Review*, 87 (1992), 100–01; *New German Studies*, 1991, 128–29; *Quinquereme*, 14 (1991), 101–02; *Quinquereme*, 9 (1986), 105–106; *Quinquereme*, 7 (1984), 235–36; *German Quarterly*, 56 (1983), 134–35; *New German Studies* 11 (1983), 146–147; *New German Studies*, 10 (1982), 128–29; *THES*, 7 July 1981, 15; *Quinquereme*, 4 (1981), 134–35; *Modern Language Review* 75 (1980), 942–43; *Modern Language Review*, 75 (1980), 452–453; *Modern Language Review*, 71 (1976), 964–65.

INDEX